WANDA COLEMAN

NATIVE IN A STRANGE LAND
TRIALS & TREMORS

BLACK SPARROW PRESS • SANTA ROSA • 1996

ACKNOWLEDGMENTS

Many of the columns which appeared in *Los Angeles Times Magazine* (June 1992 through December 1995) have been revised, original text or title restored, and, as with other essays, endnotes have been added where necessary. "City in Denial" was published as "Surviving the Riot Watch" in *The Nation*, May 17, 1993. "Dear Mama: Words Having Failed," was originally written for inclusion in *I've Always Meant to Tell You: Letters to Our Mothers, An Anthology of Women Writers*, Constance Warloe, Editor; Pocket Books, 1997. "Devaluation Blues: Ruminations on Black Families in Crisis" appeared in the Fall/Winter 1994 premiere issue and issue No. 2 of *The Woman Rebel*, Boston; Diane Glass, Editor. "Jah in Packaging" appeared in *Instant Classics* Volume 3, Los Angeles, Fall 1993. "An Interview with Nikki Giovanni" was published in *Los Angeles Free Press*, August 3, 1973. "An Interview with Bob Marley," appeared in a December 1973 issue of the *L.A. Free Press*. "Letter to Jamal" was published in *High Performance* magazine's "The Verdict & The Violence" special issue; Summer 1992. "L.A. Love Cry" appeared as "Love Cry" in *L.A. Weekly* "Best of L.A." issue, September 21–27, 1990. "Militant Looks Back at Forgotten History" was published in the *Los Angeles Times*, Tuesday, March 21, 1978. "No Way Up" was published in *Santa Monica News*, October 10, 1988. "Paying for Santa" appeared in *California Magazine*, California Christmas Carols, Nine Writers Writing, December 1983. "Reflections on a Riot—1985" appeared in *L.A. Weekly*, August 1985. "Slow Rap for Brandon" was revised and published in *Chicago Review*, Vol. 39, No. 3–4; John Wright, Editor. "Starvation Stew" was published in *L.A. Weekly*, August 22–28, 1986. "Sweet Susannah, Strange Susannah" appeared in *L.A. Weekly*, July 9–15, 1982. "A Valentine" appeared in *L.A. Weekly*, February 8–14, 1985. "Violence, Art & Hustle" appeared in *High Performance*, Fall 1993. "Voices from the Curfew Zone" was published in *L.A. Weekly*, December 30–January 5, 1989.

Black Sparrow Press books are printed on acid-free paper.

LIBRARY OF CONGRESS CATALOGING-IN-PUBLICATION DATA

Coleman, Wanda.
    Native in a strange land : trials & tremors / Wanda Coleman.
    p.   cm.
    ISBN 1-57423-022-0 (pbk. : alk. paper). — ISBN 1-57423-023-9 (cloth trade : alk. paper). — ISBN 1-57423-024-7 (signed cloth : alk. paper)
    I. Title.
PS3553.O47447N38   1996
814'.54—dc20   96-32027
                                                          CIP

by Wanda Coleman

Mad Dog Black Lady (1979)
Imagoes (1983)
Heavy Daughter Blues: Poems & Stories 1968–1986
     (1987)
A War of Eyes and Other Stories (1988)
The Dicksboro Hotel (1989)
African Sleeping Sickness: Stories & Poems (1990)
Hand Dance (1993)
American Sonnets (1994)
Native in a Strange Land: Trials & Tremors (1996)

For cousin Harry Edward Douglas
in memory of his beloved mother

Contents

A Career in Brief

LIKE MY BIRTHPLACE, Los Angeles, my fin de siècle existence is defined by the dense traffic of intersecting ideas and ambitions, the complex territorial collisions between fact and feeling, consumerism and culture, the pragmatic and the profound—all circumscribing a self who is, at this juncture, both journalist and poet. Neither is quite comfortable with the other. And what follows is the textural evidence. Yet something else is also going on. Often it is the poetic which informs the journalistic in my work and the journalistic which strengthens and substantiates the poetic. But this is not the only paradox that affects me in other incarnations—wife, mother, big sister, Black woman, Southern Californian. It is the last item on this list which distinguishes and isolates me from the majority of my Afro-American contemporaries. Poet William Everson touches on this in his Santa Cruz meditations *Birth of a Poet*:

> Nothing dies in California; it is the land of non-death...California is so new that you can almost say that nothing has died here compared to the rest of the world. There is no intrinsic knowledge in the sense of locality—our graveyards have been built within living memory.

The nature of the community I matured in was extremely tentative and vulnerable to constant shifts in the sociopolitical sand. If there were traditions, institutions and first families, I was unaware of them. The past was a rumor, the present a trial, and the future an improbability. All was transitory, of the minute. Until the Watts Riots of August 1965, there was no one other than my parents and a few inspired English teachers, outside of my grudgingly stubborn self, to imbue my life with value. I had neither the knowledge, the means, nor the money to acquire the information I needed. Completing my off-and-on college education was not an option. I was too proud to accept charity and terrified of credit. There was no local Ralph Ellison, James Baldwin or Gwendolyn Brooks to mentor me. There were no hotbeds of fledgling Black intellectuals, or intellectuals of any kind, within my reach, to thrive among. Alone, I was unable to resolve the tension endemic to the artist compelled to draw the reader into experience and the artist obliged *to perform* the experience for the reader. I had no instruction on how to resolve these and other conflicts dividing my writing psyche.

Nevertheless, I did find my guides in unexpected places; an arts studio in post-riot Watts where I was introduced to, and developed a student-mentor relationship with, Bliss Carnochan, then professor in the Department of English at Stanford University. My hunger for peers forced me out of South Central to Venice Beach, to pursue the rumor of a recently-opened arts space called Beyond Baroque. But my attendance at this, and other workshops, was limited by the availability of gas money. Writers West, a Hollywood-based workshop of older adults, welcomed my sporadic visits. And when the Writers Guild of America, west, opened its doors to minorities, scriptwriter Lois Peyser invited me into her group sessions. Other guides, nameless and diverse, would eventually school me in the smarts mandatory for survival between the margins defined by poverty and race, presuming no escape.

No matter what job momentarily fed me, my frustrated ambitions sustained me, as did my children. A tumultuous private life precluded stability and restricted quality writing time. Emergence as a poet was difficult and slow. Hollywood, notorious for its hatred and abuse of writers, was no less unkind to upstart Black writers. My opportunities were rare and invariably outside the amorphous American mainstream. In my early years as a freelance writer, a self-taught unknown, my editors seldom valued my potential, even if they thought I had talent. My assignments were limited by the going race/gender issue, the scarcity of other articulate Americans of African descent in the region, the dearth in west coast publishers, and the extent to which my benefactor deemed him/herself a sensitive and perceptive being. My assignments were usually tryouts or tests, experiments or ventures, or done on occasions when racial controversy seemed desirable, like Negro History month, or could be safely exploited to draw an issue-keen readership. There was no way for me to earn money saying what I wanted to say the way I thought I wanted it said. Writing poems, therefore, became an act of self-defense, economic futility, and relentless resentment. Poetry jammed the chasms between opportunities to express myself in prose. But, like most American bards, I could not translate poetry into rent money.

‡

In the early 70s, I lucked into a series of reviews and interviews with Black entertainers, mainly for the *Free Press*, an underground newspaper in its decline. But there were too few Black celebrities and too many starving journalists competing for their PR kits. Again, I was divided against myself. Why couldn't I also interview *White* celebrities and review their shows? The question was rhetorical. But the effect its answer had on my ability to adequately clothe and house my children was real. This, and all my frustrations, would culminate in one of the last of those interviews, written when Nikki Giovanni blew through Hollywood on a promotional tour.

Discouraged, I retreated into the underworld of men's magazine editing, then into the stultifying realm of pink collar corporate labor, sweating poems to keep my soul alive. Every now and then I struggled to write a serious essay. Most were brief, because the word-length allowed, when I managed to score an assignment, was usually less than a thousand. (I often wondered if this were a deliberate and subtle form of censorship, but I never made the accusation because I knew not only that I couldn't prove it, but that to do so would be tantamount to calling my editor a racist, thus taking a major chunk out of the hand I was stroking for the feed.) For my effort, over the intervening years, I was paid either in pennies or copies. While the journalist inside me languished, the poet flourished. By the 1980s, the *L.A. Weekly* and *Reader* were the established alternative newspapers. At last, my reputation as a poet seemed to carry weight. Editors familiar with my poetry were unusually receptive to any article or essay I cared to write, remarkably paying an occasional kill fee.

But anything resembling a measurable accomplishment would not happen until after the South Central Riot, twenty-seven years after Watts burned. During curfew, May of 1992, I received an assignment from the *Los Angeles Times Magazine*. "Letter to Jamal," was my response, along with essays from four other local writers. But the project was rejected in favor of a photographic essay; following this, I was invited to try out as a columnist. I took the offer, never expecting it to last beyond more than a handful of odd dispatches. The columns, shared with two other local writers, averaged less than seven hundred and fifty words and were usually trimmed to accommodate any accompanying art. Making my contribution to the "On The Town" column in the *Los Angeles Times* Sunday supplement, once every three weeks, demanded a disproportionate amount of time and energy, most of it spent squeezing out anything of benign interest from my psyche while quelling my overwhelming insecurity. The focus of the column was lifestyle—whatever that has become—at the end of this century. The challenge was beastly. I could not write about being a writer and poet, the largest aspect of my life. Nor did I want to cannibalize those parts of myself reserved for poetry. I was no longer interested in party politics beyond superficialities. There was only so much I could say about being Black (that I hadn't previously consistently said in my poetry) without parroting the 90s post-riot generation of Black professional pundits and academics, and my editors didn't want opinion or op-ed pieces. Wrestling this bear of a challenge proved emotionally debilitating and it was tough meeting deadlines. Ironically, no matter how those who knew me thought I'd toned down my volume, whenever I wrote out of my ethnic experience, or used idiomatic speech, those columns generated hate mail. When I dared be satirical, my supportive readers became confused. They wanted their rhetoric straight, no chaser.

If gumption, inspiration and circumstance allowed me to complete a lengthy prose article on my own (and it *had* to be on my own, without cash advance), as with my eulogy for Susannah Foster, I usually managed to find a willing publisher. But in my case, the egg, followed by an intense period of creative gestation, always had to arrive long before I could score any amount of worthwhile chicken. This kind of hand-to-mouth writing has snatched its share of substantive booty. The consistency in voice and cohesiveness of theme usually found in this kind of collection is erratic. I've omitted several editorials, all reviews, most interviews, a few of the columns, and the two lengthy literary essays I've managed to produce because they are either irreparably dated or operate outside the context and focus of this manuscript.

I've attempted to compensate for the aforementioned gaps in continuity by drawing on my poetic gift when necessary, revising and rearranging the pieces selected into a loosely suggestive chronology, or meta-autobiographical order, beginning with "L.A. Love Cry," a paean to my birthplace, and ending with an anonymously written letter, an affectionate assessment of my journey as witnessed by another. When taken *in toto*, the desired effect is a tour through the restless emotional topography of Los Angeles as glimpsed through the scattered fragments of my living memory. This, then, is a hopscotch and zigzag through my public privacies—my intermittent outcries, moans, shouts and jubilations along the route.

Wanda Coleman, Los Angeles
December 1995

Native
in a
Strange Land

Trials and Tremors

L.A. Love Cry

WHO LOVES LOS ANGELES is Los Angeles, the gospel according to Saint Who? But to love this turf is love hard and unrequited. Is to be a constant trick, a constant victim of the dry screw. Is to never be quite satisfied on deeper levels. Is to always be hungry.

Hungry for the sweet love promised.

By a city with no center, no heart, no soul—and legendary for it. A glitter queen with five o'clock shadow whose lovers don't care what sins have been committed. They keep coming back for more, longing to ensnare her/his illusive love. Love promised but never delivered.

Will you die for me?

Yes.

Where being seriously in love counts for nothing.

It's all a play, all a script, all bad film noir.

✝

Babe won't you spread those wings for me?

✝

Loving you is an S&M trip. You gave birth to me. And while I love you for that I hate you for the painful afterbirth. I hate you because you are never the same twice in the same day. You are constantly somewhere else. You are constantly someone else.

Loving your horizons while hating your gutters. Your obscenely glorious fall skies that redden as deeply as any earthbound passion. The sun a big luscious lick. A visual bliss ozoning. Soon to be followed by a moon to swoon for, heavy and broad like the exposed doughy thigh of a tired old Hollywood harlot.

Loving your chaotic sprawl yet hating to share you with others. Jealous of your ethnic diversity yet drunk with the

19

perfume of sweats that assault the nose. Hating your racism rooted deeply in southern prejudice against me my people-culture my Blackness.

Loving your outsiders. Your street racers, dragsters, low-riders, cruiser-bruisers, cowboys and crip dogs. The lonely who find solace traversing freeway interchanges. The lonely who drive slowly seeking the answer in shadowy doorways, off alleys, on gas station service lots after closing. The lonely who get off on eyes found only in the dark corners of certain clubs.

Loving your money potential. Loving your fame potential. Hating the way you make a sucker pay and pay for a slice of dream that is never delivered. Hating the way you steady pump up for the seduction. At some point the wealthy and the lucky stop getting got and get given. But you bleed the poor muthafuckas to death. And I'm bleeding for you.

L.A. you hot but you too damned cold to love.

You are one long relentless drive nowhere sometimes in circles always in heavy traffic. Gridlock is a state of mind.

You hurt me when the jazz went down. Black music has always had to go blow-to-blow to make it and the transmigration of soul into the sterile beauty of so-called classical left me longing for loves that have butterfly wings, mood indigos and the mellow smoky vibratos of too-cool DJs kickin' in Saturday night grooves from Miles to Masekela, from Baker to Brubeck, from Holiday to Hunter, from Simone to Szabo.

Loving you means everything.
Loving you means nothing.

Your nine commandments of Love:
    1) Thou shalt not get old.
    2) Do unto others before they do you.
    3) Thou shalt not yield right of way.
    4) Thou shalt honor thy real estate and insurance agents.
    5) Madness is method and mediocrity is profit.
    6) High profile talks low profile walks.
    7) The lacking in horsepower shall inherit the dust.
    8) What can't be sold is of no value.
    9) Make Believe is the only reality.

Loving you is to love a special brand of madness as sweet, as spicy and as dangerous as clove.

Loving you is to embrace the irrational and the disarranged. Is to welcome halfway house refugees and hospice hangers-on. Is to spread joy among the homeless lining corporate buildings with their possessions of castoffs, soaking up the remaining sun captured in the mortar.

Loving you is to love fast food. To eat with one hand while maneuvering the steering wheel with the other, working that arm rest. From pizza to tacos to cheese burgers to French fries to chicken chips, to garbage burritos, licking fingers at the light, holding a double thick rich malted, or something heavier, between tight thighs without hitting the accelerator. Hating your restaurants where they serve the high-priced spoilage, seat you atop the kitchen after a 50-minute wait, and throw you out if you get too loud, running after you to get your license plate number after you stomped out refusing to pay the bill.

Loving you is to embrace violence in broad daylight in South Central. Is to drive up to the service station and get gas in your brand new, chrome-finished piece of the All-American dream. Is to have some little diddy-bops half your age drive up behind you and demand your dream. Is to refuse them, to dismiss them as crazy little niggahs. Don't they know how hard you worked to get your share of the dream? Too hard to give it up. But they don't care about that. About who or what you are. Even if your skin is the same color as theirs, it's the color of your clothes that's wrong. You ain't wearing their colors. Is to be gunned down by automatic fire. Is to call for your lover, your dying words. Your lover with the deaf ears. The one who never hears your cries. The one who'll mourn you politely at the funeral.

‡

To love L.A. is to love more than a city. It's to love a language. To do lunch or done deals or do the do and there ain't much in the way of *duende*. It's to love accents that change as swiftly as the street lights in this third world gangbang. One must understand that one speaks in minutes, freeway exits, cross streets, landmarks, availability of parking and the desirability of zip codes and prefixes. In affectations punctuated by fake laughter. Over 80 tongues are spoken here. But the only language everyone understands is that sign language known as crossing-the-palms.

To love L.A. is to worship in the temple of skin, every shade from milk white to jet black. People don't wear clothes they wear images. They costume. Trend comes before comfort. The brightest and the loudest in high-tech fabrics. Our notoriously median climate frees the body. No underwear at all or underwear as outerwear. Suits are for the serious, the upwardly mobile and the established, and the poor who want to create the illusion of prosperity. Tore-down dress-down is for street-sceners and fad-conscious hipsters not to mention recent youth-kkkulture vogues.

To love you is a never-ending bitch.

You treat me bad as deeply as I love you you abuse me. You misuse me. You continually whop me upside the head. You constantly bust me for being faithful and say I'm a fool to expect gratitude. You keep me standing in line. And I want to say it's all right. It's really all right to love me back too, if only a little. But you laugh in my face if anything. I keep telling myself it's you, lover, or no one. I keep rationalizing my love for you by saying it's easier to be poor here because we have no winter. No snow as in ice as in it makes you wet without arousal.

L.A. to love you is to have my heart split open without the possibility of mending. You hurt me again and again. You hurt me with your poor your alienated your disenfranchised. And yet I still can't leave you. Still can't put you down. Like Billie Holiday might have sung, I sing my song of love to you:

> No regrets, because somebody new looks good to you.
> No regrets, Orange Town, no matter what you say or do.
> I know my love will linger when other loves forget
> So I'll hang tough and love you.
> With no regrets.

Napoleon Ice Cream Fog

ON FOGGY DAYS IN L.A., the dangers of accidents and delays keep me grounded the way they did one recent morning when my plane was stuck a full hour in Minneapolis. The pilot announced all flights into LAX delayed, diverted or in holding patterns because of fog. As I waited for takeoff, I sleepily imagined a futuristic Los Angeles rivaling San Francisco and London with a fog so dense a chainsaw couldn't slash through it. All roadworthy vehicles would be equipped with a digital radar gizmo (standard equipment, of course) that would reduce accidents by allowing the driver to navigate traffic at normal speeds as it detects stalled trucks, wayward pedestrians, wrong-way drivers and other hazards.

Rather than dispel it, the sun would exacerbate it, giving it a glassy, reflective sheen, increasing reports of eerie sightings and bizarre encounters, muffling and dulling urban violence as the fog's suggestion of a deeper, more malevolent violence drives our tenacious citizenry further into fluorescent-lit interiors. Tanning parlors and churches would experience an uncanny new boom as their congregations are revitalized. Therapists would unravel trendy fog-related syndromes, with sure-fog quick fixes, anti-fog-depression diets, and fog-fitness exercise regimens. Fog would go Hollywood with new lines of trendy fashions, jewelry and cologne. Geneticists and sociologists would clutter talk shows and the Internet arguing nature over nurture, the discussion fueled by the controversial appearance of fog-babies—all born with their eyes wide open and able to focus. Studies would reveal otherwise normal children with a peculiarly advanced development of the optic nerve.

Playing in fog was one of my favorite childhood adventures.

The fog transformed the ordinary into the marvelous, the routine into the magical, the poor into the rich. It made the ten-minute walk to South Park Elementary school fun as I leapt from the cool cement of our Florence-Graham porch into the cobblestoned romances of the 19th century. The shuffle of my oxfords scurrying schoolward, became the hurried clip-clop of a horse-drawn carriage, the pitch-and-yaw of a sargasso-swamped ghost ship. Phantoms, vampires and werewolves were alive on misty moors bubbling with quicksand—images straight out of the afternoon movies. Or TV. Like an episode of "The Twilight Zone" or "Thriller." It felt so good to be scared.

My foggy-day memories revolve around Mama, home and stuffed animals, defined by rich stews, oven-fresh cookies, hot chocolate, thick blankets, flannel pjs, hot towels and chest rubs. Everyone, even strangers, always seemed to have nicer dispositions on foggy days. Mean teachers were more tolerant; competitive classmates, more friendly. A foggy Christmas was so thrillingly spooky, even St. Nicholas took on supernatural probability.

But with adulthood and the demands of urban living, the fun has lifted. Fog is more nuisance than nuance. Still, while driving through it, I appreciate the aesthetics of objects emerging unexpectedly then receding. Drab buildings become artful facades and densely populated areas become ghost towns. Trees and bushes strike romantic poses and lion-head palms seem all-seeing sentinels at eternity's gate. I enjoy how sound and perception change when those low-level clouds drift ashore, turning every noise into a sinister thump, every street into a deserted sound stage after midnight. Fog is ever the stuff of baleful whistlers, threatening silhouettes and hidden heartbreak. Or perhaps it's just my imagination. Or maybe fog is the manifestation of Angelenos' repressed desire for winter with snow.

Off the Same Boat

WHEN I WAS A CHILD, slavery was rarely discussed in my family circle and then only askance in ominous whispers. Rarely was an explanation given for the obvious comminglings of African, Amerindian and Caucasian blood that stained our gene pool. And if a youngun got bold enough to ask that awful question, "What are we?" some testy elder would slap, "We're American like everybody else."

In my South Central classrooms, slavery eluded the textbooks and the teachers. But in the schoolyard it festered as some horrible, mysterious secret. During Saturday matinee screenings of *White Cargo, Huckleberry Finn,* and *Gone with the Wind,* it evoked embarrassment, frustration, and rage. And in the pulpit, on Sundays, it was encoded in recountings of Moses leading the children of Israel out of Egypt—the subtext being an impassioned hope that all present-day residuals would be left at the banks of the Jordan if nowhere else.

But even rarer was the mention of Whites. Except for John Brown, and an occasional Quaker, the notion of Whites being victimized, lynched or sold as chattel, was largely ignored till the civil rights movement forced national debate. Partly to temper Black self-righteous indignation and partly to correct the sin of omission, "indentured servitude" was brought to the ideological table.

A footnote in the settlement of North America in the 1700s, indentureds were an underclass of orphans, petty criminals, political/religious prisoners, and sons of poor landowners. Bound by law or by choice to a four-to-five year term, they were promised freedom and 50 acres of land (wee bit more than 40 acres and a mule). Because of these parallels to slavery, indentureship sometimes proves an effective device for fostering dialogue in communities where immigrant Irish remain at issue. Underneath the cacophony of accents, tangle of bloodlines and cultural gridlock, Los Angeles boasts at least one family which proudly claims indentured servitude as part of their heritage and has the document to prove it:

This Indenture Witnesseth, that Valentine McMenamin, Born March 13th, 1882 by and with the consent of Mrs. Catherine McMenamin, His Mother hath put himself, and by these presents doth voluntarily and of his own free will and accord, put himself Apprentice to The John B. Stetson Company of Philadelphia, to learn the art, trade and mystery of Felt Hat Finishing and after the manner of an Apprentice to serve the said John B. Stetson Company for and during, and to the full end and term of his Apprenticeship, which will be the 8th day of December A.D. 1903 next ensuing.

Said Masters expected Valentine Patrick to not gamble, frequent ale or playhouses or go AWOL, remain unmarried and generally "behave himself as a faithful apprentice ought to do."

As a child, Valentine—his father dead when he was just two—worked the woolen mills as a "blue-arm," so-named for the dye used to make military uniforms. Then, as an indentured servant, he received $2 a week during his 1899–1903 term. And while, according to grandson David, he considered the conditions repressive, they provided a trade. At the end of his service he was given a gold watch (now a family heirloom). "Freed," he stayed on another three years for a journeyman's pay. Determined to go west to make his fortune, he purchased a 6-shooter and "retired." In Spokane, he took on a Singer franchise but abandoned it for work in the Wallace, Idaho lead mines where he carried dynamite. In Tacoma, he opened his own business after working in a haberdashery. But rough economic times forced the bankrupted entrepreneur to move to L.A. in 1923.

Valentine the Hatter established his downtown chapeau emporium at 942 South Hill. Business boomed, sustained by May 15th, Hat Day (when the swells doffed beaver for the straw of summer). But when post-war L.A. went hatless, Val was forced to abandon fedoras for cowboy hats. His elite clientele included Roy Rogers and Dale Evans, William (Hopalong Cassidy) Boyd and Gene Autry. Val never got rich, but before his death in August 1951, he managed to put one son, John, through Occidental College. Grandson David recalls an introspective man who loved to drive up to Angelus Crest to spend time alone. When asked if being descended from an indentured servant had specific ethnic or cultural impact on other family members or himself, David thought it over briefly.

"No," he said. "I see myself as just an American."

♯ ♯

Got the KGGO jazz obituary for you Frank traffic jamming into L.A. from The Valley you were gone/found the next eternity behind the wheel of your scruffy Volkswagen parked at the curb all I ever heard about you was The Bad News the singer ex-wife and live-in lovers and blonde Golden State Taxi dispatcher I didn't want to know anything except that night at Pasquali's in Malibu when you slew the room it was Ray Pizzi's show but after the climax it was your ear everyone wanted to whisper in all I ever heard about was the chippin' bouts with the needle and I didn't want to know you except for the drums and I saw you levitate souls once and recall that time you came over to visit me and my ex and sat across from us and smoked beaucoup js and made with the jive chit chat and one day you and I got mean together and I had to cuss you out of my house although I did go hear you romance those drums at Jazz Safari in Long Beach and some nights we'd radio in and catch you on a cool old cut in the cold a.m. and be moved.

—"Regards Mr. Butler," written August 18th 1985

Native in a Strange Land

I GET HOMESICK. And that's funny because I've never left Los Angeles long enough to miss it. Instead, it has left me.

I was born in a ramshackle A-frame in Watts proper. Those days at the end of World War II, one whispered the name "Watts." It was synonymous with violence, death, drugs, gang warfare and the worst "culturally deprived" colored/Negro stereotypes. But most folks, like my parents, were decent, hard-working and law-abiding.

South Central was predominantly White then, and we were the first Black family on our block, part of a mushrooming Afro-American population spurred by a gradually accelerating "White flight." The building of LAX, with increased noise and traffic, opened up "restricted" housing west of the Harbor Freeway. But we stayed put. The neighborhood declined.

At Broadway, the closings of the Manchester and AAA theatres, where I spent Saturday 'noons, signaled the slide. When most of the remaining Whites left, thriving businesses and financial institutions rapidly followed them out. By the mid-60s, my home, South Central, was predominantly Black. A ghetto.

On my own, I lived in the Florence-Graham corridor. I liked the area's clement weather, several degrees cooler than the Valley on the hottest days. The streets are wide and traffic jams rare.

I earned my pennies waitressing in the bars and nightclubs that seemed to sprout on any corner where there wasn't a liquor store, gas station or church.

Few businesses were Black-owned. Public service was no service. I didn't have a chatter box in those days and Ma Bell's booths invariably stank of brew and urine, phones stripped.

Laundromats were sites for street trade. Libraries were tombs.

The last remaining banks skimped on tellers, especially on "Mother's Day," when welfare checks and food stamps arrived. Lines often ran 30-to-40 deep. Check-cashing places were worse.

My car breaking down was serious trouble. Auto repairs were unreasonably expensive and inevitably faulty. Buses were miserably slow and taxis refused to enter the area. I made hitch-hiking an art.

Survival meant higher prices for inferior goods and services. Not to mention the police. Dope was craftily dealt over counters with bubble gum and beer. Food-to-go proliferated where restaurants feared to tread. "Fresh" meat and vegetables spoiled within hours of purchase at local markets. It took extra gas money to shop outside the area. I did whenever possible.

Hell? Yes. Yet if I had my druthers, I'd live there today. But "there" no longer exists.

Since the Watts riot of August 1965, Blacks have been persistently forced out by a lack of jobs, by insurance and real estate redlining and the growth of a monster drug culture. This involuntary diaspora has been aided by the hundreds of businesses that failed to rebuild after that "long hot summer." In pursuit of better jobs and decent housing, over 75,000 Blacks have left L.A. for bedroom communities like Alta Loma and Diamond Bar, or have returned to "the New South," the East Coast or other "homes."

Even I moved. To Hollywood. I got a job in the Valley, and the daily drive to and from 120th and San Pedro Streets was killing my car. By the late 70s, *my* South Central was "disappeared" as immigrants seeking refuge from war or economic crises filled the gap created by "Black flight."

Once, in a New York restaurant, when conversation lagged, a stranger asked where I hailed from. "South Central L.A.," I answered.

He looked at me blankly. "I didn't know there were any Blacks in Los Angeles."

"*Watts*," I said, evoking images of the insurrection.

"Oh—*yeahhh!*" Suddenly I could be placed. I had my history. I had my spot.

I miss it.

When homesickness becomes chronic, I jump into my struggle buggy, set the boombox on max, and go cruisin' for the fix. Even the ghosts will do:

Usta climb them Watts Towers when I was a kid. Never could get to the top. Bought my first 45 single at that storefront usta be Dolphin's of Hollywood. That was where Mama Washington fed all the wanna-bes need-to-bes and izzes. Rudy Ray Moore usta hang on that there corner. That gravel over there is the remains of the motel where Sam Cooke was wasted. And there's where the Malcolm X Center was. Usta get down at the Kick-A-Poo Joy Room. Johnny's had the best French toast in town. That was the first clubhouse for The Chosen Few. The best story-tellin' came with a haircut at Oxidean's. Yonder over there they smoked the Symbionese Liberation Army. Caught Ike and Tina twice at the California Club. This here's known as "The Jungle"....

Street after street, I follow the circuitous map of my heart. Where my home is. As the saying goes.

Central Avenue

IT SEEMED, THEN, the hard gray sparkle-flecked cement went on forever. Foot-traffic was sparse except at the beginning and close of business days as workers went to and from jobs and, briefly, in the early afternoon when neighborhood schools let out and summer school students raided mom-and-pop stores for snacks before heading home. I spent many of those infernal eternities a.k.a. vacations, half-mesmerized by relentless heat, agitated by fumes from paint and turpentine, standing in the thin shade of the sign shop's doorway, my eyes and imagination roving the forsaken street of my father's ambition.

The minute regular school ended, Papa drafted us to work at the shop. Every morning after breakfast, except Sunday, he'd load stuff from the garage into the station wagon, then summon us out of the house. I always went reluctantly, envying my baby brother and sister who stayed home with Mama. Me and my brother George were old enough to man the phone, take messages and, in a crunch, paint a sign or two. George, the lucky one, often rode off on a job with Papa while I was left to tap my fingers on window or desk to the hum of passing cars. The years Papa struggled to keep his Jefferson-area sign shop open seemed interminable. At different times, it was located as far north as Adams and as far south as Slauson—mainly off 43rd Street—but always on Central. Papa was among a small legion of aspiring entrepreneurs who stubbornly believed some day the avenue would wake from its blighted slumber and reward them for their faith.

The sky above Central Avenue was a monotonous pale blue occasionally broken by a cloud or the silver streak of a sputtering plane. The only time it was fun to look up was when the Goodyear blimp appeared. We would laugh and point until it vanished from

31

view. Papa loved to park in front of the Coca-Cola Building and once in a while, went inside "on business." He bought gas at Garland's service station near 22nd and got his haircuts at Oxidean's barber shop off Adams, next door to that dark hollow of a shoeshine place where cronies gathered to shoot bull and breeze to the rhythm of the buff brush. I remember the mysterious-looking old Elks Hall, where befezzed Black men in tuxedos clustered out front after socials, occasionally accompanied by fancy-dressed women. There was Julia's, where my brother George and I could hardly consume our plate-sized flapjacks for staring at the stumps of fingers missing from the hands of the enormous aproned man who waited tables. Mama favored Millies for hamburgers and fries, and after it closed, Foster's Freeze. I'll remember those giant 50¢ soft vanilla cones for as infuriatingly long as it took Mama to tease them with her tongue.

This was the Central Avenue of my childhood. Only the ghosts of the famous nightclubs, chicken shacks and bawdy houses were discernible to my petulant heart. The street had declined as new-but-mostly-used auto lots proliferated, Christmas tree lots sprang up during the season, and liquor stores blossomed—all foreshadowing an escalating crime rate as poverty increased. I hated the street and its gritty undercurrent of hustle, the stone-faced adults of African descent who occasionally erupted into loud-talk and edgy unrestrained laughter, and the dismissive, calculating Whites hasty to conduct business and exit the street before sunset. A 60s Black militancy brought a spotty revival; the old Dunbar Hotel became a museum, Elks Hall became Mosque 27. Where Central crossed Manchester, one could still buy the tastiest tacos in the universe until the mid-80s.

Papa's five years gone this winter of '95. And these days, I'm rarely on the Avenue unless I'm running an errand for Mama. When friends come to visit L.A., my favorite treat is a safari through the city's underbelly. I start on the Sunset Strip for a whiff of glitz. Then, as we drive east, I tell them we'll be swinging through downtown and south into Watts along what was once my father's favorite street. It's called Central Avenue. It was the Sunset Boulevard of his glory days.

Voices from the Curfew Zone

What's the word?
Thunderbird.
What's the price?
Thirty twice.
What's the thrill?
Blueberry Hill.
Who drinks the most?
Us colored folks!

JOINING A GANG meant instant, if negative, recognition and *status*; White society denied both. In the L.A. of the late 50s to mid-60s racism dictated, as it does now, which parts of town we lived in. Even if one weren't a gangster, you were a member of a larger "gang" just by being "colored." What went for them applied to you when it came to the White authority figures.

Early on one learned to distrust and hate the police/heat/ cops. Horror stories told by adults and "bigsters" (teenagers) reinforced this fear of *the authorities*. The words "Juvi" (Juvenile Hall), "Georgia Street," and "Reese" where Black boys got heads and butts beat, evoked awed terror.

A vocal minority, Black youth gangs were greatly influenced by oldster graduates into the underworld of big money crime, highstakes gambling, prostitution and drugs. These elders schooled the youngsters in "game." One was well-mannered, if not always soft-spoken, clean, kept up with the latest styles, was polite to ladies and didn't curse in front of them. When dueling, it was the gentlemanly thing to offer choice of weapons. Assault of a lady or child was considered unmanly. Ex-convicts were considered unhip subjects of communal shame and contempt for having been

33

caught. Only the "railroaded" were thought of as folk heroes.

The Businessmen, Pharaohs, Farmers, Bartenders and others frequently sprang from stucco jungles or housing projects like Aliso Village, Hawaiian Gardens, Jordan Downs, Nickerson Gardens, etc. In the Watts-Florence-Graham-Slauson corridor the largest and fiercest were Slauson Village and rivals, Watts Village. They constantly clashed and, by the mid-60s, turf wars, betrayals, revenge killings, and assaults on police dominated the local grapevine.

Leaders were deemed toughest and smartest, with lieutenants ranked according to prowess, loyalty and access to ready cash. The emphasis was on "muscle." One messed with the cops and rival gangsters, but civilians went unmolested unless they crossed you first. Being crossed could be as minor as accidentally stepping on a toe or as major as informing to police.

By 1958 "White flight" was full-tilt as Caucasian families fled to the suburbs fearing threatened integration. While most inner city faculties remained White, the student body became predominantly Black. Gang activity on campus made school true adventure. Four South Central Los Angeles high schools—Fremont, Jefferson, Jordan and Washington—and their junior level satellites—were at the eye of the gang activity hurricane. Gang loyalty often entwined with school loyalty.

As White students became a classroom rarity, Black students went from the back of the class to the front, from Ds to Bs. Between teachers and students, the dynamics of racism played out in strange, sometimes brutal ways. Sometimes intimidating gangsters got passing grades without doing classwork. Corporal punishment was meted out via "the paddle," a sturdy varnished wooden board with holes drilled through to suck up the meat. It was reserved primarily for boys (sometimes pants-down), but an occasional girl might receive a few strokes from the Girls' Vice Principal. Bruises hid in Black skin.

"Bullshit" or racially motivated conflict would be handled after school. If a youngster felt unduly disciplined, the punisher would be confronted by angry fathers, uncles, cousins, brothers and/or partners (sometimes mothers and sisters) in hallways or outside gates. It was not unusual to witness a White adult male being thoroughly group stomped. Or for a teacher to go out to his/her car on the parking lot and find the tires slashed or the car stolen.

Music was as vital to teen-life then as it is now. White controlled airwaves continued to resist the kinds of music we thrived to at home. But by the late 50s they were giving in and by summer '61, Race music and its influence, rock-and-roll, could be heard on stations considered "our own." KGFJ, KFWB and KDAY vied for local popularity while XERB would emerge in the late 60s to attract the night owl crowd. Jackie Wilson and Sam Cooke were the major heart throbs, though there was a hot new "comer" called Marvin Gaye. James Brown was King even then (we had all seen him on the "Ed Sullivan Show"). At record hops, the good kids stuck to conservative versions of the Madison, Hully-Gully, Shimmy, Stomp and Stroll. The bodacious double-dared Walkin'-the-Dawg, The Funky Butt and The Sandwich (a boy-girl-boy affair). "Doin' the Alligator," a rigorous dance of calisthenics usually for males only, often caused rug burns to the skin. When a soloist took the spotlight, enthusiastic on-lookers shouted, "Burn, Baby! Burn!"

Jackets were an important part of belonging. Members were identified by his or her jacket, club name and *colors*. ("Jacket" is also slang for an arrest record or rap sheet.) Jackets were sported at the hops, platter parties, games, rumbles and track meets. Nicknames/monickers/"tags" were important as were high-signs and handshakes. Central focus was on male rites-of-passage into manhood (to be a Duke, Earl or King); pre-teen members were called "babies" and the ladies were "ettes." Hair styles such as marcels or conks were pampered in do-rags, bandannas, stocking caps and hair nets. Tattoos were in, but limited by degree of melanin and tendency to keloid.

Weapons, other than fists, were crude but effective: zip guns, chains, tire irons, switchblades, stilettos, razors. (I still remember how to fashion a switchblade out of Popsicle sticks and rubber bands.) Group rape was called a gangbang. Drugs were an addendum, wine was always cool. Feuds were about passion and ego. Guns were considered unfair, cowardly; and, unless turned outward against the larger society, to rob and/or kill, frowned on when used against peers. Fights instantly drew crowds from all parts of the campus or neighborhood. "Cherry bombs" going off in trash cans sent students scattering. *Eau de cologne* was the preferred liquid stink and used to bomb students assembled in auditoriums or tightly shut classrooms. Graffiti appeared primarily on school restroom walls and underground walkways. Scrawlings were primarily nasty/sexual in content, declarations of puppy-love, and logos. Fighting words were nigger, black, half-breed, funky, bastard, punk, pussy, sissy, prostitute, whore, bitch, sonofabitch and muthafucka.

Bikers were clannish and kept to themselves. The better-heeled owned automobiles and formed car clubs. They were known as lowriders. Their little mamas smoked cigarettes, gossiped about what it was like to do reefer and guzzle wine. They dared brave ten o'clock curfew to go cruising with the boys. These were the girls most envied—unless they got caught/pregnant.

Buggies lined the block when school let out. Only the best built, the fairer-skinned foxes, and the favorites (sisters or cousins) were wooed curbside. Nice girls didn't flirt and snubbed lowriders. Dark and/or ugly girls weren't asked. Another courting ritual was the love-tap. You hit or bumped the subject-of-your-affection. The bigger the crush, the harder you hit. A series of such exchanges could lead to "sweet nuthin's" or the hospital.

While a tiny elite wheeled by hot rod, the majority took the bus. Loaded with the rowdies of one gang, a bus would be ambushed at a given stop by rivals. Armed with pop bottles, eggs, rocks, anything throwable, those inside battled the sticks, 2x4s, tree branches and rocks used to smash windows. Drivers and innocent passengers were sometimes injured. Attempting to curtail South Central's gang problems, city fathers forbade gang members from riding public buses to school. Following community outcry, special passes were issued to students, and if you forgot yours at home you hauled ass and burned shoe leather.

> *Teacher teacher I declare*
> *I see someone's underwear*
> *It may be black it may be white*
> *It may be loaded with dynamite!*

As inner city violence peaked, whispers began to circulate about a man named Martin Luther King and the trouble in the deep south. The trouble was headed west and we watched its progression on television. In Summer '64, Stokely Carmichael visited L.A. trouble-shooting for SNCC, the Student Nonviolent Coordinating Committee sponsored by the concerned "Friends of." In the November elections of '64, Proposition 14, the Fair Housing Act, failed—adding to growing unrest. There was a grass roots movement afoot in Black Los Angeles, seeking new blood.

Racial tensions erupted in August 1965, torched by the Marquette Frye incident, as angry Blacks, young *and* old, rioted in the streets. KGFJ's Magnificent Montague's platter patter, "Burn, Baby, Burn!" was the battle cry of the Watts Rebellion. Overnight gang violence vanished in a surge of racial pride, the struggle for Civil Rights and Black Power. L.A.'s *colored folk* had cast off the chains of racial oppression.

Or so we thought.

Dear Mama:
Words Having Failed

COME ON, MAMA, let's go back. Return with me, thirty-odd years ago, to another of our shared instances, which today seems brutally relevant to my present gropings, current state of contentiousness, utter disorganization and chronic exhaustion. I'm worn out by wishes. And I'm factoring you into the yawns and nods. It's about time I expressed this aspect of my woeful frazzle to you, since mine is a particularly driven anxiousness which exaggerates my watchdog nature as I strive to be there for you every effing moment. And yet I must serve my own impossible agenda, too. Now that middle age is breathing down my corset, I'm so emotionally in arrears, so starved for strokes, the merest self-examination/IRS (internal revenue soulsearch) taxes me severely.

You see, Mama, I've yet to effectively manage my girlchild compulsion to be understood and appreciated. It's grown up big, dark, ugly and demanding. Yet I live better by it now, Mama. I've settled into it, like smelly foot-soiled mules as I flap around in my house of melancholy. Rather, I sweat under it, like a pair of too-tight stretch-alls straining at the thighs. The nonacceptance fits, but not without pressure. And when I'm not careful, the slightest wrong step causes those synthetic fibers to snap and send me, and those around me, spinning.

Talking about it.

No hugs. It's enough just to be near you. In case I'm needed. For you, Mama. Always. For you, no silliness is too silly. No weight too backbreaking. [Except during Papa's final slip into end-stage cancer, those last hard months when your panics, generating phone call after phone call, would reach into and snatch me out of the haze of sleeplessness. I'd throw cold water at my face, struggle into street clothes, and wear out my tires on that worrisome trek to and from the Emergency Room. Once, when I had just shut my eyes for a three-hour nap, the phone rang. I had been up two days without a wink, working against a deadline. Mama, I had just finished the project and collapsed onto the bed. When I groggily awkwardly lamely tried to explain myself, you screamed then banged down your receiver in my ear. After you hung up, I passed out of consciousness. I called you back later, sought and was granted forgiveness for that momentary glitch in my vigilance. It was evident that I couldn't have woken up to save myself. Oh, Mama, when I lose you I'll lose my only true witness!] These days, I repeatedly push myself beyond myself even as I berate the lateness and smallness of my achievements, and curse my failure to do major damage—that is, to make significant amounts of all-American cash. Yet, I'm most pleased when my accomplishments make you proud and you broadcast the news throughout the family.

Which means, I can never say no to you except in bad health or danger. Because…

…in my mid-teen years, in the 60s, it was even more impossibly difficult to maintain my self-esteem under the constant all-pervasive barrage of rejection and race prejudice. I was always too something. Too black. Too nappy-headed. Too fat. Too uppity. Too bookishly-smart for anybody's good. The National Forensics League was my ego's salvation. Original oratory was my forte. I was one of six high school students of African descent from our South Central Los Angeles campus who chose to compete in the public speech and debate society's national program of high school competitions. We were considered oddballs on our campus famous for athletes who escaped poverty through intramural sports.

Remember, Mama? Nobody but our parents ever saw us off or cheered us on. Preparations started Thursday or Friday for the one- or two-day tournaments. Sometimes you'd leave work early and pick me up at school. When we got home, you'd plow through the old cedar chest for scraps of material to patch into something wearable. Or, finding nothing suitable, wearily shop for fabric. As usual, I'd fix dinner while you napped. [There were four of us—me, George, Marvin, Sharon—but I, being the oldest, was your helpmate. I listened to your complaints about your job. I

39

quietly closed and guarded your bedroom door, shushing my brothers and sister, when you had a crying jag. I loved to surprise you with a sparkling spotless room, from venetian blinds to waxed floors, when you came home following a tough experience. I dutifully picked your corns and filed down those calluses, byproducts of cheap shoes. I hated washing and ironing the laundry, but, nevertheless, learned the proper temperature for each type of cloth, how to damp-iron, even how to properly fold dress shirts and perfect-press pleats (I spent my high school prom night ironing the leftover wash in front of the TV console. No boy in my graduating class dared ask "the professor" out. Today, in my own household, I never touch an iron except in an emergency. Everything goes to the cleaners.).] When dinner was ready, I'd set the table. Then I'd wake you at the appointed time, and you'd get up and groggily pick over the meal I'd cooked. Or I'd serve you on the couch, setting up a TV tray, where you'd relax and listen to the evening news. Me and the kids would eat at the table. Afterward, I'd put a choice plate in the oven for Papa, clear the table, and draft my brother George to towel the dishes after I had washed them. I would wipe the table and sweep the floor. George would empty the trash. While the kids played outside or watched television, you and I would lay out the pattern for my new outfit on the dining room table and cut the cloth. You'd spend almost all of Friday night, leaning into the power Singer, sewing. You'd work nonstop, with only a minute's break to say "goodnight" to the kids. I'd stay up late to assist you, to remove straight pins and refold pattern pieces. I'd bring you a glass of ice water if you needed it. Between spates of memorizing my speech, I'd read instructions aloud when your eyes "got tired." If the pattern was difficult, and you made a mistake, I'd help you snip and pick out the fine stitching. When I became bleary-voiced, you'd send me to bed.

Those exciting Saturday mornings, we'd get up early. Most times you'd never slept. I'd try on the dress or ensemble. While I packed my lunch, you'd pinking-shear and hand-stitch the hem or cuff the sleeves. Then you'd fry my nervous, damp, fresh-washed kinks with the straightening iron—all for me to "look fresh 'n pretty" for the tournament.

But pretty took considerable labor in my joyless sun-filled adolescent days when the standards of youthful beauty were exemplified by Sandra (*Gidget*) Dee, Connie (*Where the Boys Are*) Francis, and Annette (*Beach Blanket Bingo*) Funicello. Your insistence that I be well-dressed gave me desperately needed confidence. I was big and dark and ugly in a world that did not value me. My pleasant face was a perfect marriage between you and Papa. I had paternal grandmama's eagle eyes, a medium nose, an average mouth with lips of medium thickness; being overweight had been a problem since third grade. My broad-shouldered Watusi upper torso, from Papa's side of the line, was awkwardly thrown off balance by the Hottentot fullness waist-down, from your side of the line, and you made me wear a girdle. Food—greasy junk and between-meal snacks—filled the chasm created by peers who rejected me because, although they too were colored, I was the third darkest girl on campus. And of the three, I had the worst grade of hair, blessed with Papa's recalcitrant naps instead of your beautiful, long, glossy black silks, Mama. Eating, and sometimes we ate alone together, made the loneliness less lonely.

Once I was completely dressed for the day's series of bouts, had arranged the folder containing my speeches, and filled my purse with tissues and cologne, you'd give me fifty cents or a dollar for soft drinks. The house would still be asleep when we pulled out of the driveway.

Repeatedly, we six—two boys and four girls—from John C. Fremont High, went up against our predominantly White, better-educated student peers from richer Southern California schools. Sometimes our plaintive oratory, culled from the speeches of Clarence Darrow or dramatic excerpts from *The Robe*, shamed bigoted judges into rewarding us with certificates, medals or trophies. More often, those Saturday nights, we returned discouraged and empty-handed. Mr. Newsom, our White coach, did his best to rouse team spirit, and urged us to think ahead to the next tournament and beyond—but we knew he was only one man, powerless to combat the indomitable racism that repeatedly denied us victories. On those unforgettable evenings, our stunningly unfair losses rendered us tearless—stymied anger and sadness were the palpable terrors that rattled around in our silence as we journeyed homeward on the big shiny yellow-orange bus.

We knew we had been failed.

Mama, it meant *everything in the world* to see our raggedy old Rambler sedan hugging the curb on San Pedro Street, halfway up the block; to find you, sometimes half-sleep, waiting when the school bus hissed to a stop. "I tried, but..." I'd say...and somewhere in the moodiness, during the drive home, you'd manage to ignite the fuel of Mr. Newsom's words. True victory, you'd say, was in knowing I had done my best against unbeatable odds.

"Everyone wants to win, but draw or loss, fight to get on top. And if you must lose, go down fighting."

Your words were salve for my wound.

Now, in this present, whenever you've summoned me, that scenario, and those words, has replayed itself on my heart, silencing grumbles and tendencies to be contrary. Memory drives my sacrifice of time and money—there's no such animal as spare time in my jungle—to return to the home I've never lived far from, to do my best for your benefit; to interpret the law and complex legal documents, to accompany you on doctor's visits, to scratch your dandruff, to sit outside surgery during operations, to clean your house, to recommend the appropriate professionals to deal with the problem, to take you shopping for groceries, to rub your back, to pick up church dinners, to study the contraindications of your medications, to interpret confusing news reports, to accompany you to funerals, to take you to an occasional movie or concert, to drive you wherever else necessary, to hurry over after midnight when an intruder is trying to break in and the police haven't gotten there yet, to attend your church for special occasions, and to take you to visit my children, your grandchildren.

Mama, mama.

It's time I closed this particular episode from our overlapping pasts. Like always, Big Girl's gotta run. Like someone sings in the song, hard luck and trouble remain my capricious companions. Sleep deficit and an anemic pocketbook dictate my difficult lifestyle. And there's ever so much of the long-neglected I've always promised to catch up on. But I felt the imperative to make this time to reminisce. So please don't let me forget to say, "thank you" before I go.

Over these three tumultuous decades, I've borrowed, begged and haphazardly developed ways of resolving the multitude of conflicts and disappointments that continue to shape this trial I call my life. Thus far, I've found the strength to prevail. And although I'm not and never will be what you'd call happy, and although I'm not and may never be what I'd call satisfied, I'm capable. I'm dealing with our society's bloody difficult, demeaning and damning demands. I'm fighting. To win, of course. But draw or loss, I'm fighting. Much much love....

Saturday's Child

LETHARGY SETS IN. I'm in a daze. Must be that day.

Mondays? No, even when stormy, I prefer them. My bad-news-got-gray-skies days are Saturdays.

Usta be childhood weekends began before sunrise watching cartoons until the rest of the house woke up. I spent mornings cleaning my room, mopping floors, vacuuming the rugs and putting away the groceries after Mama's shop. Afternoons were either a trip downtown to the 5th Street library or over to listen to records at Wallichs Music City at Sunset and Vine. Early evenings were spent playing dodge ball or keep-away with the neighborhood kids. After supper meant gathering around the TV in the living room.

Those Saturday nights when Papa wasn't hanging with the fellas, or gettin' down at the fish fry, we sometimes piled into the Oldsmobile Super 88 and went to the Orange, the Paramount, the Vermont or the Redondo drive-in. Mama would pack a picnic lunch of ham sandwiches and potato chips with a Thermos of hot chocolate. We'd arrive early, find a good spot in the middle of the field, perhaps 5-or-6 rows back. My brothers and I would play on the slides and swings until dusk, then we'd snuggle up under blankets in the back seat enrapt by the loud, scratchy mono from the speaker mounted on the inside of the window. Mama preferred light comedies and romances, Pop was into WWII adventures and shoot-'em-ups. But occasionally they would give in and let us indulge in a double bill of monster or horror flicks.

Many firsts fell on Saturday nights: first dates and first kisses. I went to see my first Hollywood movie on a Saturday night. It was *West Side Story*. Mama made me a special pink dress for the occasion, shared with classmates. I was so nervous I broke out in ugly hives which amazingly disappeared by the time I left the theatre. But my favorite Saturdays featured concerts at the Philharmonic or languid excursions through the dinosaur exhibit at Exposition Park.

But since adulthood, Saturdays have lost their shine. Invariably I start them off cranky and rest-broken. Chances are I've been up late into the morning, and the phone, bustling neighbors slamming their gate, or some truck unloading off the alley wakes me prematurely. When this happens, I'm evil all day.

When you're working a regular job, the weekend rituals become numbingly routine, dictated by how you're rewarded for your labor. When you're paid monthly, three Saturdays are free for music lessons, morning workshops and seminars or sleeping late. Perhaps a bit of organizing, taking care of odds and ends, going to the barbershop or beauty salon. If you're paid every two weeks, alternate Saturdays may give you enough time to catch up with a friend or take in a matinee. If you're paid weekly, it's the day for whatever shopping remains to be done that wasn't done the week before.

If you've forgotten a utility bill, services are cut off on Friday evening. The weekend may start with no phone, gas or electricity until you get a check or money order into the office first thing Monday morning.

The deadliest Saturdays fall around the first and the 15th. Everyone's out taking care of business, cashing checks, descending on swap meets, doing all the things that had to wait for two weeks. Freeway traffic out of Hollywood into downtown is usually at a standstill. If you don't hit that 110 North leaving South Central before noon, it'll be bumper-to-bumper till nearly 6 p.m. But fast food and restaurant food tend to be fresher because of the rapid turnover. I like forgoing gridlock to drive north on Crenshaw, watching for the tall, nattily dressed Black Muslims hawking $5 bean or cheese pies in hot-pink boxes.

Warning: Saturday openings tend to be cattle calls. The lines are endless, the punch is watery, the wine cheap, the appetizers flat, the event lackluster. Best openings are on Thursday nights and Sunday afternoons. Funerals and most memorial services take place that day.

Saturday is the day after the night lovers' hearts are broken, the first day one must get through solo. Recent suicide statistics surprisingly report that most are committed on Sundays. It's my theory that the weakened spirit is ultimately broken by the eternity of a Saturday night spent alone, while the rest of the world is having a party.

Once in a sunny Saturday afternoon, it's good to take a family stroll along the Venice boardwalk, people-watching, then window shopping and munching one's way up and down Santa Monica's 3rd Street Promenade. Occasionally, I spend Saturdays sitting up at Mama's playing board games, crunching chocolate-chip cookies and waiting for lethargy to lift.

But my favorite Saturdays are those rare rainy ones. If I'm blessed with the time, I take my day-long pleasure curled up in bed, favorite jams wafting softly from the stereo, sipping something hot, smoking a good book.

Paying for Santa

MY CHRISTMAS PAST comes back in flashes of pain, anger, and rueful warmth. We'd tiptoe out of bed at 7 a.m. and start opening gifts. Mama and Papa would join us a couple of hours later, then she'd head for the kitchen. While Papa helped us put toys together, our two-bedroom stucco home filled with smells of waffles, bacon and hot cocoa. The four of us would break to the table, allowed to eat in our cotton pjs for the holiday. We could eat anything we wanted that day, irrespective of spoiled appetites. It was our day of unfettered freedom. Mama and Papa even did the dishes.

For years Papa worked nights, sometimes Christmas night, as a janitor for RCA Victor. Around the holidays RCA discarded hundreds of unsold recordings, and he brought some home for gifts. I once received a set of red vinyl 45s by Wanda Landowska, the harpsichordist. She was the first famous Wanda I'd ever heard or seen on television or in movies. On Christmas, Mama allowed Papa to play the 78s she couldn't tolerate on the other 364 days. The house reverberated with rhythm and blues—*T-99, Saturday Night Fish Fry, Bad Bad Whisky, Dust My Broom*—till even we kids protested. After a while we grew to love it as he did.

Throughout the day relatives stopped by. There was blue-black, soft-spoken Uncle Rich, and Aunt Lacy with her purple-tinged, silver-white hair. I'd never seen such hair. She wore it in a big upsweep atop her honey-colored head. It fascinated and repelled me. She always smelled of some exotic fragrance. To this day her image is instantly conjured up by department store perfume counters. Uncle Jimmy would bring orange net stockings full of candy and nuts. Between spates of lively chatter about their struggles as Black bridge champions, Uncle Kenneth and

Aunt Myrtle devoured all of anything Mama didn't hide.

Looking back, happiness abounded until I discovered Santa was a lie. From my poem "Growing Up Black":

one Christmas i found an invoice under the bed
at 9 i discovered Santa Claus was Sears & Roebuck
and demanded payment within 90 days

In the late 60s I followed the trend of militant young blacks and convinced my family to abandon Christmas—even Kwanza, its Black nationalist counterpart. Racial and economic disparities made celebrations of any kind seem ludicrous. Still do. But within the decade I succumbed to pressures from my children.

The result is compromise. Last year I dared heavy rains to select a tree from one of many lots on Central Avenue, as my parents had done before me. We rose early Christmas morning and spent the day at Grandma and Grandpa's with my two brothers and their families, the afternoon climaxing in a long-distance call from our baby sister. We ended our celebration with a supper of roast lamb with all the trimmings. And I did the dishes.

Starvation Stew

IT WAS THE WINTER of 1964–65. He was English-Irish, I was Afro-American and we were starting our family. He went out day-after-day looking for handiwork. I was a pregnant teen. He was from Georgia; and since the wife's birthplace didn't count in California, we were both ineligible for welfare. There wasn't much for us to do except eat, sleep, watch television and make love. Our meager finances swiftly dwindled, and life was reduced to sleep, television and lovemaking.

Our noxiously spare diet had consisted of Spam, grits, eggs, apricot jam and bread. It was down to one loaf of bread.

While he job-hunted, I watched TV, read, or made fantasy lists of foods we'd buy as soon as he got a paycheck. I constructed menus—simple at first—then elaborate Bacchanalian feasts of sumptuous involvement, including finger bowls and sojourns at the bidet.

We shared our shanty with a rat I named Irving who frequently woke us nights with noisy forages into the trash.

That night we gloomily discussed our borderline starvation status and bleak prospects. He was determined to start early the next day and not return until he'd scored by any means necessary. That loaf of bread would sustain us a few more days.

The next morning the loaf had vanished. The door and window were locked from inside. Irving Rat had done his worst. A frantic search turned up two slices of white bread at the bottom of a *Weber's* wrapper. Irving was merciful.

All day I lay paralyzed with hunger, unable to focus on TV, a book, or the menus. Visions of deep-dish apple pie bleeding vanilla ice cream and other high-caloric goodies danced in my head. I fell asleep and awoke in the late afternoon. My stomach was biting my backbone.

I went into the kitchen and stared at the two slices of bread. I went to the sink, drank four glasses of tap water, got out my slice of bread, ate it, chewing each bite twenty-eight times, and drank four more glasses of water. The rest of my day was spent fighting the urge to devour the last slice. Love stayed gluttony.

Finally my spouse arrived home a success. He had scored a job as a janitor. *And* he carried with him a 2-quart jar of home-made mulligan stew. He'd stopped by Mama's to share the news and she'd given him the freshly made "Irish goo." I hated the stuff. But that was absolutely the most delicious meal of my life—*pure dee* soul food.

A Militant Look Backwards

"WE'RE GOING TO do it," my friend said, meaning that arrangements had been made for someone to bring us guns and ammo from Canada.

"There's another person I want you to meet," he said. "There'll be three of us." I listened, my adrenaline flow giving me one hell of a high. This was it—what my comrade had just proposed was a shootout.

The year was 1969, and we had become frustrated by everything. Dr. Martin Luther King Jr. was dead. Malcolm X was dead. Huey P. Newton was in prison and, to all intents and purposes, also dead. The whole Movement, we felt, was dying. The opportunity to prove ourselves through our actions had eluded us. But now, suddenly, that opportunity arrived.

I was young, naive, militant, rash and all the other things attributed to spirited young Blacks of the 60s who looked into the crystal ball of American society and saw no future. So death and the assumed immortality of making the front page of *The Los Angeles Times* and perhaps every other major newspaper in the country appealed to my sense of adventure, and satisfied my growing ache: an overwhelming desire to be *heard*.

My friend was married and had a child, a second on the way. I was divorced and had two children. Whatever fever possessed him to want to give up his life I assumed to be a passion identical to my own. At that time, I didn't know the identity of our third member. I asked few questions. I saw myself as a soldier, ready and willing to die, no questions asked. It was proper, to my way of thinking, that no questions be asked. Romantic, yes—but I was ready to pay the price that came with making that particular romance reality; to take the lives of random strangers who knew nothing of us or our gripes with society.

The plot: so painfully simple, a cliché. Others had carried it out before. We'd get guns, go on top of a building—preferably one owned by an oil company so that our act would have some political significance—and start blasting away for as long as we lasted, until we were killed, our bodies destroyed by counterfire.

I was solemn in my preparation, and put my meager affairs in order. I was barely making a living at the time, subsisting off unemployment insurance. Rather than write a will, I made out a list of instructions à la Mama-take-care-of-the-kids: Don't let my crazy ex have them.

The thought of not being around to see my children grow up was the hard part. But what about King's children? Or Malcolm's? What about the future of Black children in America? I didn't think beyond that point.

The two of us met at the community center. The third member was late. Conversation was sparse. I asked my friend about the third member's identity. "You'll know." After a while the third member arrived. I was surprised. We'd known each other previously, while attending a post-riot creative arts workshop. We had spent many hours debating the social ills that defined us. From skin-color to economics. I had always considered him too "elitist" for the kind of guerrilla action our ringleader proposed.

We talked. We shared our ideas. We parted.

I drove away a bit confused that afternoon. Something had happened to the three of us, there, in that room. I was to understand it only years and many changes later. Suffice it to say that a synthesis took place. We had one commonality, we were highly gifted writers, frustrated in our endeavors. I wish I could offer more details, but to expose what took place in that room would be to expose the identities of the other two.

The guns from Canada never arrived. The shootout never happened. I don't see much of my two associates anymore. One went on to use his corporate job as a springboard to become a community spokesman. The other abandoned Los Angeles for New York, is a journalist for one of the nation's leading newspapers and is on his way to becoming a major social critic. And while I struggle on as, ironically, the editor of men's skin magazines, my first volume of poetry will be published next year.

These memories were evoked by the February celebration

of Black History month. That February has been designated by some state and local officials as Black History Month, and that there is a movement to bring it federal recognition strike me as ironic. Why not August? Why not the hot summer month that has received so much attention after the memorable August in 1965, when Watts exploded. August, that emblem of embarrassment, an economic albatross around the neck of Black Los Angeles. Go down to 103rd Street. Ride through, in and around. The Watts I knew and grew up in no longer exists—it has been erased as completely as a penciled error in a bookkeeper's ledger. The memories of those who died in those riots have been whited out, as neatly as an error on the typist's page.

It is 1978. This morning the rain has let up. My children are asleep, my new husband is sipping coffee in the front room. I'm sitting in the kitchen trying to recapture the past on paper, to come to terms with a long-ago incident in a community-center room. Perhaps the impetus for that incident can be found in something writer Richard Gilman once observed. In an essay, "White Standards and Negro Writing," he said, "Imagine, how it must be to know that you have not the right to feel that your birth, your pain, your joy, your death are proper, natural elements of the human universe, but are, as it were, interlopers, unsanctioned realities to be experienced on sufferance and without communal acknowledgment."

The unemployment level in Black Los Angeles has climbed several points higher than it was before the Watts Riots took place. The futility remains, although busing, undocumented workers, the Bakke case, the Middle Eastern conflict and the energy crisis are the big issues of *now*. Last night I spent the evening playing Scrabble with Mama. My children were in front of the color television set watching an episode of "What's Happening." They were laughing.

NOTE

While this piece captures my frustration in 1978 and in the decade earlier, my intentional irony has deepened over these twenty-odd years and resonates more loudly. Underscoring my youthful discontent was a second marriage which would eventually fail. Writing the same piece today, I would describe my desire to be heard as a pathological need for

acceptance, and tie that to my skin color, grade of hair, southwestern ori-
gin, and other factors defining my complex shade of Blackness. I do so
later in no less impassioned essays. Since this was published, MLK's
birthday has become a national holiday, and the anti-government
rhetoric of the political left of the 60s has become the covert anti-Black
rhetoric of the extremist right in the 90s. The leader of our little pseudo-
terrorist venture has achieved success, post-riot '92, as a nationally recog-
nized moderate community spokesman. The third member of our group
has become infamous as a Black neo-conservative social critic and major
influence on New York's jazz and literary scenes. Huey P. Newton ful-
filled his prophecy (Revolutionary Suicide) *and mine when he took a*
bullet outside a crack house in West Oakland in 1989. I'm fifteen years
deep into my third marriage. And my daughter has made me a grand-
mother.

Interview with Nikki Giovanni
August 3rd 1973

AFTER I WAITED forty-five minutes in the lobby of the Beverly Wilshire Hotel, Nikki Giovanni finally arrived for our 11 o'clock appointment. There was some momentary confusion as to where the interview was to take place. Well, upstairs in her room was the ideal; giving her a chance to change and catch her breath, I went up after about five minutes. She was getting into something more relaxed, a pair of slacks. We walked back downstairs together. She wanted a drink.

So here's the interview—condensed—minus the constant tinkling of rattling silverware, the clatter of dishes, the continuous drone of people chatting in the background, the munching of toast, the sipping of coffee and cocktails, the you-knows, uh-huhs and some other stuff. I left in most of the background conversation one gets when conducting business in the swank bar of the Beverly Wilshire Hotel.

As we're seated, the woman coordinating Nikki's tour steers Tom over to our table. He and Nikki exchange a platonic buss while I diddle with the tape recorder to be sure it's working.

VOICE: He's at your disposal, dear, until we're ready to leave.

NIKKI: I don't have a disposalment vanity. I always like to say, "Do you mind?"

VOICE: Well—as long as it's nothing ridiculous that we have him doing…

NIKKI: Well, I'm glad to see Tommy. He's competent, professional and sweet and I like him. Tommy's an old friend, and I feel better now that he's around to look out for me.

(*Laughter*)

NIKKI: Let's make it for 8:30 Wednesday.

VOICE: ... order ...?

NIKKI: I would like coffee—

VOICE: C.'s free. She's coming over now.

NIKKI: Oh good (*turning to me*). This is the *Playboy* magazine? The *Playgirl* magazine?

ME: It's supposed to be the first Black men's magazine. The nude layouts, the whole thing.

NIKKI: I'm not going to deal with it.

(*Laughter*)

ME: It's rough to deal with.

NIKKI: When I start my women's magazine, Tom, I want to have you pose nude for my centerfold.

TOM: All right.

NIKKI: If Burt Reynolds can do it?

ME: Right.

TOM: Right.

NIKKI: I tell you who put everybody to shame, though. George Maharis. Did you see the nude photo of George?

ME: No, I didn't see it.

NIKKI: God, that boy's really hung! He's really hung. I looked at that and I said—wow!

(*Laughter*)

NIKKI: It's a nice picture and he looks kind of shy. I mean his face looked kind of shy.

VOICE: Excuse me, please.

NIKKI: We just had a Black women's magazine....

VOICE: ... John Butler ... magazine ...

ME: *Essence* might take off in that direction one of these days.

NIKKI: I worked at *Encore* ... I had ...

ME: That's nice (*meaning the publication*)....

NIKKI: ...well we're hanging in...I mean you're not gonna always work...(*waitress brings coffee*)...Oh! Isn't that precious. Coffee! The staff of life, no matter what they say about bread! It's coffee. This is really crazy.

NIKKI: (*to Tom*) I'm glad you decided to come and bring some sanity—we fought one uphill battle.

TOM: I can imagine.

NIKKI: I feel—all the way.

VOICE: Well we all had this shit straightened out before you got here. We needed you last week.

TOM: (*to the waiter*) Oh, no!...I need some hot sauce, please.

WAITER: Excuse me?

TOM: Hot sauce.

NIKKI: (*to me*) I can talk to you.

ME: I have a bad habit of being very honest in my interviews and sort of putting down what happens.

NIKKI: So how come you're doing this?

ME: I'm doing it for the *Free Press*. I'm a free-lance writer.

VOICE: Oh! You're doing it for the *Press*?

VOICE: I guess not....

NIKKI: I can't get over that crack....(*to me*) I just had a marvelous interview.

TOM: Is there a napkin over there anywhere?

VOICE: Pumpernickel bread.

VOICE: There's plenty.

VOICE: Put butter on it.

NIKKI: They have more upstairs.

ME: I was reading over some of your material. I hate to go on interviews and ask people questions they've been asked a million times. I don't know if there's any way to avoid that. You've been interviewed to death—my God!

NIKKI: It's a good thing I like it, huh?

(*Laughter*)

ME: I'm hip.

NIKKI: Don't ask me about women's lib and we'll be okay.

ME: I don't have that down here, now that you mention it.

NIKKI: If you don't ask me—'cause I'm just tired of hearing that question.

ME: In fact, I guess I was going to ask you everything but that.

NIKKI: That's good.

ME: I always like to ask people things of basic interest to me, rather than—just the readers.

NIKKI: I like the old-fashioned selfish interview.

(*Tommy chuckles*)

ME: You're in a position, I would assume, to probably have hassles I can relate to. That's what I want to know about. For example, being single and raising a child. Being in the same system myself and having twice the load, I'd like to know how you deal with it. It's not the hassle of the children themselves so much as the hassles society lays on you. For example, here in L.A. getting a pad is next to impossible unless you have a lot of bread. Especially in the Black part of L.A. Going out with guys is a hassle. Baby sitters are a hassle—unless you have family. Do you have comparable hassles?

NIKKI: No. I haven't.

ME: Do you have any job hassles—I mean as a Black woman?

NIKKI: Personally I don't have any of those problems. Sometimes I have problems with the baby sitter. I've been very fortunate. And I know that's a charmed existence in terms of finding good people. But the rest of those things—you hire a little old man, preferably—about 60 and you make him find your apartment and pay your rent. You know—that kind of thing. I don't look for jobs. I'm fortunate. I would say I'm certainly aware that there's a terrific problem—and I think there's a problem that probably most Black people face. I think that as Black people face it, Black women will be the beneficiaries. Because the situations that I do have and you have are not unusual situations.

TOM: (*into the phone*) I want to get an outside line.

NIKKI: It's more women who have children and are divorced or widowed or unwed mothers...so it's kind of phony.

ME: Unreal.

NIKKI: Not unreal. Phony. To be phony is not to be unreal. It's a phony issue of a phony morality. If I were a landlord—which I'm not—and I was going to rent my home, my apartment, I would look for an unwed mother with a child, 'cause I know them to be the most stable people in the community. The most unstable are young married couples, right? In terms of how they spend their money. You may or may not get your rent from them. But a mother with a child is always gonna pay her rent on time. She's gonna be there for a long time. It's just their own male chauvinism that makes them say there has to be a man around.

ME: You'd be surprised. Some of the landlords that turn you down are women.

NIKKI: I wouldn't be surprised. Again, it's because your life is a comment on their life. If I was to put my life as a hassle in respect to my child—it's that people who got married and had children, who are unhappy and look at somebody like me who didn't get married and has a child and is very happy. They say, "I'm not gonna let her get away with it!!" "I'm going to punish her for being happy." If they would look at me and I was miserable or burned or regretting my situation, I would be all right. They would say she's having a tough time but she's struggling through. As long as they can look at me and I'm happy it's annoying because they paid a high price, indeed, for the right to have children.

TOM: Four, five, nine. Nine one—wait a minute—four-six, five-nine-zero.

NIKKI: I think that at least in my situation that's part of it. A lot of women get married and they're stuck with the guy. They're very angry when they see single women with children. They sometimes go right on and seem content with the situation or in some cases—in my case in particular—I courted that situation. I saw it and said I did not want to get married, or some ol' bullshit. That's the way I like to live my life; it makes me happy. And they say, we must punish her. Of course, being Nikki Giovanni, it's exotic; so that I'm really relieved of a lot of those hassles. Because people say, well that's really cute. Well, Nikki can get away with it.

VOICE: Pete S.

NIKKI: As long as people can look at your life as a …

VOICE: What are you doing? What are you doing?

NIKKI: … comment on their life, they have a problem with your …

TOM: I've been on vacation, man...

NIKKI: Understand what I mean. If you cry the blues to your friends they're really happy with it. But if you call them up and you say, well I'm pleased today such and such happened—they don't want to hear it.

ME: That's true. I'm discovering that, to my dismay, with friends I've had for years. All of a sudden I can't talk to them. Not that I'm any different, but circumstances change. The same people who were ready to die side-by-side with you in the ol' days of the "revolution" all of a sudden change.

VOICE: What's the photographer's name?

ME: It tickled me—at the press party Friday—talking about the church. The feeling you got from it. I found that surprising. I guess it depends on the realm of one's experience. The way you put it was (*drowned out by ringing telephone*).

VOICE: Charlene? Charlene? Is she there?

ME: I found there was a price tag on the welcome in the church. The Black church in particular. That welcome was extended for an introductory length of time and withdrawn if you didn't have something to offer out of your pocketbook.

NIKKI: I can't comment on your experiences. Only mine, or conglomerate experiences. One of the things I went through at Reverend Cleveland's church Sunday, which is the Cornerstone Institution Baptist Church—I think that's the name of it. One of the things he said in his sermon: "You know what keeps people who want to accept Christ out of Church? The church people. The church people. The Christians are the ones that keep you from joining the church." I think he's right. It goes back to the hypocrisy or phoniness. If they can't accept you—if they can't feel better than you, they—what—I don't know how to explain it—it doesn't bother me. I understand. On that level—I understand people on that level. But it seems like the history of mankind shows everybody needs to feel better than somebody else. It seems to be a weakness. It seems to be something that...

VOICE: ...in a few days...

NIKKI: ...something I don't see the necessity for. It's a useless emotion.

VOICE: ...San Francisco...the *Chronicle*...

NIKKI: I may not be much, but I'm better than whatever. White people say, I may not be much but I'm better than any Black person. Jews say I may not be much, but I'm better than any Christian. Catholics say, well I may be poor but I'm better than (*garbled*)...Black people go through their various stages. Black society has a very structured pecking order....

(*Laughter*)

NIKKI: Whether it's the church, the school, the community—whether it's anything, somebody has got to feel somebody is below them. If you meet an alcoholic, he'll tell you, "but I'm not a wino." If you meet a guy who smokes pot, he'll tell you but he doesn't shoot.

VOICE: Either Jerry K. or Ron...

NIKKI: ... everybody's got to feel like whatever your field is, it's not as low as anybody else. I just happen to find the church, to me, an institution worth working with. I feel they're no better or any worse. I tell them that. For the most part I will stand by my statement. I have gone into many churches, not just as Nikki Giovanni, but as just another woman....

VOICE: When you go to San Francisco you don't want her to do much work up there, right?

VOICE: ... All I want her to do...

NIKKI: (*to them*) All I want to do is major majors.

VOICE: Okay. Well, these two stations I have right here are major stations.

TOM: Can you do the two interviews there?

NIKKI: Can you put it all in one day?

VOICE: One day. You don't have but one day for work and one day for pleasure.

NIKKI: I don't care what you do. One day, and that doesn't mean one day plus three hours of the next.

VOICE: Yeah. Okay. One day. All in one day, man—but don't jam it up, okay?

NIKKI: He can jam it!

VOICE: ... it's in San Francisco.

NIKKI: Just so it's one day.

VOICE: It's the *Chronicle*...can meet us at the hotel...

NIKKI: What I'm saying is, I've never been in a Black church that the initial thrust is not welcome. On the other hand I've never been in a militant meeting that the initial thrust was not, "What the hell are you doing?" And I think once the initial thrust is over they extend themselves and it becomes something else. See what I mean? Everybody's not going to welcome anybody. Everybody didn't welcome Jesus. Everybody don't love Nixon. You have to give them that. There is always somebody who says, I'm glad you came to my church.

VOICE: KPFA. Oh, okay. KPFA. What about the morning... if that's possible—you'd like 7:20—is that right?

ME: On your album there's mention of Fisk University—autobiographical, right? I mean you did go to Fisk?

NIKKI: I went to Fisk.

ME: How do you feel about your son's education?

NIKKI: It's premature to make a determination. I'm a classicist. I happen to believe the classics are very important. I would want Thomas to learn the classics. I would like him to have a classical education, and to have that balanced by the realities of the world, which is to say that if I had my choice—if there are no major changes, I'd like to have Thomas learn Latin and Greek. I would also like him to learn Russian and Chinese in terms of language. I would like for him to read not only...

VOICE: Two, nine, one, four...

NIKKI: ...so-called great poets. There are quite a few of those I think he should read. If you're familiar with Shakespeare? (*jumbled*)...Richard Wright, Langston Hughes, (*jumbled*) so on that level, classical education with Black knowledge. I was that kind of teacher. I think that what is beautiful about being Black is that you can get the best of everything. I think it's important that when we learn science we have to learn not just that Newton discovered a theory of relativity or whatever he discovered—you know what I mean? But that he was a White man and that this theory had been explored—for example I'm interested in the pyramids—the Black men—the highest scientists had to go into that. I would not let Thomas study Egypt as part of the Middle East. I think classical geography—I think that's what you're stuck with—whether the White folks like it or not. I think...

VOICE: What I want to tell you is...

NIKKI: ... of countries. So the people study Africa. I would like him to have the choice I didn't have, which is to study African history. I'm particularly interested in pre-1500. And I think that's something we'll be exploring together because I'm not extremely knowledgeable. I just know basic things like mathematics. There's a reason for calling them (numbers) Arabic. I want him to know they come from the Arabs. I want him to know—and I think it very important that I teach that to him—the first number is zero. It's a small thing. I know that mathematicians who teach math, well, it's not a small thing cause the first number is one. But it's not one. Because the first number is one and you can never go beyond nine. The first number is zero and that represents the sun. The nine planets represent the universe. And as you couple the sun with the planets you get an infinite number of universes. And that's how numbers were made.

VOICE: What's happening with...?

NIKKI: That's the Black system. I look at numbers in the Black way. I want him to learn things like that. There would be arguments, I'm sure, because I get that from educators. I call it classic, and they say no. Gospel is classical music. Jazz, at this point, is classical. All classical music is not just Debussy. We have classical music. When you start to deal with the classics you have to deal with Black classics.

ME: Have you noticed in literature, the total absence—with the exclusion of the last six years or so—of the Black woman? Reading everything I can get my hands on, I began to feel this overwhelming void—this absence of myself. We aren't there, in their words. There were no works like Simone de Beauvoir's *The Second Sex*—(*jumbled*).

(*Laughter*)

ME: I read all 700 odd pages...

NIKKI: Congratulations.

ME: I read it in a relatively short time, because my drive has always been to find that with which I could identify. I couldn't find it in the pages of her book. Joyce Ladner has finally done...

NIKKI: *Tomorrow's Tomorrow?*

ME: Have you read them?

NIKKI: I didn't read Simone de Beauvoir. I started to read Joyce's book. It's not an approach that interests me. That's not a comment—I hope that doesn't get distorted. I know Joyce Ladner and I like her, but I'm not interested in a sociological approach to Black women. I'm interested in an emotional approach...I didn't grow up with Black literature vis-à-vis Black literature....

VOICE: ...oh, we're sitting in a bar, doing an interview...

NIKKI: ...the last couple of years we've been able to (*jumbled*)...

VOICE: 12:30 for lunch. Oh! That's groovy! That's good. We can have lunch here—okay. About four of us will be at the pool...oh, no!!!

NIKKI: ...warm, the emotional approach. I could read Louise Merriweather's *Daddy Was a Numbers Runner*. I can read Toni Morrison 'cause I like an emotional approach.

VOICE: Excuse me. This is Roberta. She says why don't we come over to the pool and finish our business there?

NIKKI: Tell her—ask her what we get if we do?

(*Laughter*)

VOICE: Nikki says what do we get if we go over there? (*to Nikki*) A big kiss.

NIKKI: Oh, for a big kiss...

VOICE: Okay. We'll be over. Bye...

NIKKI: But—what I'm saying—is—you all go on and I'll join you.

VOICE: ...can you imagine!

VOICE: ...un-huh...

NIKKI: This is a question that's difficult because the answer is arrogant. Okay. One, I know Black women. Two, I know what I'm interested in finding out. Okay? So that what I'm interested in most when I'm learning something is the emotional...

(*Laughter from another table drowning out her voice*)

NIKKI: I don't give a shit how many statistics show...

VOICE: Can we get a drink from the bar at the pool?

NIKKI: I couldn't care less. What I do care about is the relationship...

VOICE: Where is the pool?

VOICE: It's on the other side.

NIKKI: I care that that little girl in the (*garbled*) was raped. That her mother could hold her. I care that that gets represented in literature. I don't give a shit how many women have how many babies and how many of them died. It means nothing to me. But it means the world to me that a little ol' lady could write a poem called "Conversation" about—that girl could sit there and talk to the old lady while they rocked and she chewed on her (*garbled*) snuff. That's what I want to read in literature. I find those other things boring, to answer your question. To answer your question about it? Not a goddamned thing! I tried to find a nice way to say it but there's no nice way. It's just boring to me—just boring.

VOICE: An interview...

ME: You're moving a lot. Mobility means money. Are you working full time with your album and NikTom, promoting your books? Is that you whole life? Your whole employment?

NIKKI: Career. It's not quite proper to say employment. It's more proper to say "career." I have a career. I'm trying to build a company, 'cause it's not built yet. People are sweet, people don't think and people don't know. They say, who else are you going to put on your label? They don't realize I don't have any capital.

VOICE: It's a weird country...

NIKKI: I'm being very selfish, but I can hire myself for nothing. I've done it several times because I believe in what I'm doing. I did a concert in Philharmonic Hall because I've always been interested in promotion. I produced it myself because nobody else was interested. I went to a couple of producers, and one person refused to return my call. Another person said it was a foolish idea. The third person said, I'll do it but not at the Hall. I wanted the Philharmonic because it's a beautiful hall and my input into my community has been beauty and has been truth. That means everything that I do and everything that I'm doing should be the best I can do....

VOICE: I'd like you to meet...

> (*Note To Reader: Here I have deleted about what was transcribed as a two-page description of how Nikki set up the concert, got the tickets, sold them and had a successful concert. But at this point, it got boring to me. Boring. I can't help it, but it's just plain boring!*)

NIKKI: (*speaking about the successful way it eventually turned out*) I was very proud. (*Oh–it's not fair to leave out the fact that she stated she wasn't able to make much money, but she did it for the pleasure of doing it and not the bread.*)

VOICE: Excuse me just a second. When Walter comes over, you'll join us by the pool?

NIKKI: I'll join you at the pool. Don't let her get away.

VOICE: She's (*not referring to Walter*) gonna split at one, though.

NIKKI: I'll join you—I'll be there. Are you gonna take this, Tommy?

TOM: (*looking at his Bloody Mary*) No, no—the waiter will bring it over.

NIKKI: No—these books and stuff.

TOM: Judy'll bring it over.

ME: May I be so bold as to ask for an autographed book?

NIKKI: Those are Judy's books.

ME: Oh, okay.

NIKKI: When she comes back you can ask her. They're not mine.

ME: Okay.

NIKKI: People trip out on money. Every time they see your name in the newspaper or see your face on TV, you're rich, you know? Here I am just filthy rich—you have so much money you don't know what to do with yourself. It's difficult to explain, and I don't even know why I continue to fight that battle. You cannot work for money. And I don't think you can work for prestige or fame. I think you can only work for what pleases you. You know?

(*Suppose money and fame please you, I thought.*)

NIKKI: 'Cause there's no guarantee you will get money, prestige or fame. And it would be very sad indeed to have sold your soul and have nothing. If I have nothing, I still have my integrity. If you ask me why I did any number of things—why I produced that show, why I wrote that book, why did I produce that album. I can tell you why. I had an argument with a young man who runs the record company here, because he didn't think I knew what the hell I was doing; and he was mishandling it very badly. And I had a meeting with him and I expressed extreme disappointment with the way it was being handled. And he started to give me some okey-doke. And I started giving him statistics. He said, oh, 'cause they think everybody's creation is a creation of a mixer, the creation of an engineer, creation of echo—you know what I mean?

They think of you as being a record and a product. They don't think of you as being a person who's doing things because you believe in them. I wouldn't mind being rich. It would make me happy. I would like it, as a matter of fact, because I find money makes life a lot easier.

ME: I'm hip.

NIKKI: It does. And very honestly—I'm not righteous like this. I wouldn't sell myself for money. I wouldn't let somebody say, well, it's a lot easier if you have a limousine, so if you do what I want you to, I'll let you have a limousine. 'Cause it would be useless. I don't have an automobile. I have a bicycle. And my son and I get around by bicycle, which is very comfortable indeed in New York. Other times I take a cab. I don't live where I could live. I'm sure I could probably afford a better apartment. I live in public housing. It's a very nice apartment. I would like to have a brownstone someday. I grew up in the Midwest and houses and backyards are very big things and they still mean a lot to me. But I would be foolish to sign a contract for 30 to 40,000 dollars and buy a home and then be unable to control what I do. It would be meaningless, so I wait. I didn't sign a contract with Atlantic Records. I formed a company. So that I didn't make any money and I fired one of my business managers who expressed the fact that it was foolish for me to do it that way. I thought if that's what you think about what I'm doing then obviously I don't need to pay you everyday to hear your voice. So I fired him. He was very upset and we have a lawsuit going right now. He's suing me. He said I fired him improperly. I couldn't see it. I would rather not have any money—which I didn't get—and have a company maybe one day my son's—it would mean something maybe ten years from now—it would mean something if we do get a capital foundation. Then my son can do something. He doesn't have to hire himself out to anybody. He can work for himself and that's what I'm excited about.

ME: You're very adept in handling people who are trying to hustle you.

NIKKI: You fire those you can't handle and get rid of the rest of them. It's no problem. I'm generally pretty honest, but you hear things. I say that to the kids. I have a young readership, the kids are very talented. They're very anxious to be what they think is famous. It's not that they don't want to pay any dues. They don't even understand what dues are. They think all you have to do is be a star. Nobody can make you a star. People can hassle you and prevent you from being fully realized when you think you ought to be. They can never stop you because they are only middlemen, and as long as that talent resides in you, you have the responsibility to yourself and your people to deal with that talent. Once you've made a mistake—my first album—I made it with a brother. It's the last mistake I've made like that. He just decided he'd rather not pay me because he owed me a lot of money and it would be a hassle in his life if he did.

ME: Cold shot.

NIKKI: Very cold. I said, so you realize you've made a slave of me if you don't? He said he just couldn't handle it—"I just can't see paying you that amount of money." That'll never happen to me again. That's why we formed NikTom, 'cause I don't want to have to go around shooting people. And that made me too angry. I didn't want to shoot—it just made me angry. I know that I'm not going to rip off myself. I know that I'm not going to refuse to pay anybody else. I don't haggle with other artists, 'cause I know what they go through. That's why I think integrity is what it's all about.

ME: Okay. One more. Uh—you also mentioned at the press party how you used to go to groups and read poetry and carried two guns; so I just took that to mean, so you went through that "movement" phase.

NIKKI: I used to live in Delaware. Those guns got stolen. I don't think anybody who lived in Delaware didn't have guns. It's frontier.

ME: Frontier?

NIKKI: It's plantation. It's awful—I think, an awful place. I was very comfortable. I thought the best thing for me to do was to move. But—uh—I've never shot anybody. It wasn't on that level. I just didn't want anybody coming into my house.

ME: There was a period of about five years where the movement was strong, with the meetings, poetry readings, that kind of growth period. I wonder how you saw your time in the movement...

(*Waiter arrives*)

ME: Hello, Walter! Fancy meeting you here!

WALTER: Hi! Hello.

VOICE: What—why don't you take Walter over to the pool?

At that point I knew it was time to split, so I clicked off the tape. We talked a minute longer, but I don't remember what was said. In the end, I left feeling a bit dissatisfied. Celebrity interviews are hell. This is the last one I'm gonna do. Later for this shit. Some people may be lucky enough to live a charmed existence. I'm not one of them. Besides, I have my own career. And interviewing "stars" is not part of it.

Later.

Devaluation Blues: Ruminations on Black Families in Crisis

I.

Is as Does

good Black men are scarce as the dodo. in private
the women of my generation complain—
"where are the good men?"

they can't all be winos and junkies
they can't all be priests and hermits
they can't all be mercenaries dying in foreign intrigues
they can't all be Hollywood hustlers
they can't all be happily married
    prison riffraff
    sadists
    men who've chosen men

        —from my poem, *At Liberty*

     ♯

Increasingly, Black females are
being left alone to rear the children.
They, along with the myth of the so-called
"Strong Black female," are crumbling under
this impossible burden. Nonetheless,

the survival-units become dominated
by adult female presence and all of the
children are feminized, males and females alike.

—Cress Welsing, *The Isis Papers*
Third World Press, 1991

≠

Loneliness is skin deep. I try to conceal it, but there is a kind of man who can smell it on me as if it's an odor. He knows that my options are few and that my choices are dictated by circumstances beyond my desires. This kind of man is dangerous because he will use my need against me. Especially when our tentative love relationship begins to sour. Especially since I have children to raise. Especially since my children are not his.

He is a Black man. He is what I want. But he will not give himself to me. He says he cares deeply for me. And I want to believe him. But even in the privacy of our nakedness, during sex, we never seem to be alone. There is always another between us. This other who climbs into bed with us is as old as the Middle Passage. It is neither male nor female, yet both. It speaks in one tongue to me and in another to him. It divides us against one another. It is an idea. A construct of negative images, false assumptions and profound lies. When it talks, we listen.

He refuses to baby-sit even in emergencies. He likes my kids, but they're my kids. He discourages them from calling him daddy. He always avoids answering my phone. He seldom stays overnight and rarely, if ever, brings a change of clothes. We never go anywhere, unless it's to a bar or some place cheap to dance or to a movie. If that. He mainly likes to come over, lay up with me and watch TV. The kids and I spend the holidays alone, which means we spend them with my family.

≠

During the Civil Rights Movement, and during the Black Power struggle of the 60s–70s, the phenomenal strength of Black womanhood, which sustained her oppressed people, was touted in Black history celebrations, political rallies and feminist forums. From Sojourner Truth and Harriet Tubman to Ida B. Wells and Biddy Mason, from Rosa Parks to Barbara Jordan, Black women and their remarkable fortitude, endurance and forbearance were acknowledged as sustenance for an esteem-starved people. The strength, sweetness and beauty of the "black pearl" were lauded in song ("precious little girl, let me put you up where you belong") and in poetry:

> first
> a woman should be a woman
> first,
> if she's anything.
> but if she's *black*, really black
> and a woman
> that's special, that's
> realspecial

> —from *We Walk the Way of the New World*, Don L. Lee
> Broadside Press, 1970

This sixty-ish sentiment is nice, but what exactly does "real-special" mean today when many bright-skinned Black women still find it necessary to emphasize their non-Black lineage, passing for anything but Black, in order to work successfully as dramatic actors as opposed to comic, in television and the movies; when dark-skinned women, and/or women with strong Negroid features find that a nose job, contact lenses, breast implants and artificial hair woven into their real hair makes them more attractive to their White potential employer (and/or lovers)?

The unresolved resonance of Slavery further complicates the already complex nature of relations between the sexes. The act of enslavement has served to humiliate, demean and *dehumanize* all Blacks—male and female alike. Black men were stripped of their ability to protect their women, or psychologically castrated.

The ultimate devaluation of first the Black male and now the Black female has served to weaken both—coercing them to assume the only postures that will allow the entire race to survive. Under intense and artificially generated social pressures, he (with few exceptions) is forced to accept his passive-aggressive socioeconomic status as a son-of-a-bitch; and she is forced to accept her aggressive socioecomonic status as a bitch—those both have been effectively reduced to animal/subhuman level.

The Black male has fought valiantly to save his manhood, constantly under assault, and thence his humanity. Kept out of the power structure, he has managed to make his stand on the only grounds, if shaky, on which he's allowed to stand—sports, entertainment and any entrepreneurial pursuit that's little if any threat to the economic status quo. In his music, from the beginnings of the blues to hiphop and beyond, the Black male has persisted in reshaping his image (I'm a man—spelled M-A-N), if not always profiting by his creativity. The explosive effects that the expression of this repressed manhood has on the dominant culture always show themselves in the form of a new cultural fad. By its very nature, the fad itself (as in bebop, hiphop/rap, each accompanied by the kind of fashions they generate) is little more than irrepressible bluster, posturing and posing.

In her struggle to regain her human dignity, the Black woman has had far less success. Maintaining her self-image as a desirable mate has been a Sisyphean feat. (Even entertainment superstars like Oprah, Whoopi, and Janet haven't been able to escape this cruel reality.) Without her man to "cover her back," the unmarried and the unmarriageable Black female was/is particularly vulnerable to the erratic whims of the White male/White society. Her survival, and the survival of her children, particularly those born out of wedlock—whether the father was Black, White or Other—has been predicated on her ability to either bend or break under these bizarre social circumstances. The kind of strength of character required to overcome this assault on her psyche and her body has led to the development of four distinct defenses:

The first was to declare herself a lady or diva—equal to upper class White women, the Southern Belle, the Mayflower Blue Bloods, the descendants of royalty—and if at all possible—to find her way to the periphery of their society. Otherwise, she created a world of her own in which she and those like her would hold court as queens, princesses and duchesses.

This led her to emulate the White female, adopting any measure no matter how strange (starvation diets, clamping her nose, straight-ironing her hair, lightening her skin), muting and mutating her own natural beauty. Additionally, she learned to mimic accents and manners of speech, cultivating an appetite for a culture that excluded her race. She had to become a fake. (Adopting an African mode of "ladyship" might boost her ego; but, despite the Alex Haley fantasy, many Africans who've immigrated to America look down on Blacks-of-Slave-Origin, regarding us as "akata" or "cotton pickers.")

72

The second defense by the Black woman was to shroud herself in traditional middle class values—to prove herself worthy of respect by engaging in social and civic activities (teaching, nursing, church work), which would elevate her above the common riffraff of her own race as well as "poor white trash."

This posture demanded she distance herself from the majority of Black men since they were circumstantially prevented from attaining "equal station." Unless she was lucky enough to either hold her man with her sensitivity, sexual prowess, *fear* (by use of superstition and cult religious rites), or her intelligent wit, she was destined to find herself in a "shack-up" and of little better marital or moral status than her lower class sistuhs.

The third defense was to declare herself a social equal (frequently the physical equal) to any man, and worthy of respect because it was fully earned without help from anyone. This was not that difficult a choice since slavery had well-prepared her for this workmanlike (warrior) posture. This resulted in social isolation and alienation, frequent and dissatisfying sexual liaisons without necessarily scoring a mate, or having to share a man with one or more women. Attempts to hold her man or substitute for him by having a baby "for him" usually failed either to end his womanizing or to improve her life.

The fourth defense was to further devalue the worth of her already demeaned person, her own body/sexuality/pussy—completing the already-begun process of dehumanization/defeminization. By doing so, she also affected a strange reversal, imbuing the lowly status of whore with a functional dignity above and beyond the romantic notions White males reserve for the concubine.

But it is this fourth posture and last step that has, over the generations, proved the killer—the unwitting self-cheapening of a life which, in the larger society, was already dirt cheap.

II.

Yet the language of family values essentially ignores many racial and economic issues. Before a true discourse/dialogue on "family values" can take place in the broader culture, the issue of human value and the Black subculture must be resolved.

The obvious implication in *Newsweek*'s "A World without Fathers: The Struggle to Save the Black Family," and other media sources, is that the endangered African-American family can solve its own problems independent of the larger society. Yet all evidence testifies grimly to the contrary.

Statistics from the 1990 Census Bureau report reveal that since the 60s the number of children living in poverty has drastically increased. From 1973 to 1993, the total number of poor American children rose by 47%, in spite of the so-called period of "sustained economic growth" which occurred in the 80s. These figures substantiate the argument that the said growth was more dysinformational hype than actuality. The American family unit, as a whole, was being deconstructed by greed. Even the number of White children below the poverty line increased by 53%, with 116% for Latino children (factoring in immigration) and a 27% rise in the ranks of impoverished Black children.

The reasonable assumption is that if the children are poor, the parents are also poor and unable to elevate themselves or their families above the poverty line. The more parents go into poverty, the more children are born into poverty. But when these statistics are presented in the media, no direct correlation is made—as though the children exist independent of the family unit. In the same census report it is estimated that there are now 37 million poor people in the U.S., nearly a fifth of the population. The typical household income for White Americans was over $32,000 in 1992, with $22,000 for Latino families and roughly $18,500 for Blacks. The reasonable deduction is that Blacks remain at the bottom of the U.S. economic chain precisely because we are victimized by a complex social dynamic, fueled by racism, that purposefully intends to keep Blacks from achieving social parity—ever.

According to an August 24th 1993 *Los Angeles Times* article, seventy percent of juveniles who are arrested nationally for criminal offenses are Whites, yet Whites make up only 35% of those in custody. Black juveniles make up only about 25% of those arrested, but 44% of those in custody. Out of every 100,000 White youngsters in the nation, 287 are in custody. But for every 100,000 Black youngsters, 1009 are in custody. FBI statistics show Black juveniles are arrested at double, triple and sometimes five times the rate of their White counterparts. Black juveniles are arrested for a disproportionate number of serious and violent offenses, which carry tougher sentences, but Black juveniles receive stiffer terms for drug offenses, motor vehicle theft and burglary than Whites charged with the same crimes.

The article goes on to give public officials' assessments of the reasons for this increase in Black juvenile arrests: since Black children make up a disproportionate share of the number of children in poverty, they have fewer social options such as recreational facilities, decent schools, community centers and *stable families*.

What happened to their parents—the Baby Boom Generation of Blacks who were forced to back down off their "Black power/Afro-centric" push for self-determination in order to survive a series of economic recessions which began immediately after the war in Vietnam and under which the nation still gropes for recovery? The failure of many Black communities nationwide demonstrates that Blacks remain dependent on "the system." Any belief Black Boomers had that the American Dream could be attained by adhering to traditional American Family Values (a hard honest day's work for honest pay, commitment to wife and children/fidelity, respect for God/The Father, moral/righteous behavior as its own reward, do unto others as you would have others do unto you) was sorely misguided. At the same time these very tenets were being undermined (in the larger culture) in the daily news (the end of the industrial age/high unemployment, the sexual revolution, the rise of the conservative and the religious right, the decline of the humanities in deference to white collar professional money-oriented studies, the obfuscation of race as a critical issue).

Between the eruption of Watts in the Los Angeles of August 1965 and the South Central L.A. uprising in April/May 1992, the operative phrase "Law and Order," popular among politicians, was eased out in favor of "Crime and Violence." Encoded with the latter phrase is the racially-specific on-going assault on the Black male by the two-headed (state and federal) criminal justice system which disproportionately punishes any Afro-American unfortunate enough to come within its purview.

The responsibility for the Black family has fallen squarely on Black women. To evoke stale, romantic images of American tribes in which women are warriors, tend herds, construct housing and rule the marketplace while still managing to raise healthy children does not sufficiently lighten her burden.

Encoded in Dan Quayle's loaded use of the phrase "family values" was the racist implication that morally superior White America sets the standard for the said values in a way similar to that in which the White missionaries brought God to Africa. This, along with Quayle's reference to Murphy Brown giving birth out of TV wedlock, accounts for the popularity of this phrase. But, as numerous African and Afro-American scholars have pointed out, God existed in Africa long before the missionaries arrived. Likewise, Blacks-of-Slave-Origin have family values rooted in a history that precedes American Slavery.

People living under oppression always develop social formations which appear to the surrounding culture to be excessive or pathological.... A people is not destroyed by its history. What destroys a people is physical annihilation or assimilation, not its family life.

—Laura Carper, *Dissent*, 1966

It rarely goes deeper than sex. Which is good but indifferent. There are certain things that he won't do. He'll ask me to go down on him but he won't go down on me. Or he'll go down on me but he won't do it very well. Or we don't do that oral thing at all because his Mama told him that you should never shit in the same pan you cook in. He doesn't need to know my friends. And he'd prefer that I not need my friends. He doesn't want to hear about my job. He'll listen to my problems, if he's not too beat himself or too stoned, but he knows that I'm a big girl and will work through them on my own without his help. The way I'm accustomed/conditioned to doing.

I have to be careful not to put any pressure on him. None at all. He gets skittish under the least bit of weight. If I ask him for help or advice he always knows somebody, but avoids specifics like name and phone number. He doesn't mind spending money on me for entertainment, and gets generous in front of people he wants to impress. But I take care of the food and the bills all by myself. If he cares for my feelings, he might bring the kids a toy or two, if it crosses his mind. But there are no such things as birthdays.

We live in a transitory yet relentless present. There is no discussion of my past and no discussion of our future together. We just are. Day after day. In the cozy jazz of his solar rhythm. Before long he will ease his way out of my life, if he doesn't simply walk out and never come back. He'll find ways to lengthen the time between visits. And before long, there will be someone else beside me. And while he'll be a different man, his pattern will be the same.

Reflections on a Riot—1985

IT TOOK EFFORT to view news coverage devoted to Watts twenty years after the infamous "long hot summer." Had things changed? On the night of August 13th 1985, CBS presented a retrospective which featured Mayor Tom Bradley who fumbled when asked what issues had led to the riots. The ex-cop and ex-councilman suddenly suffered a cloudy memory. I screamed obscenities and turned it off.

"Haven't you heard? They've been rioting three days!" My brother met me on my parents' front lawn.

"What riot? I ain't heard about no riot."

I had walked the long blocks between 88th Place and Broadway to 89th Street and Central. Nothing was happening except starvation. My husband, myself and our firstborn had no food to eat. I walked because we couldn't afford to burn gas in the car unless there was an emergency. Eating did not constitute an emergency, and as previously noted, we didn't qualify for county aid. Women didn't count as head-of-household and my husband was a nonresident.

"You all better hide," my brother warned. "They are attacking _anything_ White."

"Oh."

My husband was White. He'd come west, toting a guitar and wearing bib-overalls, with Jessie Jackson and Stokely Carmichael, three trouble-shooters for the Student Nonviolent Coordinating Committee (SNCC). Stokely left L.A. after a brief visit. My husband met me and stayed. He was a twenty-two-year-old "cracker" as he liked to call himself. As a grassroots organizer, he was upset that L.A. Blacks seemed more interested in socializing than political consciousness. He was an avid supporter of Martin Luther King, an intimate of Jesse Jackson and an original Freedom Rider. Things were not happening to suit him. Not only couldn't he find much trouble to shoot, but he couldn't keep a job, especially once his employers caught sight of me.

In spite of his disappointment, tension in Black L.A. had been building for well over a year. We were aware of the racial violence taking place across the country. And many of us shared an expectation that "civil unrest" was on its way west. We knew about the continual assaults by Whites upon peacefully marching Blacks; Black soldiers who had fought and died for their country were denied burial in all-White Veterans Administration cemeteries. We were less than second-class citizens. Like the American Indian, we were wards of the U.S.

Today we are not quite first-class citizens. Today we have over a hundred Black mayors nationwide. Whites no longer stare at Black hair in its natural state. Our entertainers can cross over if not too negroid. There is Martin Luther King Jr. Hospital and Drew Medical Center. A long-promised shopping center recently opened in the heart of Watts where there is still no major restaurant, no movie theatre (east of the Crenshaw area) and insufficient low-income housing. Black L.A. has the EXACT SAME PROBLEMS it had twenty years ago including gang warfare, police brutality, high unemployment and inadequate health services and *segregated housing.*

Circa 1964 Black awareness in L.A. was spearheaded by support for Proposition 14. It was the big issue of the day. It went down to overwhelming defeat. The majority White electorate sent a resounding message: NO FAIR HOUSING. The inspired anger simmered in the Black community for months and was the primary fuel for growing racial tensions—tensions ignited that August 11th when Marquette Frye was arrested for drunk driving.

Now there was a riot going on. Stores were closing as merchants fled. There were shortages as supplies ceased coming into South Central. Fresh produce, meats, eggs, dairy products, even toilet paper became scarce amid panic buying. Mother gave as much as she could spare then drove me home, fearful of my being on the streets alone.

Within hours the action spread to our neighborhood. The National Guard set up an outpost at 88th Street within full view of our second story bedroom window. All Whites and light-skinned Blacks mistaken for Whites were being forced out of the "cordoned off" area. My husband didn't dare go out in daylight for fear we'd be separated. There was little to do but watch the televised coverage. Frequently we saw the same scene unfold on the streets below as took place on camera.

Looters carried truckloads and armfuls of goodies through the alley to the rear of our building. It was one big crazed party with buildings going off instead of fireworks. Then rumor reached us that a young girl had been killed when a stray bullet penetrated an apartment building just north of our location. That night the baby slept in his tub under our bed, fortified by brick. We were afraid to use the crib.

After dark we visited venturesome neighbors for details on the looting. Most prized were cases of expensive liquor, china, silverware, rugs, drugs, jewelry and guns. Someone had broken into a gun shop and all weapons had been spirited away. Looters would come to the door begging brief respite, a drink and a bite to eat, after which they'd return to the fray. It was rumored that Black militants were flying in from out-of-town to organize. Black leaders began appearing on camera with pleas for a halt to the violence. The rioting reached Crenshaw. Beverly Hills was over the rise. *Burn, baby, burn.*

By August 17th it had burnt itself out: millions lost in property damage and the priceless lives of thirty-four people. Thousands were wounded and injured, hundreds jailed. Black consciousness exploded in Los Angeles.

In a television interview this past August 13th, Marquette Frye was asked if there would be another riot. "There will be!" was his response *after* he hedged. I beg to differ with Mr. Frye. The Black community has been *defused* since Watts erupted. Some of it has "relocated" quietly in search of jobs and housing. And political consciousness is at a significant low, corresponding to all-time highs in gang and drug activities.

No. There will not be a riot soon. Not like that last time.

NOTE

Every year, since 1965, as the anniversary of Watts approached, someone would ask me if "you Blacks" were going to riot. This question usually followed some terrible incident, such as Jonestown or the officer-involved killing of Eulia Love. By the time I wrote this, I was thoroughly sick of hearing the tiresome question. Since the reporter's question to Frye implied that a riot was imminent, or within days, my answer was based on that assumption. I would not call the seven years that transpired before the Rodney King verdict "soon." And, indeed, the riots which followed were quite different, even if the root causes were the same.

No Way Up

NAN'S LETTER CAME that morning and read like suicide. I got on the phone and told her electronic message service I'd be there by noon, uncertain if she'd get word.

Our friendship goes back nearly fifteen years, to our late twenties. We met as co-workers, magazine editors in the semi-sleaze world of cheap men's magazines. Both of us aspired to the dreamy height of literature as famous authors.

Those who knew us puzzled over our friendship. We were such opposites: she was bright, cheery, terminally optimistic. I was hard-boiled, quiet, dismally realistic. A few years my senior, she was a child of the 50s, romance-crazy, nostalgic for the pop-rock stars of the period, impressed by the trappings of entertainment glitz and upper class glamour. I was a child of the 60s, militantly political, cynical about men and history, a denizen of the gritty underbelly of L.A. She had never married and had no children. I had two children and was on my way to marriages two and three. She's White and I'm Black.

Our common ground was gossip, ambition, lust for the power of the printed page. We were both working class poor struggling to make it big.

Leaving the job that had brought us together, we stayed in touch over the years. I entered the pink-collar work force, moon-lighting as a poet and sometime journalist. Nan enjoyed modest success with a coffee-table book on cinema, unsuccessfully pursuing scriptwriting, and continuing work on her magnum opus—an autobiography. While I busied myself with readings and grants-manship, she chased script editors and agents. We were on fairly equal footing in pursuit of our career goals until Nan was confronted by two illnesses: alcoholism and diabetes.

Complicated by the harsh economic realities and social reversals of the 80s, Nan's life took a persistent slide downward. Courageously, she confronted and overcame alcoholism. The diabetes was another matter. Proper diet was unfeasible on her "no budget." She was unable to maintain a job. She was fired from one editorship when her passion for controversy superseded the conservative notions of her publisher. Her last chance as editor of a celebrity-watch magazine was blown when her benefactor died unexpectedly.

Armed with a hundred copies of her resume and indefatigable faith, she contacted every likely publication. The response was nil.

Forced to go back to waitressing, Nan found it demeaning. An occasional diabetic crisis and the threat of coma began to further undermine her shaky status. She sought help, but it was repeatedly denied from one bureaucracy or another. She wasn't crazy enough for institutionalization. Disappointment and depression affected her job performance. She spilled things. She dropped things. She mixed up orders. She was repeatedly fired, one waitress gig after another. She went from working class poor to borderline homeless.

When I arrived that noon, Nan was in a horrible state. She cried hysterically for forty minutes as I consoled her. She had contacted the few friends she had left—none of whom were able to offer the kind of financial assistance she needed, but all doing better than she. I was the only one to respond.

She was holed up in a high-rise hell as run-down as anything I'd ever seen. There was no running water and she was forced to use the jane at the local service station up the street. She had no phone. The place was furnished with the remnants of what she hadn't pawned and stuff she had found in the streets. Her cat was severely flea-bitten and in serious need of attention from a vet.

Her major problem of the moment was her typewriter. Between severe bouts of depression, stress, the poverty and the diabetes, Nan was losing her ability to type. She made constant and repeated errors. Her speed, never above forty words per minute, had fallen to twenty. She tearfully declared she would never finish her autobiography. She'd been feverishly reworking it for months, and was in the midst of further revisions. In order to finish a clean draft, good enough to show an agent, a correcting electric typewriter was vital. Then she showed me the sores on her fingers. Drying her eyes, she told me her unemployment check was unusually late.

I had two twenties in my wallet. I gave her one. Pridefully, she insisted she'd pay it back though I insisted it wasn't a loan. Then I made a promise I wasn't sure I could keep. I suggested she do the best she could with her present machine. I had a little windfall in the works. It wouldn't be much, but maybe I could *loan* her a couple hundred to get a correcting typewriter. While my halo was glowing, my stomach began to churn. I was a long way from affording my generous offer. I still hadn't achieved the lofty literary life I fantasized about.

Nevertheless, Nan visibly perked up, and slowly, her old cheeriness began to shine through. She thanked me and offered some instant coffee which I accepted. Then she gave me a few freshly revised pages of her script to look over. In no time, we were chatting away again, jawing about editing, The Business, and our still-promising futures. We sounded like the dynamic young women of the naive old days, when we were in our late twenties, eager to blow the socks off the writing world.

NOTE

Nan would never make it as a writer. The 90s would bring the rejection of several manuscripts and scripts as well as continual firings from waitress gigs. One night in October of 1993, Nan slipped into a diabetic coma, collapsed and died.

Sweet Susannah, Strange Susannah

there it was
the night blood clotting the moon
and the evening wasps were swarming
as if indifferent to our pleasure

and some sunk and some swam
and even song is this
prayer is just what you make it
or make out or in of it
o my god
i can see the still moon in memory
and know there are places where stars are forgotten
but i shall never forget that
i have been happy
one time

—Susannah

Susannah Foster was one of the most incredible White girls I've ever known. I introduced her as that to my other friends: "When she's out of the fog, *man* is she sharp!" She spent her last days in the intensive care unit at Hollywood Presbyterian Medical Center. She was there a little over three weeks.

Susannah knew (loved) Donovan in London.

Susannah was one of Warhol's Chelsea Girls.

Susannah always laid claim that the legendary Josh White, the black folk guitarist, had been her "play" step-dad.

Susannah met Coltrane one snowy night on a sidewalk in New York and was able to confess her fanhood. She glowed whenever she told this story.

Susannah didn't like being called White. She said she was Rom (gypsy). She wrote music and played the guitar. She was a romantic, into jazz, R & B and rock & roll. She spoke French and Esperanto. Susannah's voice was wry, sharp and mid-range soprano. She spoke with a jazz lilt. Susannah didn't make five feet. She didn't weigh 80 pounds. I've seen, as I've too often said, healthier looking 80-year-old women.

Susannah had brilliant carrot-red hair. Goo-gobs of it. This past year it had thinned to malnourished lifeless wisps. She had cut it and it began falling out.

Allen Ginsberg personally let Susannah into his 1982 January 15th standing-room-only L.A. poetry reading at the First Unitarian Church. She had done a reading with him years ago in Europe. He remembered her. "Crazy Suzie" wasn't easy to forget.

She spent one "fantastic" night with poet Jack Hirschman.

She had once written letters to poet/novelist Charles Bukowski.

Susannah was a street mime.

On March 13th, the Saturday night before she went into the hospital, Susannah did a reading with John Thomas, Mike Roth and a couple of other local poets at the Echo Park Methodist Church off Alvarado and Sunset. She had organized this reading herself. A little over two years ago, Tim, the director there, started a coffee house series called The Basement that featured musicians and poets. When Susannah sang you could hear that her voice used to have something, but the something was squelched by a throaty rasp that worked well when she read her poems aloud. At the reading that night there weren't many people. Susannah was good but weaved as though stoned. We couldn't tell if it was dope, booze, illness or a combine of the three. She'd had pneumonia six times in the past two years, a statistic she liked to quote as an explanation for her "condition."

Susannah liked to announce herself as an ex-junkie and/or ex-hooker depending on how much propriety she determined needed offending.

She had been a "rock star," then a groupie. Susannah Campbell was her stage name. She had spent time with Mick and the Stones and Lennon and the Beatles in London. I didn't know who was talking, the booze, the codeine or Susannah. I usually deferred to Susannah because she seemed to value my friendship so much. And I couldn't believe that the hippest White woman I had ever met was always a "spinner-of-tales."

Susannah voluntarily ran a welfare hotline for years, advising recipients about their rights and how to establish a case, etc. She had taken a hard fall from the heights of rock & roll and had ended up on AFDC (Aid to Families with Dependent Children) in order to support her daughter, Bella.

The first night I called the hospital, March 15th, the charge nurse asked why no one had called about Susannah. Didn't she have any family? She was listed as Susannah Campbell, and few of us knew her as that. I told the RN I was a friend and that she had no family here in Los Angeles that I was aware of. On that first visit, my man Austin and I met Michael, Susannah's roomie, in the lobby. Susannah's neighbor-friend, Maya, was with him. She carried flowers. They donned masks and went in first. We waited. She could only receive two visitors at a time. She was sedated. She had been too hard to handle, pulling out tubes and being obnoxious in general. She didn't seem to realize how sick she was. Austin and I started to go in, but I saw her through the glass door. What I saw was enough. "Susannah's bought it," I said later when I talked to others.

Michael was in a dither and didn't know what to do. I copied some numbers from Susannah's phone book, trying to figure out who was important and who wasn't, recalling friends and relations and what she had confided about them. That night I started making calls west coast and east. By the end of the week the hospital was complaining. They were being deluged by calls for Susannah. Just how many brothers, sisters and cousins did this woman have?

The first time I saw Susannah was in one of the lobbies of the big pink Beverly Hills Hotel. I spied this thin, tipsy little red-head making her way across one of the lobbies outside the banquet room, drink in hand. The drinks were free. Assessing her with my graphic eye, I could see remnants of what had once been devastating, classic Erin beauty. She stood out, strikingly clad 60s fashion, in a black dress and black Mother Hubbard hat revealing a fringe of carrot-red hair. She toted a big, black carpet bag. I knew my photographer brother, George, was always looking for models. I thought she would make a marvelous subject. We ended up juxtaposed on two love seats. I approached her, "Have you ever been a model?" She slurred, "No, I ain't no fuckin' model." I got real hot and decided I didn't need this bitch in my life, nor did George. I shined her on.

We were there for a fund-raiser; Women's Equal Rights Legal Defense and Education Fund (WERLDEF), Gloria Allred's new alternative to NOW. My friend, Kika, one of WERLDEF's founding board members, was responsible for my being there. During the evening she kept telling me that I *had* to meet Susannah. Kika was full of praise and stories about Susannah's political acuity.

Kika Warfield was a VISTA worker in the mid 70s and had met Susannah at a NOW meeting in 1977. Kika headed the NOW Committee for Women on Welfare (WOW). The committee represented 400 Western-area women. One time Susannah figured out how to prepare enough spaghetti to feed a thousand professional women at a University of Southern California benefit for NOW. She was the only one in the group who knew how to fix meatless spaghetti so that it tasted like it had meat. On another occasion, in Fall 1978, and even though she was afraid of flying, she consented to be flown to Washington D.C., where she testified before a Senate committee hearing on welfare rights. She had not wanted to go, but the committee had specifically requested a *White* welfare mother. She had lunch with Strom Thurmond after an articulate "blowing" of Senate minds.

Susannah was adamant about her activities as a welfare mother and called herself that proudly. She had lobbied for free bus passes from the RTD for welfare mothers and adequate public child care so that women could opt to work their ways off the rolls. In November of 1978, Gloria Allred left NOW to form WERLDEF. Many women, dissatisfied with the treatment accorded minority women and poor women by the NOW hierarchy— Kika and her WOW group including Susannah among them— made the split along with Allred.

Finally, she and I were introduced. It was the red-headed little bitch from the lobby. She came on like we were meeting for the first time. Maybe she was so drunk she didn't recognize me as the same Black woman from earlier. I concluded I didn't want to know Susannah. Later in the evening we watched as Susannah staggered from table to table dumping salt shakers, silverware and uneaten chicken into her carpet bag. "These people are so wasteful!" she complained over and over.

She was driven to the hospital Sunday morning March 14th by her roomie, Michael. Her AA friend Mardy said Susannah was popping codeine right out of her purse those first couple of nights in the hospital. "Yeah," Kika said, "her purse was her drug store."

♯

it was nonexistent as a lantern dusty
with unuse. or the dress i never wore because
it outdid my face
and the lovers i never had
because they outdid my heart.

but it was predictable

when i woke this morning
this morning
the moon and the sun
were sharing the same sky

—Susannah

She and I had poverty, bad men, bad experience with success (she as an actress and rock star and me as a TV scriptwriter), poetry and politics in common. We were also both born on the 13th day of our respective months.

Susannah used to say she was a witch. She practiced "white" (good) magic.

Susannah was always giving when she had so little to give. She gave my oldest son her lovely folk guitar. Susannah knitted a cap for my youngest son. It is blue with an interweaving of reds and yellows and a tassel on top. It embarrassed me to take the few pieces of garish (I thought ugly) jewelry she foisted upon me. I took them anyhow with mumbled you-shouldn't-haves and buried them quietly in a dresser drawer. She once gave me a "magic ring." It would bring the wearer success. I was going to pass it on. I wore it. I made the cover of the *L.A. Weekly* in the company of Gloria Allred, and then the ring cracked and broke, so I was never able to pass it on.

Susannah lived in a small California bungalow, one of three

on a lot, in Echo Park off Berkeley and Colorado. She rented the little one bedroom house for the incredibly low sum of $150 a month. Stepping into Susannah's crib was like stepping into a 1967 San Francisco crash pad, the Summer of Love. There was the ever-present ambiance of burning incense, scented painted candles and beaded drapes. When coming through the door, the first things you saw were Susannah's books. Four levels of improvised book shelves occupied a third of the west wall of her front room. A battered old stereo with two speakers, one at each end of the shelves, was nestled between clumps of books on the lower shelf. Underneath the books was her massive collection of choice folk, jazz, rhythm and blues, and rock LPs, featuring Coltrane, Holiday, Parker, Miles Davis, The Beatles, The Stones, etc.

Beyond the door to the kitchen, bathroom and bedroom, on the northwest wall, was a table where her TV sat. Crammed underneath the table was a used green file box that her neighbor Norman had given her. Next to this was a closet in which she kept her clothes, scrapbooks and guitar. Next to that, on the north wall, was a high corner-bed that fronted as a couch. It was covered with multi-patterned quilts and lush pillows. Above that, on the wall next to the closet, was a beautiful old oakwood looking-glass with a crescent moon cut into its crown. In the southeast of the front room hung her assorted hats on a rack and beneath that, a wooden bench. The south wall was occupied by a mock fireplace that, in recent years, had been turned into an electric heater. Above it was the mantel where she kept assorted figurines, kerosene lamps, candlestick holders, unopened letters to be returned to sender, matchbooks, etc., all atop lace doilies. Against the wall adjacent to the mantel and between it and the bookcase was an armless old chair with its bottom falling out. It looked like a precarious sit but was very secure. Underneath it, hidden from view by torn upholstery, was an old black clarinet case. Inside this, Susannah kept her sheet music and songs.

Her special part of her main room, however, was the northeast corner. This was where she did her writing. She had situated several heavy boxes and a couple of old trunks so that they were neatly stacked next to a small stand against the east wall, right next to the corner-bed, creating a nook. There was a huge round table with two chairs making up the third aspect of the nook, with the opening just wide enough for someone small as Susannah to slip into the cranny, sit and work comfortably, everything within reach. The boxes, the stand and the trunks housed her poetry, notebooks, drawing pads, etc. and a small desk lamp. On the high round table was her Smith-Corona, a lamp, pencils in holders, paper clips and other writer's paraphernalia, ashtrays, letters and bills.

On the walls, in this room as well as in the brief passageway leading into the kitchen, there were photos and paintings. Most of the paintings were done either by herself, her grandmother or Bella. Her grandmother had actually been a New England artist of local note, Elena Campbell French. On the wall above her work table, Susannah intermittently scrawled the names and phone numbers of friends in black ink. On the remaining wall space between the curtained, shaded windows, she taped up notes to herself, lists of places of interest, notices of local events and photos.

Susannah had a lot of stuff in this 9 x 12 rectangle. There were two red and blue mock oriental rugs covering much of the hardwood floor. Mid-room there was a small, low mahogany oriental-like table covered with a crocheted mat dotted with sculptures and ashtrays and not much else. She usually sat at it when preparing samples of her "stash" for "get-high," or meals for friends. Susannah loved showing off her culinary artistry. A gourmet cook, she'd feed you until you were stuffed but rarely, if ever, ate a bite herself.

Beyond the front room was a tiny bathroom with an unshuttable door, and a tiny alcove containing a built-in breakfront where she kept her art supplies and assorted other items including loads of baskets. One of her favorite places to shop on "the other end of Sunset" was Creative Handweavers, and evidence of their industry was all over the place. Bella's room was the single bedroom in the back next to the kitchen. Capping off the '60s feel of Susannah's place was her large, mainly red, rainbow-colored cat, China. The overall effect was one of a well-ordered, slightly funky Bohemian doll's house with a prevailing atmosphere of warm welcome.

One of the best times I had with Susannah: me and Kika at her crib, sippin' beer and "rappin' that rap," Susannah flush from her return from New York. She'd been shoplifting in Neiman-Marcus, she said, and among the spoils was a little lovely jar of black caviar. She offered it. I didn't want any. Fish eggs—yeccch! The things White people eat! The few times I'd had caviar,

including a caviar pie, I found it gruesomely greenish and taste-
less. Susannah insisted. With bread and crackers. Twenty minutes
later, I was eating the spilled little black things out of the rug after
having consumed the major portion of the jar, to her delight. I
didn't know what good caviar was about—tiny, very black and
damned out-of-sight washed down with cold beer.

don't let me lie down till i die
no more noise to the moon
forgive me if you can
settle this impatience
yes. settle it
and leave me still to lay eggs
and other artifacts

behind me
once in a while
i see shadows
coughing out their perturbed infinity

and once in a while
i see stars
and it's not from a sum of blows
no. it's not from a sum of blows....

—Susannah

On the morning of March 22nd I got a telephone call.
Susannah was asking for me. But by the time I got there, she
couldn't talk. She was awake and sitting up in the hospital bed.
The white tentacles of the respirator were bandaged to her arms.
She had been on the respirator eight days. There was no improve-
ment in her breathing. I told her about the goings down. Her
mother-in-law taking Bella for care, maintaining her pad, notifying
all concerned. I put yes and no questions to her. She couldn't
write. The RN held a pad before her and gave her a pencil. She
seemed strong enough and held it. But what she wrote was totally
incomprehensible. Graphic swirls. Except for one word, "my."
I made Susannah laugh by telling her about the time I bit
the doctor when I was in the hospital. I didn't tell her I was a kid

at the time, so the image was funnier. Both she and the admonishing RN laughed, Susannah in spite of her tubes. And I told her it was the first time that I had pneumonia. But it wasn't. I had encephalitis. My necessary distortions came without premeditation.

My last goodbye to Susannah was a little kiss on the forehead that same visit. Me and Austin went downstairs to the car. He cried, "I don't want Susannah to die." I didn't either. But I'm more pragmatic about things than he is.

They did a brain scan. There was talk about damage. A toxicity transferred to her brain via the blood. Hard liquor, drugs, self-abuse. What the years have done. What this woman has done to herself. What being on welfare does to self-image. Diagnosis: pneumonia, endocarditis, abscess of the lung, meningitis, shortness-of-breath. When the doctor called me, he said that even if Susannah survives all of these illnesses there will be crippling damage. *But there is hope.*

On that same evening, within four hours of our visit, Susannah slipped into a coma.

Four days later. In my dream that morning I saw Susannah rise from a hospital bed and smile at me. One eye was blue and one eye green. She winked at me with a big smile. She looked healthier and her hair had grown out a foot and a half and was fanned out from her head in wavy shocks of carrot-red. "Boy, Susannah," I said as I gave her a hug, "I'm glad you made it!" The dream image burst and altered into something else. When I woke, I was filled with remembrances—when I was 18 and the world full of peace-love possibilities.

Susannah suffered what's known as 60s damage.

if you are somewhat of a celebrity
don't be too surprised.
i am a long term casualty of my generation.
incapable of decision among other things.
people now like to observe my nocturnal habits
especially the ones who are now teachers and lawyers and
never see me after seven p.m.
we came from the gutters and the hills in which we trusted
no formalities were defined.

—Susannah

She seemed frail, hapless, a victim of massive on-going culture shock. Machines alienated her totally. As much as she hated to fly, Susannah hated to drive. She was afraid of cars. She walked or took the bus. Susannah had been mugged and raped on a couple of occasions. At one point she became so paranoid she would not leave her house. She alluded to this period often although she never went into much detail. The horror she expressed over her trauma, and her significant silence, seemed to answer all possible questions.

Occasionally I am haunted by Susannah's tale told over lunch and drinks at La Villa Taxco in August of '81. She described the overdose death of a man she'd loved. She had tried to save him but couldn't. I don't know if this was truth or metaphor.

One day Susannah showed me photos of herself when she was ten years younger. There was a young man in some of them. He was blond and as beautiful as Susannah. They looked like the Anglo version of the perfect couple. She refused to tell me his name or anything about him. Her husband, Gray, was Caucasian "dark," someone later told me. He and Susannah were married September 19th, 1973, in Las Vegas and drove to Los Angeles for the honeymoon and to further their musical careers. Gray played the trumpet. He left her shortly after Bella was born, two years into their marriage.

Susannah still kept the crushed roses from her bridal bouquet among the wedding announcements. In eight years of separation they had never divorced. Susannah always spoke of him vaguely. Gray lives in another state with a Black woman, a former friend. The betrayal upset Susannah very much. She showed me a letter she received from Gray's new woman and asked my opinion. She thought it was strange. I agreed. It was strange. But then, much of what surrounded Susannah seemed tragic and strange.

Of English and Scottish ancestry, Susannah was her mother's only child. She had a younger half-sister and half-brother by her father, who divorced her mother and remarried. Susannah got along well with her step-family and loved them deeply, I am told. Susannah's mother was a polio victim. Susannah used to say her mother was "the *real* poet in the family," having been published and fairly well known. On my last visit to Susannah, while she was still conscious, I sent her a message from her mother: "You're the real poet in the family." Susannah smiled.

Susannah's parents were both chronically ill and unable to

travel. Her other kinfolk couldn't or wouldn't make the trip from back east. Who was gonna see to her business? Her friends quickly rallied. We all made plans to maintain Susannah's household and look after Bella, her daughter, in case her story had a happy ending. And we began to learn more and more about Susannah, seeing her through each other's eyes.

Susannah had desperately wanted to be involved in *any* part of show-biz and jumped at any opportunity. As an official witch with the title of Witch of the Wicca, she had participated in an occult theater group, Z Budapest, in 1978. But even the creative coven could not tolerate Susannah's alcoholism and she was ousted from the play production. A friend told me that Susannah was devastated by this action as she had always wanted to be an actress. At age 19 she had attended the Academy of Dramatic Arts in New York. She dropped out and went to Europe for two years.

when i was young i went to France
and it was like a christmas tree
can you imagine a whole country with colored lights?
or that's the way it seemed to me.
i got lost on the metro and wept for thirty seconds
and was saved in a language i couldn't yet understand
and the stops said etienne marcel
which was for etienne de croux and marcel marceau
and i was a mime and knew i wouldn't lose my
innocence
and there was a chestnut creme and pommes frites
and buckets of the most wonderful rain
and people singing on the rue de la huchette
and the best cake
and the best scrambled eggs in the world at the cafe tournon
at three a.m. when poems came as easily as eggs
and love was round each corner
no waiting.
i did not lose my innocence.

—Susannah

She first came to California at age 21 in 1965 and returned in 1973. Susannah was a floater and in the intervening years traveled widely, living briefly in San Francisco, in New York's Greenwich Village and in Chelsea at the infamous Chelsea Hotel.

Kika told me that Susannah did attempt a career as a professional model. The man in the photos I romanticized over was a gay model who had been picked by the modeling agency to pose with Susannah. The agency felt that they made the "perfect American couple."

Susannah couldn't cut it flatbackin'. Susannah couldn't score big as a booster (thief). But as a junkie she succeeded royally and as an alcoholic she was top of the heap. Her friends Betty, Kika and Monica had tried their best to save Susannah. They confronted her about her alcoholism at a WOW meeting in late 1978. Susannah was shaken, upset and angered. The experience caused a rift between Susannah and Kika. Monica washed her hands of Susannah in late 1980. She couldn't bear witnessing Susannah's destruction.

ten years ago there were investigations
i held the simple needle to my arm
without question
i savored the quick pain
wished i had married a doctor
so much simpler than eavesdropping on time
and taking shady turns with the street
always looking over my shoulder
but stoned to the bone
that's what i was

i held the needle to my lips
and then watched the sweaty blood appear
i noticed not the strike of flesh and metal
merely waited for relief.

i have my souvenirs
three needles in a silver box
i named them the way i used to name trees

—Susannah

While stardom eluded her, Susannah was exceptional as a poet. She claimed she had published a small book back in the 60s. She had never pursued poetry, but still wrote. She had refused to show me her work at first. I coaxed her, and finally she did. I raved over it and encouraged her to start doing readings, send the stuff out and try to get published. She took my advice, although slowly. A group of poets called The Poets Gathering run by "the twins," Tani and Dran Guthrie, met at The Basement one Saturday night a month for poetry readings. Susannah got involved with them and later won their 1979 and 1980 Jucumba Springs writing retreat poetry contests. She took a poetry class in Spring '80 with author Sam Eisenstein at Los Angeles City College and ended up editing *The Citadel*, the campus literary magazine, for one issue. On December 19, 1981, she appeared on "The Poetry Connexion" on KPFK, a program co-hosted by Austin Straus and myself. She read from her work and talked a blue streak. Her man Stu sat silently supportive in the studio with us.

I convinced Susannah to send her work to a small press in Santa Cruz. She did, and three poems were accepted and published in February of '82 by Stephen Kessler in his *Alcatraz 2* anthology. It featured poems by Charles Bukowski, Fernando Alegria, Nellie Wong, Cesare Pavese, Julio Cortazar, myself and a number of other heavyweight subculture bards. I also suggested she get a book manuscript together and send it to Kessler at Alcatraz Press. She was working on the book up until the day of The Basement reading.

you had your chance lazy doll
you've lived with some pretty messy instincts
you drank wine until you were full
but still not drunk enough to forget the distances.
you saw too much.

you had your chance mirror child
to lash and even lurk about
you hid and watched them with unreason
you faltered at the first dance
your dress was tight
and snow was falling on your hair

you had your chance
and broke your promise to it
you began in passion and ended in hunger.

—Susannah

My hands were hot and palms unusually red for days after my visit with Susannah. I couldn't figure out why. And on the morning of March 29th, it occurred to me that Susannah might end up like Karen Ann Quinlan. The moon must have been coming down on me. I became increasingly edgy, uptight and hard to get along with, yelling at the kids and arguing with Austin. It had to be all the mess over Susannah, the phone ringing steadily day and night, the concerned and sometimes teary inquiries of friends.

Susannah, I am alternately angered and hurt by your sorry state of affairs. You've gotten next to me. I didn't think you'd bother me so. Maybe it's because you're the first in what I regard as my peer group to pass away. Maybe it's because when old people die, one feels it's a part of a natural rhythm; but when someone young dies, any possible potential they had remains unfulfilled. If the good die young, Susannah, I want to go ancient, evil and ugly, and in my sleep.

Susannah was clean as far as booze was concerned four days before going to Hollywood Presbyterian. She'd found some AA buddies, Mardy and her husband. And her heroin habit, I was told, had died when her connection was busted. And after "cleaning up" eight years ago behind her pregnancy with Bella, she was not so bad, until lately. Rumor had it that she was *chippin'* (going back on H bit by bit). Her decline was quite marked even in the few years I had known her, but her physical slide hadn't really started to pick up momentum until those last six months. Until Shirley died. Until she broke up with Stu.

Shirley was Susannah's neighbor and most-times baby-sitter, a slight, dark brown-haired woman in her mid-40s. She and Susannah played poker a lot for extremely low stakes, if any. Shirley usually won. She had a daughter 16 and was alone—that is, without a lover. According to Susannah, Shirley was prejudiced and totally uncool. By exposing Shirley to her friends, especially Kika and myself, Susannah had managed to quick-cure Shirley of her racism, unhipness and political narrowness.

Poetry was also a whole new world to Shirley. She had

discovered it through Susannah. I last saw Shirley in late February 1981, a year before her death. Susannah called me around 9 o'clock one night in a panic. She'd talked Shirley into trying marijuana. Shirley drank hard liquor but wasn't into smoke. Susannah suggested Shirley try it to help her appetite. Shirley couldn't eat. Cervical cancer. She was wasting—sunken cheeks, the pallor, the bones beginning to show through skin. Shirley was in so much pain she'd try anything. Susannah didn't have any smoke and neither she nor Shirley had the bucks to lay out on a lid. Cancer did not inspire credit among the local dope dealers. I happened to have a generous stash on hand, so I rolled up several Js of the high-powered sans and took it over to her. At Susannah's Shirley looked a lot worse. She palmed the Js and asked how much. I said gratis. She gave me a deep sincere thanks and went home to bed. Later, Susannah called to tell me the smoke helped. Shirley's appetite immediately improved and, in general, she bore the pain better.

During Shirley's dying and shortly after her death, I heard a lot from Susannah. Susannah said that when Shirley's eyes began to hurt they knew her time was near. Close to her time, Susannah was banned from seeing Shirley by the family. Shirley was too weak to protest. Frantic, Susannah called me almost daily. She received reports that the dying woman was asking for her. Still, Susannah was forbidden a visit. After Shirley died, Susannah received guilt-laden hasty apologies from the family. They requested Susannah write a eulogy for the funeral. She did. And got totally ripped after the service. When I saw Susannah two weeks later, she was physically more shot than I'd ever seen her. She'd put a lot of herself into seeing Shirley pass.

After Shirley's death, Bella had nightmares about Susannah dying. She begged Susannah, "Mommy, please don't die." Of course, Susannah answered that she wasn't going to die. Bella, Susannah's beautiful seven-year-old daughter, is with her grandparents in La Mirada. She was Susannah's heart.

This unsigned poem was found among Bella's birth announcements and is dated 1/28/75. It is not written in Susannah's hand:

AMBIVALENCE

How can I bear this stricture—
my body translated once again
Into my daughter's child?
How can I stand this male assault
Upon her small blond bones
Into my own white ones?
Can I endure
the pain faced by her?
Why am I wild
with hate for the child
I long to be—
extension of me?
Who am I to grandmother or
To utterly adore
the not yet born?
This child will be
more than the heart of me
It will be the cracking
of my very loin—
Too old for such pain
Too wondrous glad
for this new use!

On Tuesday, March 30th, Susannah's mama called me long distance. She said she had talked to another doctor on the case. Poor "Suzandie," brain stem all messed up. She was an erratic, wonderfully explosive young thing. *There is no hope.* They expect she'll die soon and the tubes will be disconnected. Loved dearly. Dearly loved. The mind that created all that beautiful poetry is gone.

I got a chill. I got a glass of wine, put on soft, mellow jazz and R&B. My head spun. Code blue. I refused to cry. For whatever reasons, I had never had to explain being Black to Susannah. Whites I've met with that kind of understanding I'm able to count on two fingers. *Susannah, do you know how rare friends like you are?*

Barely ten minutes later Stu calls. Haven't I heard? Susannah has come out of her coma. I go hot and cold, flashing both hope and doubt at the same time. He's been talking to her.

Of course, she can't talk. But he's communicated. She can move. She's detached from her body. But she can *move*. The right eye open and shut. Open and shut. She raised her right arm. Of course, she's still in intensive care. She's still in danger. She's still…

They won't allow Stu to stay as long as he's stayed with Susannah before, for hours at a time. They've cut it down to minutes. He told them he was her husband but they found out otherwise. He's glad for whatever time. Any time. He tells her about things. He plays her tapes. Tapes from Bella. Music. He tells her over and over that he loves her. They are back together again.

Dear Stu, they say she'll be a vegetable. Will you take care of her if? Will you love her if? Dear Stu…

But I can't say it. And I tell him to keep me posted. It has been impossible for me to visit the hospital every day and I call every other morning or evening. It's time, I decide, for me to go to the hospital and see what's going on myself.

Stu had been in and out of Susannah's life periodically. She had known Ron Burkholder and Stu was one of his best running buddies. One of Susannah's last published poems, *a sacred treason*, expressed her horror over Burkholder's alleged PCP-related death at the hands of the Los Angeles police on August 4th 1977:

> and he says
> forgive me
> for they know not what they do
> and i say damn them all
> for what they have done to you
> and i research their pistols
> find blanks in one of the murderer's
> hidden all this time
> and i found the fireworks
> as unpleasant as visiting the morgue
> but i found you cold
> and left you there
> i did not tell them you had a good
> excuse for dying.
> the helicopters circle
> they are trying to catch me now
> somehow they discovered my meat
> my sacred scarcity
> and they eagle in…

i am not long for this foolish chase.
let me climb the lamppost
and smile while they kill me.

—Susannah

I met Stu one night in late Fall 1980 when Kika and I had fallen by Susannah's. Falling by Susannah's was getting to be a pleasurable pastime for me, as it was for most people who knew her. People were always trippin' through. Kika had been Susannah's roomie for a while, between apartments, and was planning to bunk there that night. Stu came in while we were talking and laughing. He had a bunch of monster smoke and white lightning. Kika and I got royally ripped, and then we both discreetly and somewhat drunkenly retired to my place, seeing how Susannah and Stu were radiating some heavy love vibes. She was blossoming in their relationship, but like those things are apt to do, it went sour. The reasons? I don't and probably will never know. Susannah claimed she couldn't write with him hanging around. I was willing to accept her explanations if she wanted to make them. But when she came to a party I gave in February, I could see death all over her. Whatever Stu had been, he'd been life for her. And my eyes saw that.

A typed, faded, unsigned note found among Susannah's old letters:

For Susannah

I hate you I am angry and because
I love you so I am waiting for
you to return so I can tell you
(your understanding is so beautiful)
this is a strange kind of pain
I wonder if you'll have the same
kind soon
You may tell me all about it
because I understand
we are such quixotic victims
of our own likenesses.

The note is torn in two.

Wednesday morning, March 31st. At the hospital Susannah was smaller and paler. Her skin was gossamer, the veins and arteries blue and red canals etched along her limbs. She seemed in peaceful deep sleep. The RN was completing an injection as I came up behind them. Stu was standing next to the bed. He looked at her, loving, longing, anxious.

I looked at Susannah. *Ah.* Her hair was brown. In death, Susannah's truths came to light. Her hair had grown out a foot and cast off the henna. Susannah had not come out of her coma. Not ever. All responses were involuntary.

Susannah went into cardiac arrest Saturday night, April 3rd. It took two hours to resuscitate her. I found out about it on Monday morning, April 5th.

Tuesday morning just as I was leaving for work, someone called. Susannah was dead.

Susannah Foster a.k.a. Andrea Campbell Cox expired at 1:45 a.m., April 6th, 1982, seven days shy of her 38th birthday. Services were held the following Saturday, April 10th at the First Unitarian Church. She was cremated and her ashes returned to her family.

Last night, another dream of Susannah.

She is ugly, gnarled, bent, her hair weedlike fire-red thatches, her skin rotting, putrid, her face full of pain and horror. I don't sleep well, thinking about her and all the parallels.

Tonight the moon is full, Susannah. It rose from the east, plum and red tinged. Now the sky is clear and cloudless. Everywhere, stars. When the moon reaches its apex, it becomes a white disk in their midst. It's a perfect night, Susannah. And the moon, Susannah, the moon!

<u>*Revisiting Welfare*</u>

ROUNDING THE CORNER we spot them immediately. At 7:45 in the morning there are dozens of people outside the building. The line is a block long. We look for parking within a reasonable hike. A visit to the County Department of Social Services was horror enough in the old days. Things were supposed to be better in the 90s.

"What's going on?" I ask my girlfriend.

"Something about fire regulations, I think."

Anger washes over me, accompanied by disgust. My mouth is suddenly dry. We park four blocks up the boulevard and walk back slowly. No reason to hurry. My day full of urgencies is evaporating right before my eyes. I thank the shoe god I've worn flats.

A roach coach is stationed out front. It hawks over-priced hot and cold junk for consumption by the desperate or nondiscriminating. We wade through assorted individuals, to the end of the line which has snaked along the block and twisted around the corner like opening day at the Cinerama Dome. I'm rudely reminded of the lines seen on the 6 o'clock news; hungry, fur-clad, ex-Soviets anxiously waiting their turns, outside in the cold.

Here, the cold part is that these people all have "appointments." (Doesn't that mean you don't have to wait?)

My girlfriend spies a pay phone up the street. "Wait for me, I'll be right back!" She leaves me to hold the fort. I survey the crowd, people of every size and color like some skewed queue-up for a new age Ark. In my day, recipients were mainly us Afro-Americans with a smattering of Latinos.

Today there are Asian-Americans, Jewish-Americans, and more White folk than before. I study the faces. Some have sleep gathered in the corners of unwashed eyes. A couple are blue-bruised and bandaged. Collectively all mouths are down-turned. I spot a homeless man gathering up his belongings from a doorway. Comparatively he looks prosperous.

It doesn't matter if you're sick or disabled, you stand and wait. I wonder if any of these people are dying of some misery other than financial embarrassment? How many have full-blown AIDS? I imagine the outrageous indignity of getting up out of my death bed to zombie down here so I can fight about getting last month's Medi-Cal stickers, cut off because of some bureaucratic clerical glitch.

A horn honk interrupts my reverie and I'm seized by a sudden dread. "Suppose somebody I know sees me standing here?"

The line's turned the corner and I see the front of it. I try hard not to overhear the conversations going on around me through the screams of crying infants. I try to pretend I'm not here. I'm acutely aware of coughers spitting phlegm, of the oppressive odors of overchewed fruity gum and stale cigarette smoke.

Mercifully the women in front of me speak Spanish, so it's easy to tune them out. Behind me, a tall, brown-haired lanky White guy, in a T-shirt and baggy shorts emotes loudly.

"Yeah—like, man it went all the way up there and around," he points. "I showed up at seven in the morning, man. Time I got to the front it was closing. Hadta come back the next day. Ain't that a bitch?"

When my friend returns, I find out that all she has to do is deliver some papers.

"Sounds easy. Why can't you simply drop them off?" I ask.

"I have to take them to window 5. Which means we have to stand in line again. I can't do that unless I can get inside."

"This is ridiculous!" I complain.

"What choice do I have?"

We notice an officious-looking Armenian-American man walking the line, handing out numbers. After several people have left the building, a new batch is filtered through the mag scanner metal detector. A Chinese-American man moves along the line with slates on which names have been scrawled. He pulls the recipients out of line and escorts them inside.

A Mexican-American man also moves along the line. He's expensively dressed, carries a clipboard and a seductive smile. He stops at the two Spanish-speaking ladies in front of us. It doesn't take a translator to figure out he's hustling clients for a school that teaches English to new arrivals. He sees me listening, turns toward me, and asks me what country I'm from *en Español.*

"These colorblind United States of America," I say, bursting into laughter.

California Running

NAME YOUR VEHICLE. The road has its own rhythm. Name your music. The road'll take it in and give it back as your heartbeat. Some call it white line fever or wanderlust. Driving the length of California is exhilarating and fraught with beautifully eerie moments: night suddenly defined by banks of lights glowing on slow-moving rigs; heavy rain on an incline, forcing you to pray through it, and grip the wheel; a full moon hanging on the horizon so long it seems to be rising from the west.

Something about La Costa that tempts me to take the time to do the regular stuff: pose by a giant redwood or the Golden Gate Bridge; forgo a burger stop to lose my head in the clouds at Nepenthe's in Big Sur; gawk at the silk-clad spooks haunting San Simeon, then wind inland to overdose on walnut maple fudge in Solvang. The big challenge is to soar straight through to Malibu, stopping only for refills of gas and java.

Ultimately, direction doesn't matter. What counts is *the ride*: weaving down from Eureka in and out along the 101 and PCH; beelining up Interstate 5, cresting into Bakersfield dead-set on Fresno; zooming past Victorville north along the 15, Vegas-bound; Del Mar-busting, headed south for Baja. I call it the California run. It's in my blood. And I plan to do it as long as I'm do-able. Black lady rebel with a car.

Wasn't it summer '55 when James Dean caught the light where the 466 meets the 41 up near Paso Robles?

Road dangers are legendary, many exacerbated by the ever-present temptation to break the safety barrier. For some of us demons-on-wheels the 55 m.p.h. speed limit merely increased the thrill of outrunning stormy thunderheads at Tejon-Lebec, sky-driving near Big Sur or midnight fog-surfing in Santa Maria. Dead man's curves and flame-engulfed tunnels aside, the baddest danger sometimes lies at the vanishing point of one's thoughts, as it did on one recent trip I made alone.

Headed up-coast to the Santa Cruz Mountains, burning rubber, I averaged an illegal 85 m.p.h. It was smooth cruising news. At confident moments, I dared as much as 110. One eye on the road, one on my wristwatch, I was pleased at my excellent timing. Having left L.A. in the wee a.m., I made San Luis Obispo at sunrise. I figured I could make the whole trip in under six hours. The going was gr-r-r-reat until San Jose.

R&B blasting, I roared up behind two teensy compacts crawling parallel to each other at 50 m.p.h. I slowed and waited a quarter-mile for the bug in the left lane to pull over and join the gnat on the right. It didn't and wouldn't. There was no on-coming highway and a sheer drop on the left. On the right, the shoulder was too soft and too narrow for me to pass.

Furious that my road-rhythm had been broken, I began to anticipate bumpercide. These guys had to be doing this deliberately. They had to know each other. This was probably a stunt they pulled regularly on us poor unsuspecting speeders. Let the California Highway Patrol give chase and bust me by law, but God help anyone else who cramps my driving style.

I moved over and tailgated the car in the right lane for another quarter mile. He wouldn't give an inch. I could hear the drivers' dufus laughter. I decided to make them clean their seats.

I slowed to 40 m.p.h. and fell back a dozen or so car lengths. Then I jammed the accelerator to the floor, revving up to 75. I rammed my 4-door half-ton monster down the middle of the road, charging past the two compacts. They were too small to effectively hog the road, the space between them making a breezy escape route. I laughed all the way into Santa Cruz.

The next day my husband called, upset. He had received something that looked like a ticket. It was from the CHP in San Jose, and addressed to him, since the car is registered in his name. What had I been up to?

"A vehicle registered to you has been observed by a concerned citizen in violation of: 21658 (a) V.C.—UNSAFE LANE CHANGE: Your cooperation in obeying the rules of the road is requested." Signed by a captain commander, it stated that no further action was being taken. Lucky for me.

I try. Seriously. But the roadrunner in me is hard to tame.

On my trip back down the coast, I took the big dare. I ran the 101 straight through to Malibu. The trip was considerably less eventful and my timing was slightly off. But I managed to do it without stopping except for gas, java and, uh, two CHP citations. For speeding. What else?

Parlor Politics

DURING THE 80s economic upswing, I was hired by a private hospital in Hollywood. As a working-class-poor Black primary wage-earner, a Baby Boomer with three children and a landlady to support, I needed the steady paycheck. But after nearly four years, I was stymied by the institutional racism, sexism and cronyism. I was relearning a difficult lesson: my coworkers who most eloquently voiced the going politically correct rhetoric were the first to fail practice of their own gospel. But by the time I decided that I'd had enough, a recession had chilled the climate of artificial prosperity and I was afraid to walk away from basically decent work.

Trapped by the limits of my pink-collar salary, I couldn't afford an attorney and doubted the labor board would take my case. Finally, in late spring of '89, I took my complaints to Betty, the highly recommended employee dispute counselor (hers and all names followed are changed). An African-American by-product of affirmative action, she was proud of her ivy-league education and white-collar position. She was, I was told, extremely sympathetic "to us," meaning women and Blacks. I found Betty pleasant and coolly professional.

Central to my grievance was Etta, our departmental diva, with whom I shared an office. Our jobs, while different, were inextricably yoked by the complexities of medical billing. To be fair, Etta had devoted twenty years to an institution which hadn't always treated her justly. But, having maxed out her bootstraps, Etta wanted all Blacks coming on staff after her, no matter how qualified, to likewise struggle. Fifteen years her junior, I adjusted quickly and worked tirelessly. My swift progress proved an affront and a threat. Blinded by confidence, I ignored warnings that Etta controlled a spy network used to rid the hospital of undesirables. I explained to Etta that I was not after her job or status. She apparently did not believe me. Etta was extremely protective of her popularity with patients and doctors. She orchestrated groundless "confidential complaints" against me across the institution. When those failed, Etta stopped speaking. But the conflict festered and eventually culminated when Stella forced a showdown in our White supervisor's office. Our supervisor seemed indifferent. But when calm reasoning failed to assuage Etta, I launched a stream of epithets that sent my challenger running from the room, palms protecting her ears, slamming the door on my laughter. From that day forward, our office became a tomb filled with the stinking corpse of her rage.

But hers wasn't the only ugly I endured. I found myself iced on a regular basis by the Latinos in reception whose clannishness negatively affected appointment scheduling, staffing hires and employee relations. At that time, an English-only campaign, appetizer to Prop. 187, was being waged in a California predicted to be the first ethnic majority state in the union, predominantly Spanish-speaking. Emboldened, the Chicanos directed their quiet militancy against anyone not Latino. I was spoken to only perfunctorily until they discovered my daughter had a Spanish surname.

Another kind of silence fell between the White female professionals and the support staff, mainly women-of-color. The avowed feminists were always eager to talk sexual harassment, economic disparity and unfair promotions. But activism was rare and overshadowed by covert racism. In the basement Xerox room, White males and ethnic others languished in long lines but White females waltzed in, flipped their hair, and scored upsies. Frequent gatherings in lunch and conference rooms embarrassingly broke down along gender and race lines. The White male professionals sat together as did the White females. Blacks, Latinos and others sat separately together.

In a building complex riddled with numerous corridors, it wasn't unusual for anyone to turn a corner and abruptly become privy to intimate talk while unobserved. One morning, I came up behind my White supervisor and a blonde crony as they trailed my coworker Nola, who walked yards ahead of them, out of earshot.

"Look at those buttocks! Absolutely disgusting," my supervisor tsk-tsked.

"*They* all have derrières like that," the other woman smirked. "No bone. Makes it easy, though, when you have to hot pop 'em in the rump."

Sweet-natured Nola, a 45-year-old built like a teenager, was oblivious to the hostility her unconcealable hourglass figure inspired. A 17-year nursing veteran, her firing followed six months of relentless criticism of "job performance."

Betty raised an eyebrow, apparently revolted by this last vulgar characterization of the atmosphere in which I was smothering.

"Are you all right?" She passed a box of tissues and I blew my nose.

"Yes," I smiled grimly, collecting myself.

Without blinking, Betty succinctly acknowledged my complaints as valid but implacable. "Then," she said flatly, "I think you'd do best to find another position outside this institution."

I left her office, stung and uncertain. Two days later, I again turned a corner, an unseen observer. This time, the two women who laughed and chatted arm-in-arm were Betty and my diva-nemesis, Etta.

✝

Reflecting on my situation, I concluded that any satisfactory resolution of my problem within the institution wasn't going to happen. I had invested nearly five years on the job and was reluctant to abandon the regular paycheck. And I was acutely aware that, should I seek other employment, I'd have to confront yet another politically correct social issue—ageism. Ironically, my approaching maturity could prove as much a barrier as my race and gender, here in Los Angeles, the youth-culture capital.

I had limited means and no savings. Nevertheless, I quit during a staff meeting at which I denounced the institutional isms and the individuals who perpetuated them. Afterwards, I toasted my departure over drinks with two coworkers, Jorge and Ione. Within months the former would die of AIDS, the latter would train for my old position as medical secretary/transcriber and combination billing clerk. Etta, of course, would be promoted to department supervisor.

Unemployment insurance, not enough to cover food and rent, ran out quickly. And no new job was forthcoming. Three years would pass, including the Spring 1992 civil unrest of South Central L.A., before I again earned enough money to raise my family to the poverty line.

Remembering Lee

IT'S 1989. I'M SITTING in Woodland Pattern, a bookstore and cultural center in Milwaukee, talking to my host, thumbing idly through a copy of *Temblor*. He asks me if I know Lee Hickman, the editor. I tell him we used to be very close, but parted company over literary politics. He tells me he's heard Lee's tested HIV positive. I get the chills.

‡

The last time I see Lee is at the screening of French student Sophie Rachmuhl's film *Innerscapes: Portrait of 10 L.A. Poets* at UCLA. We avoid looking at each other and do not speak. The next to the last time I see Lee is at a reading at a Beverly Center bookstore. Lee walks by, I say hello, he snubs me and says nothing.

‡

Lee is the only one of us to be nominated for the *Los Angeles Times* book award in poetry. He doesn't win. I don't know if that matters to him. My former girlfriend has poisoned Lee against me and we're not speaking anymore. I'm disappointed that Lee wasn't decent enough to pick up the phone and jam me himself. Whatever lie it is, I decide to let it stand between us.

‡

There's a new crisis going on in the Middle East with a local upsurge in Arab-Jew hostilities. Someone has spread the false rumor around town that I'm anti-Semitic. Lee calls concerned about one of the poems I've submitted to *Bachy*. It's a poem about self-image and in it I refer to myself as Egyptian. Irritated, he asks if I identify with the Arabs. I don't ask him why he asks because I don't care. I like Lee for Lee. So I give him my context for the poem: I was once mistaken for Egyptian by visitors from the region traveling through L.A. and felt complimented at the time. But do I identify with the Arabs, he persists.

"Well," I said, "Both Arabs and Jews are Semitic peoples. And if you stand between brothers when they're fighting they'll turn on you." This isn't what Lee wants to hear, but I'm not into saying what people want to hear. Stymied, he sighs and hangs up.

I'm standing around waiting for the reading to kick off. Lee strolls over and we exchange warm hellos. Then he asks me how my first book, *Mad Dog Black Lady,* is doing. I tell him I don't know but I've only gotten three reviews so far, pretty much raves, but they were only seen locally. I ask him how the *Great Slave Suite* is doing.

"Most critics hate it but it's gotten thirteen reviews so far—all over the map." He smiles broadly. He knows he's piqued my envy.

Up at Lee's new apartment on Griffith, back in the early 80s, we watch the first documentary video tape of our maturing literary scene—another failed attempt to get any documentation on the new Southern California bards on Public Broadcasting. Before leaving I tell Lee that one day those video tapes, and the poets on them, will be very important. That we're *the* generation. Like Hemingway and Gertrude, like Virginia Woolf and Bloomsbury, like Henry and Anais, Kerouac and Ginsberg. We're a group a movement a happening. I'm not bragging, I'm describing what I believe, the place where I've invested my future. Lee buries his hands deep in his pockets and goes into thoughtful silence as he walks me to my car. The night is clear, the stars twinkle, I can see the observatory from where we stand.

"I've never thought of us quite that way, Wanda."

I'm surprised and not sure I believe him. I'd always assumed Lee had more ego. My laughter fills the street. "Think about it Lee, we're literary L.A., baby."

Lee comes over in the afternoon to interview me for *Bachy*. My husband Steve listens awhile, becomes anxious and then goes for a walk. Me and Lee get high, enjoying our conversation. Every time Lee corners me, I manage to squiggle out of the verbal trap. But sometimes it's awkward. The toughest question Lee asks is about failure. I understand this is one of the significant questions of his acting life. I don't believe that failure is as big a tragedy as Lee thinks.

‡

I've heard it through the grapevine Lee's got everybody worried. He's talking depressed he's talking failure he's talking getting old he's talking anger he's talking it's so hard to be turning forty-five like use a .45 to take yourself out on your 45th. Given my socio-economic stats I think I'll be lucky to live so long. I drive out to see him. There's a birthday cake and wine. He's in the cubbyhole at the back of Papa Bach's. He's uptight looks cornered hasn't slept. My cheeriness is forced and we tiptoe through banalities and chitchat about the next issue of *Bachy*. After the well-wishing runs dry, I wish him many more.

"The older it gets the better it gets," I said, one hand behind my back, fingers crossed.

‡

Lee tells me he's hanging out with this terrific family, the Pillins—William, Polia and son Boris. They're these wonderful potters. Have I seen their work? I haven't. He's excited about the interview he's doing with Bill who's also a poet.

‡

I'm over in Echo Park so I decide to drop in on my girlfriend at her new condo. When I get to the entrance I hear all this commotion, tusslings, gasps and grunts like somebody's fighting right up against the door. Shocked and concerned, I grab the knob and discover it's unlocked. I push the door inward. It opens a couple of inches then stops, causing a startled duet of squawks.

"Who is it?"

"Wanda!"

"Oh, wait a minute! Wait a minute!"

There's more scuffling, scrambling and healthy laughter. She opens the door in a black silk slip, tossing back her red-brown hair, smiling so hard her face is breaking.

"We were so hot we couldn't wait long enough to get to the bed upstairs," she explains.

I look around and there's Hickthang, barefoot and bare-chested, pulling up his pants and zipping his fly. I thought Lee only loved men. He blushes in answer to my astonished stare.

"I guess I'm sort of—bisexual," he stammers.

My girlfriend and Lee come with me when I drop by my brother's crib to pick up some photographs. Lee spots some nudes of Kathy, my running buddy from years back. "They're beautiful," he says. "I'd like to publish them. With some of your poems." I stare at Kathy and remember our falling-out over a man. I'm still troubled by the pain. "No," I say.

Then I take a book from George's case and show my girlfriend and Lee the astonishing drawings collected by an art lover who'd committed suicide just months before. The world they reveal is bizarre and twisted.

"I believe this is what the world really looks like," I say.

"Yes, I know what you mean," Girlfriend whispers.

"Yes," says Lee.

I'm hard up for another umpteenth time. I put my last two bucks in the gas tank and head out from Watts to West L.A. I hear John Harris is looking for an editor over at Papa Bach's. I need the job something dire. I've been hanging at Beyond Baroque for years and know John Harris from there. I decide it's worth a shot. When I get there Harris seems embarrassed to see me. It's awkward. I get through the interview but know the odds are zip. A few days later Lee calls and asks me to send poems. He's got a great new job editing *Bachy*. I'm happy for Hickthang but sad for myself. I end up working days for a Beverly Hills dialysis outfit and moonlighting as a bartender.

Lee sees me for the first time: he walks into a room in late August when the evenings are just starting to cool. I'm introduced to this stranger who I've only seen from afar. He's about my height, a different breed, but *vavavavoom* there's this draw this pull this gravity. We've never been formally introduced and I've always wanted to meet him. I get in his boy-face and it's handsome and flush, eyes the color of mischief fully on me getting into feeling and I'm only half-focused on what he's saying. I'm too busy watching his hair now silver now blond now sandy now ash now alabaster now white now platinum now salt & pepper. I notice the shirt he has on, one of those burnished western plaids I thought I never liked until he wore it and he's got on faded light-blue dungarees which I didn't think were hip until he wore them. And he's got on range-rider boots, looking the above-average shit-kicker. He's smiling while he talks, a small tight smile favoring the right or left, lips parted slightly to suggest private pleasure. Then my lover Steve comes up, a jealous study of the way Lee and I throw off sparks.

"You poets," he snorts, "I didn't know your world existed."

The first time I hear Lee read I fall in love with his voice. It's a standing room only reading at Beyond Baroque. It is 1969. I've seen him from a distance. He never pays me any attention. But that's okay. He speaks/his voice a reedy temblor. He speaks/a melodious effusive burst. He speaks/a dramatic basso cantante. He speaks his father's dying.

He speaks his own.

NOTE

Lee Hickman died of AIDS on May 12th 1991. This piece was written for Jacaranda Review, *as one of several remembrances by poets who had known him.*

Jazz Blues

"DON'T THINK I could live in Los Angeles," Patricia said, quiet horror audible in her dusky voice long-distance from St. Louis.

"Why's that?" I was poised to defend my home turf against carjackings, lung-degenerating smog and civic unrest.

"Y'all's funny about music and I hav'ta have my jazz."

I was zapped, had no comeback. I love a multitude of sounds but Afro-American music in nearly all its variations heads my list. Especially jazz. Whenever I'm able, I indulge, be it a saxophone summit, drum fest or piano bar.

But yes, jazz has always had it tough in L.A.

As Patricia and I disconnected, unsettling memories flooded in: under the stars, at The Hollywood Bowl, Dexter Gordon plays 14 notes for the cheering mob, slightly more generous than Miles Davis, who manages 12. At the Universal Ampitheater, everyone else swoons while I bust the exit as Bobby McFerrin intones "The Itsy Bitsy Spider." At the Vine St. Bar & Grill, I can't hear Mark Murphy because I'm boggled by his silk fuchsia shirt belted over white-on-olive swim trunks. A few months before, I ran across him at Sweet Basil in New York, and he was the essence of natty snazz down to his nines. What happened?

Are these incidents evidence of deep-seated cultural contempt? Do jazz folk sometimes mute their artistry to cater to assumptions about L.A.? Have they been told Angelenos don't know beans about jazz? Yes, they are, they do and they have.

'Tain't necessarily so.

America's primo original art form was birthed by the pain of racial oppression. Once "jass" left the stoops, bawdy houses, and back streets, it became elite, sophisticated and undanceable. Duke Ellington and Count Basie took it into concert halls, yachts and opera houses. Lena Horne, Nat (King) Cole and Daniel Louis (Satchmo) Armstrong infused it into pop culture via TV and movies. Holiday and Parker made it scary. Dizzy, Dolphy, Miles and T. Sphere Monk elevated it to avant-garde. Mingus and Shepp made it philosophical. Coltrane and Sun Ra made it cosmic. Ornette Coleman (no relation) deconstructed it.

Today, despite the Marsalis brothers and the admirable persistence of Max Roach, "new music" barely survives in Black communities. South Central is no exception, unless rap is included. Many older afficionados argue that rag is a contemporary jazz form.

Locally, more traditional forms of jazz are kept alive by such luminaries as Buddy Collette, Lynn Carey, Charley Hayden, Nels Cline, Horace Tapscott and Thomas Tedesco. Small social groups like BEEM (Black Experience as Expressed through Music) encourage a new generation through scholarships and achievement awards. And on Degnan Boulevard, misters Kamau Daa'oud and Billy Higgins regularly introduce newborns to The World Stage. Nearby at Marla's, the young bloods in fedoras-with-attitude get deep into serious.

Most L.A. jazz, though, comes with gray whiskers, overcooked pasta and the aura of grantsmanship. Audiences are distinctly older and distinctly lacking in melanin. It's gone from all-night jams to midafternoon brunches and teas, from sizzling on bandstands to fizzling in galleries and museums, banquet halls, university and community centers.

Still, I'll take my jazz any way I can. While the new scene may seem more cult-like than countercultural, it appears to be growing. It's comforting to note that there are goo-gobs of enthusiasts willing to buck Southern Cal's hostility to anything that doesn't have a twang or a yodel. Venues are as diverse as At My Place, Barnabey's, Birdland West, Dodsworth Bar & Grill, and the Jazz Bakery.

I prefer my tonal experiences straight-up with a champagne chaser in an anonymous heavy-breathing dark. I like intimate public rooms, filled with strangers couched in velvet, oozing melon-colored damask, reeking of expensive perfume mangled by cigarette stink, talk kept to a whisper.

Look close. You'll find me near the back of the room, gloating over my newly autographed LP. Some of my best nights have been spent gettin' tore down by Herbie Hancock, uplifted by

Randy Weston, knocked over by Dorothy Donegan, inspired by "Little" Jimmy Scott and shazzammed by Betty Carter. Right here in L.A.

NOTE

Los Angeles remains an entertainment industry town where celebrity eclipses serious art and stage shows are plentiful. Jazz, like poetry, still has difficulty competing for attention. Audiences tend to be elite but enthusiastic, the venues pricey and short-lived.

Laughs for Sale

THE POST-RECESSION 70s crushed in on me. I jumped behind the wheel, desperate for release, if not escape. I headed for the strip and L.A.'s hottest comedy stop.

Free parking was a cinch. My eyes scanned the marquee. I wanted a whiff of the newcomers. Unknowns took chances, and even when bad, usually proved fascinating. Besides, talent nights and off nights were all I could afford. And management didn't complain if I nursed my one-and-only drink through the entire set. Nothing's tougher on a comic than a cold empty room.

I breezed through the door after the *pro forma* I.D. check and teensy cover charge. On the bar, two comedy stars quietly minded their shot glasses. In the main room, my eyes swept the wide crescent for a cozy squat. To sit up front was to risk being foil to somebody's shtick, being coaxed onstage for a major embarrassment, or getting an unexpected cleaning bill. So I'd sit mid-room or snare an unreserved booth. Wrapping myself around my increasingly watery Cuba libre, more cola than rum, I lost my private worries in the public personas of the laugh-makers.

Rudy Ray Moore was forbidden fruit and Lenny Bruce overdosed before I lost my baby fat, but catching Mort Sahl live at the hungry i, on San Francisco's North Beach, a decade after the Beatnik hayday, jump-started my love affair with laugh houses. Once I caught an unannounced Lily Tomlin breaking-in fresh gritty material. Late one night I saw an electrifying performance by Freddie Prinze, days before he shot himself in January 1977. As comedy clubs mushroomed in the 80s, intimacy gave way to trend, and then a new wave of nontraditional comics—but in these barely post-recession 90s, as rampant greed breeds self-censorship, the guffaws are fewer and further between.

╪

We arrive on time. Parking is terrible and expensive. I have reservations for my daughter's birthday, certain we are going to catch Bobcat Goldthwait's act. Then, while paying for our tickets, we discover Bobcat isn't on the bill. But it's a special evening so we stay, mollified by one recognizable name, a young Black comic starring in his first movie.

Inside, we discover seating is first come first served. Then why did we have to stand in line for an hour when we had reservations and there was no earlier show? Reservations, we're told, are the management's body count. Not enough? Then the show is cancelled. As for the line, customers double as involuntary shills, a draw for walk-ins.

There are barely 30 people in a room that'll seat 150. We're sandwiched into the far right corner, making for uncomfortable neck craning. My husband points out that the joint isn't exactly jumping, but he's forced to ask for our money back before we're reseated.

We're invited to play the raffle. Prizes will be awarded over the phone, we're told. My husband sends back his gin-and-tonic, asking the bartender to please put some gin in it. Patiently we fill out our little red raffle tickets and put them in the paper-maché hat. As we chew on pasteboard-flavored munchables and slurp over-priced drinks, the show begins.

From beyond the stale—out trots one retread after another. A couple have mined news headlines for source material but instead of caustic, witty insights, or imaginative send-ups, we're fed high school-level pap—not even as good as elephant jokes. No risks taken here and (gasp!) no four-letter words or, censor forbid, strong lingo. Two are so unoriginal they manage to tell the same joke in the same set. Applause is polite, punctuated by tee-hees and an occasional moronic HA! from a heavy drinker up front. I manage to get off a couple of solid boos despite my husband's disparaging elbow, and my daughter's chastising, "Mom!"

Oh, for the caustic smarts of a Mort Sahl, the imagination of a Jay Leno, the savvy wit of a Steve Allen, the razor tongue of an Eddie Murphy, even the rude nastiness of an Andrew Dice Clay. Our evening is nearly saved by the young comic, who skirts

Pryor-like slams of White folk, for funny, poignant and rare glimpses into the Black psyche, and one hard-drinking holdover from the Smothers Brothers era. But even they fail to dispel the blatant pathos of mediocrity dying to be discovered by talent agents for TV sitcoms.

♯

"Congratulations! You took part in our club's door price lottery! You're a winner."

"Great. What did I win?"

"A free evening of fun at our club with a maximum of 15 guests. Your drinks are provided free, but your guests must honor the 2-drink minimum."

"Hmmmm. Uh—well, thanks, but no thanks."

"You don't want your prize???"

"Some other time." I hang up.

'Twasn't a bit funny, McGee.

Starcrossed Encounters

IN 1950s L.A., it was our family duty to show visiting kin the stellar parts of town. Mama and Papa would don Sunday best for the obligatory tour of Hollywood, stopping for the mandatory comparison of hand, foot and hoof prints at Grauman's Chinese Theatre, then heading into the hills to tour the homes of the stars.

It wasn't unusual to occasionally catch celebrities at home, like the time Uncle Ben and his bride not only got to eyeball his famous piano-shaped pool, but exchanged gracious small talk with Liberace. Or to discover a celeb or two chowing down at the next table over, like the time my parents found themselves ogling the Mills Brothers over fried chicken and mashed potatoes.

But these days, try and find a real, live celebrity when you need one. Increasingly rare glimpses are more apt to occur in a highly ordinary context, the unglamorous realm of daily commerce:

—I'm among the anonymous Beverly Hills office workers hurrying to lunch, when I see a horror-film legend heading toward me. I'm only carrying a coin purse, so an autograph is out. A simple greeting will have to do. "Hello, Vincent Price," I say softly as we pass. He's deep in thought and my words startle him. He walks against the light into oncoming traffic as brakes and onlookers screech.

—I gasp over my Hilton dinner roll, staring at Myrna Loy and Gloria Swanson seated one table over. I squeeze in as others ring their table and join the chirping about enjoying Loy and William Powell in those charming old *Thin Man* movies and Swanson as the immortal Norma Desmond in *Sunset Boulevard*.

—Impatient, I cut off the slow-moving luxury car on Beverly Boulevard, cursing the driver to an eternity of right lanes. In the rearview mirror, I recognize t.v. personality Charles Nelson Reilly.

—Racing along Sunset, I'm inched over by a huge red Cadillac convertible, "Kung Fu's" David Carradine behind the wheel.

—Late to a social event, I bump the fender of a Rolls Royce, narrowly beating it to the last convenient parking space. Dionne Warwick steps out to see if there's any damage.

—The car is in the shop and I'm on foot. As I board the bus in front of Brentano's, a white-haired, ruddy-faced man, clutching a leather writing caddy, excuses himself as he jostles by. It's science fiction author and *Moby Dick* scriptwriter, Ray Bradbury.

—I'm entering the lobby of the Taft Building in Hollywood when the blur I recognize as Karl Malden pushes past.

—As I exit the City Hall elevator, I hear the clatter of heels and hold the doors. Barbara Bain and companion leap inside, disappearing as the doors snap shut.

Less elusive than personalities, places prove the more reliable tourist fare. The Watts Towers, trendy Melrose, Ports O'Call, the Rose Bowl, Universal's City Walk, the Faith Dome and the Crystal Cathedral rank high on a list that also includes the more notorious landmarks including the Ambassador Hotel where Robert Kennedy was assassinated, the Manson Ranch, Marilyn Monroe's death house, the carport behind Sal Mineo's Holloway Drive apartment, the old People's Temple building, and more recently, the 1992 Florence-Normandie flashpoint, the nightspot where River Phoenix collapsed and the Northridge earthquake damage.

But when disappointed glitter-seeking cousins complain about the tarnish, we gently explain that even with paparazzo determination, they'll be lucky to see one star, let alone two. What the folk from back home reluctantly realize is that it's easier to spot a star among the veggies at Pavilion's than up on Hollywood Boulevard.

—At Big and Tall Books/Cafe, comic actor Bill Murray slips in to peruse the stacks. My teenager seizes the opportunity to tell him the latest joke making campus rounds.

—Speeding down Gower towards Astro's, on my way to score a cheeseburger, I spot actor Henry Winkler exiting the Paramount lot.

—"Whatever you do, don't ask him about his days as Bud," the bee-hived Valley party hostess cautions before she introduces me to Billy Gray—formerly of 50s sitcom "Father Knows Best." "Talk to him like you'd talk to the average person."

Say It Ain't Cool, Joe

BOY-OH-BOY, there's Joe, sportin' those Polaroid peepers, looking rakishly Mediterranean with hot blonde babes and hotter cars. His hair looks like Mu'ammar al-Qadhafi's. The tuxedoed dome-nose has all the sleek arrogance of a Shah exiled to Malibu.

Guilty. I like Joe Camel. And I don't smoke. Not out of the closet anyway. And Camels? Never. But...

In Afro-American street parlance Joe the Camel is a *player*. Life is a game and he's winning it. He runs in the fast lane. And he's about as Black as music business, and as gangsterish as it comes. The cat—er, dromedary—is too cool Old School. (Consult your *Digital Underground* on TNT Recordings.)

If I didn't know better, I'd say Joe was patterned after one of my father's old cronies. The Doc was the original "crip," meaning physically challenged. But that didn't stop any action. He hustled his way around South Central with one crutch on his best days, a wheelchair on his worst.

According to his own legend he had lost one leg in World War II. But rumor was that he'd sacrificed the gam in some unsavory back-alley adventure.

In spite of his cop-and-blow existence, Doc always sported highly polished wing-tipped kicks, though one shoe was always curiously devoid of mass. As Mama would say, he was "sharp as a tack." And generous. One of his philanthropic pleasures was formal-dress tea parties, where he gave us munchkins a crash course on etiquette, Mesta-style. He paid polite attention to me and charmed my little socks off—the adult who takes a child seriously is always an attraction.

Doc smoked. He carried the first gold cigarette case I ever saw. It was impressive to watch him slip it from the pocket of his pin-striped vest. Thing about Doc was that, no matter how vulnerable he might've been, he was not to be pitied or messed with. A gat was concealed in the creases of his threads.

And therein lies the appeal of Joe Camel as a clever selling gizmo and tobacco kingpin's dream.

Underneath Joe's Cheshire-cat macho is a deeper message. Joe's not just another lung-collapse peddler. He's a self-respect maven. In rural bottoms and urban ghettos nationwide, rife with runaways and bored, unemployed youth, there's a serious shortage of self-esteem. Like Doc or Joe, you can fire up a coffin nail for instant attitude, the quickest, easiest way to strike a pose.

Face it. Joe Camel has lifestyle appeal. He's rich and he's infamous. And he runs with the pack. There's Joe the suave, white-on-white betuxed academic. If you ain't got it you can fake his "smooth philosophy" by lighting up. Or you can rack 'em up for pool shark Joe 'cuz he's about to run the table.

In his stingy fedora, Hard Pack Joe and his Wide cousins have all the Hollywood charisma of William Bendix breathing down Robert Mitchum's neck in *The Big Steal* or Brando in *The Godfather*.

Beachcomber Joe has done his share of Venice Beach schmoozing, no doubt sipping Long Island iced tea on the volleyball court. Calypso Joe opens the doors of Club Camel on some tiny Caribbean isle where the cane grows tall and the money laundering is easy.

Joe's crimey, Eddie Camel, was a bead-wearing, applecapped, paintbrush-totin' long-haired flowerchild in the 60s. But today he's a loose-lipped, slack-collared, tam-topped, neo-Bebop jazz drummer. Bustah (note the idiomatic black spelling) Camel undergoes a similar transformation, and only his electric guitar remains the same.

I can't resist poking fun at ol' Joe. But underneath the fun, I'm clear on all the negativity that allows him his success. The birth of his cool is, unfortunately, linked to the birth of survival strategies that have allowed the Black male to withstand the relentlessness of racism. It is the cool personified by men as diverse as Malcolm X, Miles Davis, California politician Willie Brown and Ice Cube. To be cool is to be laid-back black.

But Joe Camel is offensive. Not only because cigarettes may cause heart disease, emphysema, and complications during pregnancy. Not only because cigarettes can be addictive and debilitating, but because, at root, old Joe's seduction campaign is plain-and-simple racist.

You dig?

Trouble in Paradise

SENSITIVE AND SOCIALLY responsible, David and Sheila exchanged vows in the late 80s and, eighteen months later, announced plans to divorce Los Angeles. The birth of their first child forced them to re-evaluate long-held concerns about the environment, the economy and ethnic tensions. L.A. had become too much like David's native New York City. When Sheila scored a job in Eugene, Oregon, the deal was done. We wished them luck, and secretly speculated about our own escape.

We kept in touch. But David had become so abrasively cheery, I could barely stomach our occasional phone chats. He and Sheila shared household and parenting duties while David completed his degree, something he couldn't afford to do when "back in ol' L.A." When I retorted "Seen one tree, seen 'em all," David challenged my urban callousness and dared us a visit.

On that virgin trip, David's praise proved gospel. Eugene was the deep ecology heartland where the organically grown, the recycled, and the bioengineered thrived. David and Sheila rubbed it in a little, extolling the squeaky-clean air, the laid-back traffic, the *real* farmer's market. Their four-bedroom hillside home had a pool, sauna, jacuzzi, fireplace, two skylights and his-and-hers carport. The monthly note was half the rent on their two-bedroom Santa Monica apartment. No screens or curtains obscured tree-enshrined windows. And no one locked their doors, house or car, day or night. No burglars, no gangs, no street violence.

The region teemed with easy-livin' ex-Californians, mainly retirees. But we couldn't distinguish them from the natives. After 10 blissed-out days, we drove back to L.A., struggling to hold on to the spirit of Eugene. But it had dissipated by the time we hit Ventura and descended into the hell zone at rush hour.

This year, four summers later, craving to repeat our Eden-like experience, I phoned David. He was delighted to have us. We—husband, son and a cooler full of sandwiches—arrived the week of July 4th. What we didn't know was that Ol' Man Trouble was ahoof in tie-dye heaven.

Having gotten his degree, David found good-paying jobs in Eugene nonexistent and was considering moving back to L.A. Sheila's love affair with her job had soured with the denial of a much-needed raise. The pair still kept doors and windows unlocked despite three visits from prowlers with expensive tastes. While the air remained squeaky-clean, local law enforcement had developed an uncanny appetite for issuing traffic citations.

Others also complained. A black journalist told me "the Ku Klux Klan rules south of the Columbia River" and that racial incidents were hushed up. One Berkeley escapee, an American of Norwegian descent, bristled when describing xenophobic regional politics and carped about "the disparity in cultural diversity" causing her daughter's difficult adjustment to schools "straight out of Mayberry U.S.A."

Ex-Angelenos were everywhere. After complimenting a chef on his culinary savvy, he said he'd relocated from West L.A. An arts fair potter had just closed his Beverly Hills studio. At a party, we met a Hollywood photographer. And so it went. The Bach festival was sold out and we'd seen all the current film releases before leaving L.A. so there wasn't much doing except relaxing poolside, reading and conversation. The hottest topic was the O.J. Simpson murder case. Eerily, Eugene seemed more an annex of L.A. than a getaway from it.

Under a cloud-flecked July 8th sky, we joined hundreds of fun-seekers at the 25th annual Oregon Country Fair. Entering the idyllic grove, we were transported to a 60s Dionysian love-in. Bare-breasted dryads romped, behorned satyrs pranced, harlequins flounced, and hedonistic revelers paraded through the throng wandering the maze of booths and performance stages.

Nevertheless, we couldn't recapture the stress-free Eugene of our past. The tensions we had fled reverberated around us. The festiveness seemed forced, a throwback to a peace-love era untarnished by the specter of HIV. The resonant crises in Bosnia, Haiti and Rwanda rendered the food flavorless. That afternoon we cut our trip short, bid David and Sheila adieu, and returned to the urban nightmare we hadn't left nearly far enough behind.

School for Thugstas

YES. L.A. REMAINS A city in crisis.

Many Angelenos still suffer post-traumatic stress syndrome directly traceable to the events of April/May 1992. The evidence appears daily in local newspaper headlines, on TV and radio broadcasts, in reports of economic unrest and sporadic violence. Plus, there are the pressures of electing a new mayor. Who will best serve El Pueblo de Nuestra Señora la Reina de Los Angeles de Porciuncula? Who will be our cutting-edge champion? Our Great Multicultural Hope?

Cynicism aside, amid complaints of continued decline and failed recovery, there's still the huge glimmer of opportunity for the enterprising, culturally savvy, budding entrepreneurs of South Central. How about a school that teaches the well-heeled the ins and outs of hard-core urban warfare?

Instead of calling out the National Guard or lobbying for federal aid, why not build an educational institution that capitalizes on gangbanger glamour? Imagine. An academy where the curious, the uninitiated and the over-30 have the option of a six-month short course or a 20-year-to-life aggregate of comprehensive and diverse studies, from the technical to the creative, as this abbreviated syllabus suggests:

BLOODS, BROTHERHOODS, CREWS AND POSSES: Breakin' down culture clubs and group power. Trendy gats and full-auto discussed.

'CHINES AND RIDES: Uses and functions of the automobile in major and minor busts. Bump-and-rob, drive-by, carjacking and swooping.

132

DOPE-SPEAK 2000: Current street slang with D-stroy survey of 50s DJ platter-patter and 60s to 90s funky lingo for sampling and mixing jive enrichment.

DEF HEIST BIZ—WAYS TO MEANS: Scoring, concealing, flashing, laundering, fencing, stashing, tooling, packing, ditching and plea-copping.

DOZENS TO DO-WOP TO HIP-HOP: What every boss free stylin' psychotic raptivist needs to T-lash potential upstarts into an iambic spazz. Dissin' seriously.

JUMPIN' BAD AND WASTIN' MUSHROOMS: How to hang. Initiation rites from the group-bang to rollin'-and-poppin'.

DIVAS, HOMEGIRLS AND BITCHEZ: P-power, aggressive resistance, gangsta feminist thought. How to be a Single Momma without really tryin' (to marry the MF).

ROGUE MOVES AND MOTIONS: D-veloping vogue attitude and props etiquette. Hand signals and handshakes. Buffalo stance, bogarting and steppin'-off baaad.

STYLIN' AND BOMBIN': The history of graffiti and the art of tagging, from restrooms to underpasses. How to treat spray-paint poisoning.

SWITCHBLADES, RAZORS AND SHANKS: The art of wielding blade and trimming matters to size. Wedge cuts and scalping.

THREADS AND DREADS: Attire for all occasions. How to properly cuff for concealment. Bugle Boys and baggies, T-shirts and tank tops, slickster togs, do-rags and headgear.

Z AS IN ZONING: Code of conduct when arrested. Frisk stance, kris-skrossing wrists, T for taser, the zen of lying prone during baton practice.

Such a curriculum would be guaranteed to transform the most egregious dominant-society jerks, nerds and dweebs into Monster Mack Daddies, Downwithit Vatos Loco and OGs. And it would be a unique way to reverse the demoralizing negatives of chronic unemployment, persistent drug trade and alcohol abuse, illiteracy and miseducation, and clashes with the justice system.

A chain of these cultural "cool schools," like private academies specializing in English as a Second Language, would bring vast *legitimate* revenues into Black and Latino hoods, fueling the local economy while simultaneously employing ex-felons, rehab program internees, half-way house residents, and penitentiary furloughees—dramatically X-ing out institutional recidivism and street crime.

Certainly such schools would draw an impressive, first-class student clientele of scriptwriters, journalists, novelists, filmmakers, actors, corporate executives, and, without a doubt, scads of television talk-show hosts. Set in authentic no-income environments, these learning-skill centers would stimulate additional economic growth by encouraging development of specialty stores such as one-stop combination jewelry and weapons boutiques, and restaurants serving gourmet *nouvelle* gangsta cuisine, like chili-over-chips Dijon or *shiitake*-dog *panini*. Quicker than you can say "Ice-T," South Central would go from D-pressed to boom.

Kickin' it.

Under the Weather

'TIS THE SEASON. Rain or sun.

The house is inhabited but dark, and the air inside is hot, stale, and claustrophobic. Intermittently, a hacking cough or sneeze can be heard amid muffled wheezes and rales.

In the bathroom, near the overflowing wastebasket, the floor is littered with the foil and plastic remains of sinus caplet containers. Sticking out of the wastebasket, bottom-up, is an empty bottle of antiseptic mouthwash swimming in aspirin tins, phlegm-stained tissues, and a chalk-crusted blue bottle of liquid laxative and analgesic.

The bathroom counter is cluttered with a giant bottle of vinegar, a box of tissues, several vials of alcohol-free expectorant for chest and head congestion, and assorted throat lozenges. Next to those are several bottles of vitamins—C, B complex, and E—all in crystalline pure, yeast-free gelatin capsules. In the medicine cabinet, squeezed between the aloe-plus-lanolin soap and the cotton-tip swabs, is the combination echinacea and goldenseal herbal extract and the fiery vaporizing ointment.

In the kitchen, trash is piled up in one corner, dirty laundry in another. The sink is plugged up with gray soapy water two evenings old. Dishes, silverware and pans cover the length of the counter, spilling onto the stove. The coffee maker has been on for hours, the decanter choked with stewing herbal tea bags. The refrigerator is bulging with lemons and oranges, cranberry and apple juice, seltzer and tonic waters. The shelves are packed with boxes of instant soup mix and cans of bouillon.

There's a war on, and we're not winning. But if all remedies fail, there's an elegant slim-necked bottle of extra smooth brandy (80 proof), mellowed in aged oak, sequestered next to the matchbook collection on the mantel. By the phone, the Rolodex is flipped open to the number and address of the family doctor....

Jokes about Southern California climate aside, there are only three seasons: spring, summer and flu. My husband, my son and I considered ourselves lucky to get through the holidays without anyone falling ill. It promised to be a banner year, but just as we were starting to feel invincible, it struck.

I was dismayed as my husband, who boasts radiant health because of his tough Brooklyn upbringing, moaned, "But I'm never sick!" as he collapsed onto his studio futon. He apparently got the bug at work. Immediately, I raided the nearest supermarket pharmacy section for my reliable combatants, spending a fifth of what it would cost, in time as well as cash, to see the doctor. After a quick study of contraindications, I supplied my husband with what would probably work best for him and then put aside my own precious stash, loading my purse for trips outdoors.

"I can't afford to get ill!" I groaned, frantically waving the calendar as if I were waving a cross at a vampire. Its pages were glutted with urgent appointments, social engagements and rapidly approaching deadlines. My husband and I had kept apart for a week in an effort to save me from the clutches of this troublesome, acute, debilitating, pandemic disease.

But the conflagration has spread. Last night, our hefty 14-year-old lost his supper to a "tummy ache," his first since infancy. And despite ingesting sickeningly sweet syrups and bitter pills to a fare-thee-well, I've come down with it, too. Hard.

Unlike many children of the 50s and 60s, I still have my tonsils. I live in dread of sore throats and their complications—pharyngitis which could possibly indicate an acute tonsillitis or that horrible-sounding complaint my great aunt used to warn us kiddies about, "the quinsy," which is an abscess of the tonsils. Don't hear much about that one these days. There's also the threat of laryngitis. And I have a tendency to lose my voice.

Now this mean virus persists, well into its second week of evil, and we've finally called to see the doctor but his assistant said she's down with it too, and that we might as well save our money, stay home in bed and drink plenty of fluids.

Next year, maybe we'll get flu shots, as I swear we will every year. But I'll probably forget, lulled by the sunshine and blue skies that promise invulnerability.

Achooo!

Would somebody please pass the brandy?

⨎ ⨎

I fainted twice in the woolly 80s: At the start of the decade with my third husband's first kiss and at the end of it, when I heard Huey Newton was murdered. The suicide of Abbie Hoffman got my biggest whoowhee since Phil Ochs went out. I spent the rest of the 80s cursing or saying "I told you so." Even the death of the astronauts was no surprise. What made this Cassandra angriest was the rise of Krack Kulture Kiddies—the new KKK—except most of them were Black and incorporated crack cocaine into our Black Tongue/music and popularized "dope" as buzzword for hip/in/with-it/trendy. The resurgence of open racism, increasingly bizarre serial killings, job-related homicides, the advent of AIDS (symptoms of the chronic social apathy, political jaundice and economic impotence infarcting the American heart) have been major gross-outs. The toppling of the Berlin Wall was terrific, but continued crises in Africa, and Central and South America bode ill for international relations in the 90s. The two temblors that shook the South Bay and the Big One that assassinated Soviet Armenia, worked my nerves. But what shook me into a three-day stupor, mesmerized by CNN/C-SPAN/ABC, the remote-control unit never out of reach, was the late-afternoon Hollister earthquake that shook the Bay area October 17th 1989. Robin Ortiz, one of my older son's former Marshall High classmates, died while working in a Santa Cruz, California delicatessen shop.

—from "Blown Away in the Eighties," *L.A. Weekly*, January 1990

Beneath the Milky Way

"COME HERE HONEY—I want to show you something."

My husband takes my hand and leads me down the hallway at the Chateau Marmont. We're on a getaway. We stand in the vestibule and look down on Sunset Boulevard, out across the extravagant light-strewn vista. Hard to believe it's winter. Directly below, the boulevard is noisy with rock club doings. Limos, luxury cars, and taxis pull curbside to the *bomp-bomp-bomp* of disco house, empty out passengers then zip away.

"It's like a Max Beckmann," I say with a sigh.

"More like a George Grosz," he whispers. Starstruck but exhausted, we call it a night, then:

"Honey, wake up! It's the Big One!" he shouts. "We've got to get out of here!"

The building shakes, sways, shimmies. It's seconds before I realize we aren't at home. I find some matches and, in the fits and starts of flame, we dress. The manager arrives with a flashlight. We grab our things and follow him downstairs, avoiding fallen plaster. Frightened residents, still in pajamas, gather in the lobby. We run to the garage, get our car, and venture out onto the dark boulevard. It's unconfirmed, but one radio reports the epicenter may be Northridge.

The only lights are from the headlamps of early morning traffic. No sounds except for the sirens of emergency vehicles. East along Sunset, hundreds of people line the streets. Traffic signals are out so we drive cautiously. Then we get home and step out of the car. Startled, I look up. My husband does likewise.

"Lookathat! There *are* stars up there!"

✝

It's August 1994 and Comet Swift-Tuttle is news again, making its splash near the constellation Perseus. The meteors can be seen without telescopes, say news reports, and prime viewing time is between one and three a.m. It'll be family fun, we think, but our teenager opts out. Last year's sighting was a big fizzle as we craned backs and strained eyeballs. Nothing above but the usual ho-hum twinkles. This year he's so unenthusiastic he snubs us and goes to bed early.

Nevertheless, we map out the comet's path, get our field glasses and climb to the roof, eager to enjoy a skyful of shooting stars. Alas, the city's glow mutes all. Undaunted, we jump in the car, hit the 170 north, then exit west into North Hollywood. Two hours later, reports come in on two Unidentified Comet-Gazers oohing and aahing at the intersection of Rhodes and Cantara.

✝

It's 1995 and July 4th falls on a Tuesday, but it's only the weekend before and bursts of fireworks dot the summer twilight as we exit the 101 east at Manchester. We're on our way to Mama's in Florence-Graham, rife with A-frames, bungalows, and stucco havens on modest lots—now Crip territory. As we ride, I remember afternoons when these streets echoed with the whistle from Helms Bakery vans and the tinkle-jingle from the Good Humor ice cream truck. There were still a few White families left.

Every time we pull into Mama's driveway, my eyes are drawn to the hole left by the bullet that pierced the north wall inches beneath the dining room. Then I look to the neighboring house on the right and am silently grateful for the Latino family who gentrified the old crackhead safehouse, replaced bars, sandblasted graffiti, planted flowers and shrubbery. Briefly, I recall the five-year-old girl up the street, killed in a post-riot drive-by. Mama called last night to tell us the police had knocked, once more, on her door. Her neighbor across the street was beaten to death by gangsters while trying to protect her grandson. Had she seen anything? No, she hadn't.

Just now, all's quiet. A few houses down, youngsters are shooting off fireworks. I remember the brouhaha over property values when city fathers announced expansion plans for what would become Los Angeles International Airport (LAX). And I'm reminded of those scorching summer eves when we neighborhood kids stopped in our street play, eyes searching the panorama, ears prickling as the sky spit thunder, our tiny fingers arcing to follow the silver streak breaking the sound barrier at Mach 1, turning gold in waning sun.

As we park, we notice how eerily luminescent the eastern sky has become. It's filled with scores of large white orbs moving swiftly toward earth.

"Lookathat!" My husband gasps and points.

Yes, those lights from airships descending. Do they ever look like stars.

Astrology to Go

SEEKING HI-CALORIC satori? Having a fat attack? Aching to satisfy pre-health-fad lusts for the highly salted, sugary, spicy, crispy, crunchy, gooey? Southern California offers quintessential junk food junkies a borderless diversity in gastronomic delights. (*Warning*: keep your favorite antacid, anti-flatulent, anti-hypertensive, anti-toxin, anti-diarrheal agent, and antiseptic gargle handy, or consult your physician.) This fast-food forecast will help you when selecting health-unconscious goodies compatible with your sun sign:

ARIES (March 21st–April 19th): Gyros and fishburgers temper your fiery ego. California-style thin-crust pizza offsets ambitious and combative moods. Sushi—for vitality when romantic. Pasta salads and chicken quesadillas to better direct forceful energies. Sloppy Joes if you need to think it over. D-Zert: trail mix.

TAURUS (April 20th–May 20th): Cheese steak caters to your self-sufficient and practical nature. Potato chips and coleslaw increase discriminatory powers. Fried chicken and Chicago-style pizza liberate the easygoing aspect of your conservative outlook. Dodger dogs and shrimp fried rice break bullish routines. D-Zert: cupcake.

GEMINI (May 21st–June 20th): Macaroni salad incites your go-getter id. Mild chili when feeling overly sensitive. Rib tips and lox-and-onions appeal to your versatile tastes. Beef tongue on rye demonstrates your appetite for intellectual stimulation. Baked beans and veggie tempura fulfill your love of mystery. D-Zert: cannoli.

CANCER (June 21st–July 22nd): Tuna melts and tacos fuel your dreams. Chorizo-and-egg burritos and cheese dogs when you need change. Chef's salad when wanting to explore unknowns. Barbecued chicken when persistence matters. Fish-and-chips to gratify your deepest fantasy. D-Zert: fried ice cream.

LEO (July 23rd–August 22nd): *Mee krob* and *machaca* burritos arouse your derring-do. Ham-and-Swiss on rye when feeling expansive. Grilled chicken inspires your drive for success. Chili fries and turkey salad spark leadership qualities. Spinach lasagna flatters your dignified manner. D-Zert: French pastry.

VIRGO (August 23rd–September 22nd): Broasted chicken and shrimp scampi challenge your contemplative nature. Pork *bok choy* for when you have time to take time. Teriyaki beef sparks your ingenuity. Loaded dogs and *carnitas*—because you prefer fact over theory. The Reuben sharpens your mental acuity. D-Zert: baklava.

LIBRA (September 23rd–October 22nd): Louisiana hot links and pastrami dip satisfy your need for variety. Beet salad and *pad thai* complement your harmonious, creative nature. Bean-cheese-and-onion burritos spur romance. Shoestring fries help you unwind. Chicken wings always lift your spirits. D-Zert: fresh fruit.

SCORPIO (October 23rd–November 21st): Chopped liver and subways augment your native problem-solving skills. Tamales calm your demanding appetite for the different. Mustard dogs and deep-fried shrimp subdue emotional extremes. Roast beef on white with mayo perks up your energy level. D-Zert: churros.

SAGITTARIUS (November 22nd–December 21st): Fried clams and kraut dogs stimulate your enthusiasm for the philosophical. Onion rings and green Jell-O salad bring out your freedom-loving aspect. Rotisserie chicken when feeling romantic. Meatloaf sandwiches sate your love of pragmatic ideals. Fried tofu tones down those dangerous tendencies. D-Zert: chocolate chip cookies.

CAPRICORN (December 22nd–January 19th): The BLT enhances your organizational skills. Bacon burgers reveal your chameleon-like nature. *Taquitos* and jalapeño dogs best suit your tendency to penny-pinch. Gourmet potato salad boosts those low-energy periods. D-Zert: candy bar.

AQUARIUS (January 20th–February 18th): *Larb* and *chichirones* keep you ahead of the mob. Garbage burritos and club sandwiches fill the urge to pursue scientific curiosities. Corn dogs and carrot-and-raisin salad evoke the child in you. Patty melts mute your inclination to be argumentative. D-Zert: fruit turnovers.

PISCES (February 19th–March 20th): Ketchup dogs and falafel offer stability when you're preoccupied with superficialities. Eggplant pizza and curly fries appeal to your empathetic nature. Crab excites loving tendencies. Chinese chicken salad and tostadas satisfy a proactive imagination. D-Zert: cheesecake.

Bust a gut!

Afro-American like Me

As I'VE SAID, *Black* was a fightin' epithet in my South Central school days. By the late 60s the militant outcry was, "There's no such country as colored!" And Black had become beautiful. This upsurge in racial pride seemed new but was only another phase in a war for recognition hard-fought since the first American slave was drug ashore.

Unlike other groups, what we Blacks call ourselves has resulted in a centuries-long identity crisis. W. E. B. DuBois, instrumental in the Niagara Movement, later the N.A.A.C.P., reclaimed ethnic self-esteem via Ethiopia, a reference so popular by the 30s that comedian W. C. Fields used it as a derogatory euphemism "Ethiopian in the fuel supplies" (N-word in the woodpile). Nevertheless, evoking Mama Afrika—Egypt, Nubia, even the Belgian Congo—elevated our race far above Negro, capitalized or not, the Spanish word for black. By the time I reached high school we were called Americans of African descent in mixed race classrooms, but nigger still ruled at recess.

By the 70s Afro-American was the widely accepted label because it locked our landless people to a land mass. But by the end of the 80s, Jessie Jackson and other Black leaders proclaimed African-American the preferred term for pragmatic political reasons. Yet this rechristening further complicated the sticky discourse it was meant to end. Black Studies programs that initially scrambled to rename themselves Afro-American now grapple with African-American, not to mention "Africana Studies."

As a writer, I use the terms Black, Afro-American, and Black-of-Slave-Origin interchangeably, depending on the context and the space allotted. I happen to favor *Black* because it's short. But nearly all commercial U.S. publications refuse to capitalize (or dignify) the word, citing matters of style. If I want a capitalized term I'm forced to use *African-American* because the establishment has decreed *Afro-American* out of vogue.

Overall, the term African-American dissatisfies me because it whitewashes my history, and equates it with that of newly arrived immigrants, muting present-day residuals of slavery and its inequities. When lecturing on this touchy topic, I ask:

"Who were the first Black American leading male actors who were not athletes!"

Hands go up immediately. "Sidney Poitier and Harry Belafonte!"

"They're islanders," I correct, "not American-born Blacks-of-Slave-Origin."

There's sharp intake of breath followed by a chorus of ooooohs.

‡

To avoid confusion, I propose that *Afro-American* be re-adopted to distinguish American Blacks-of-Slave-Origin from Black immigrants from Africa, and that the term *African-American* be used only to refer to the latter. Substitution of one for the other blurs strong cultural differences. Africans naturalized as U.S. citizens should also have the option of self-identity, as should Black Latinos and Black Asians.

Emphasis on my slave origin assumes the African connection, but I do not wish to be identified as an African, or Oglala Sioux, or Johnny Reb—other parts of my genetic lineage. Thus I also reject New African, another new label. If I must suffer categorization, I prefer to do it as an Afro-American.

"*A nation of immigrants*," is my other PC peeve. It sounds politically correct but denies the uniqueness of the Black experience. And its pain. Granted there are similarities, but my forebears had *no choice* in coming to America. Tracing ancestors back to "The Continent" was a fad following Alex Haley's *Roots*, but most Blacks can only go back three to five generations. The trail stops where the Atlantic starts. Unlike some folk, I'm not ashamed of being descended from slaves. Regardless of who sold whom as "black gold," my great-great-granddad did not flee a war-torn country, defect from an oppressive government, or violate the border to seek work. He was not an indentured servant or flim-flammed into building the railroads. A Mississippi slave, he

purchased his freedom with his sweat and intellect and then
headed northwest.

≠

"I don't understand you Blacks in America," frowned the South
African, a recent Apartheid escapee. "You're too preoccupied
with proving yourselves human."

"The U.S. Constitution excluded us as chattel," I say by
rote. "That's why there's this never-ending debate about what we
call ourselves."

"Aaahhh!" he smiled and nodded.

On Hold for Dear Life

EMMMMMBUZZZprrrrinnnnnggggg.

Hello, you have reached your National Public Services General Disaster Emergency Hot Line. If you are a first-time user, please be patient and listen carefully while our newly expanded service is explained. Following this explanation, you will be instructed on how to take full advantage of this miraculous technological advancement.

Due to budgetary considerations, a hiring freeze, and our sincere desire to satisfy a growing public mandate, we have initiated this new telephone help line so that we may continue to serve you faster and more efficiently, yet maintain our reception team of underpaid, sleep-deprived, stressed-out, emotionally challenged individuals, downsized to minimize wasteful, low-paying positions.

Please press 1 to hear this entire message repeated in Spanish. Press 2 for Korean. Press 3 for Farsi. Press 4 to hear Vietnamese. Press 5 for Armenian. Press 6 if you have a hearing loss and wish to have this message amplified. Press 7 if you have a Brooklyn accent. To repeat these options, press 8. Press 9 for additional options. Press your star key to return to the original menu. Press your pound sign to continue.

You have pressed pound. If you have been victimized by a disaster of federal proportions, such as flood, hurricane, earthquake, pestilence or tax audit, please press 1. If your disaster falls under labor, industrial, or environmental concerns such as exposure to illegally disposed nuclear waste or chronic unemployment, press 2. If your disaster is personal and involves a member or members of your immediate family or community and can best be served by city or county facilitators, press 3. If none of

147

these apply, press 4 and hold for an operator.

You have pressed 4. All available operators are handling other calls; however, *do not hang up*. While you are waiting, you will be entertained by this month's musical selections. Press 1 for operatic favorites. Press 2 for country & western. Press 3 for jazz. Press 4 for rhythm, rap and blues. Press 5 for easy listening. Press 6 for classic rock. Press 7 for alternative rock. Press 8 for psychotic silence. Press 9 to review this menu. Press pound to return to the previous menu.

You have pressed 9. You have pressed 3.

Prrrrringggggg. Prrrrrriinnnnggggg. Prrrrrrinnng. Click!

You have reached the Auto-Response line for your region. When you hear the beep, please enter your Social Security number, driver's license, or passport number. Listen carefully for the beep. It will not be repeated.

Blaaaaaaaapppp.

000-00-0000.

Zzzzzzzzhissfizzle.

We're sorry. According to our records, there is no such number. Therefore, you have either misdialed or do not exist. Please hang up and try again or press 9 to return to the previous menu.

Thank you for entering your numbers correctly. Please enter your five-digit postal ZIP code. Thank you.

According to our records, you reside in a substandard residential area currently undergoing rapid economic fluctuation. For the proper assistance please listen carefully and follow these instructions closely. If you are single and have a median income, press 1. If you are a single head of household and have a median income, press 2. If you are a married couple with more than 2.5 children and median income, press 3. If you have an above-median income, press 4. If you are uncertain about your income, press 5. Press 9 to repeat this menu. Press pound to return to the previous menu.

You have pressed 5. Please hold.

"Hello, this is Ms. Answer. May I help you?"

"Are you a real person or another recording?"

"Hahahahaha. I'm a real person."

"It's been thirty minutes! I can't believe it—"

"Excuse me! Another call's coming in. Please hold."

"Bbbbuttt—"

Mmmmmmmmm. Click. Blurp. If you'd like to make a call, please hang up and try again. If you need help, please hang up and dial your operator. *Beep-beep-beep!!!*

<u>The Evil Eye</u>

LOVE CONQUERS ALL? *Imagine factionalized living in a post-strife-torn city where those who marry across barriers of class, color and religion are discreetly tolerated in sophisticated settings but constantly denigrated in the streets. Imagine yourself–if you dare–in my skin, unable to go anywhere, day or night, without anticipating trouble.*

We duck into a mid-Wilshire hang for appetizers, find the music enticing and ditch the buffet for a few rhythmic twirls. We're unaware that we've become an issue until we sense the laserlike stare of a young Black man dissecting us as we crisscross the dance floor.

I'm the object of his vibes. In the darkness he doesn't notice I'm at least 12 years his senior and sport a wedding ring. He's blinded by the sight of a mixed couple and huffs around us in a hostile orbit. We shine him on. Not to be ignored, he rudely thumps my man's shoulder. Huz grimaces and shakes his head. Youngblood stomps off to a dark corner, an altercation brewing.

Our fun spoiled, we make for the exit.

While Huz nurses his frozen yogurt at a Glendale mall rest stop, I step into a luggage boutique. I answer the ugly glare of the Semitic owner with an awkward nod, then examine the stock. I decide on a slender, wine-colored tote. At the register, I present my check and requisite IDs. "Credit card or cash," he admonishes.

Thrown, I leave, angrily swallowing epithets.

"Did you find anything?" Huz asks.

"Yeah, but my check was refused. I'm too Black for 'em."

"Ridiculous. Come on, I'll get it for you." He marches me back into the shop. "My wife was in here to buy a briefcase. Where is it?" Flustered, the owner reaches under the counter. "Sweetheart, is that the one?" I nod.

"We'll take it!" Authoritatively, he plucks a check from his wallet. Without a word, the owner bags the case. "I told you they'd take a check," Huz says when we get outside.

"Yeah," I smirk, "from *you*."

‡

We bogart through heavy traffic to the nearest pump at the Melrose self-serve station, unintentionally cutting off another car. My man jumps out, tugs the recalcitrant nozzle to the rear, wrestling to unlock the gas cap. There's a screech of rubber and scream of brakes. The incensed driver roars up on our bumper, threatening my beloved with below-the-knee amputations. Unintimidated, Huz shouts, "You dirty mutha—!"

The driver, an American of African descent, inches taller and outweighing my man by 30 pounds, mushrooms out onto the blacktop. Succumbing to heat and gridlock-inspired tensions, Huz continues the tongue-lashing. The driver, insulted by being bad-mouthed in front of his family, silently goes into his trunk for a tire iron.

I scramble out of the car and buffalo up behind my man. The driver is surprised. That I'm Black matters and uncomfortably complicates his rage. A grudging truce ensues. The driver lowers the tire iron, and we finish getting our gas. But there are no apologies.

‡

I'm satisfied with my giant hot *caffè latte* to go, but Huz wants a real breakfast elsewhere. At his favorite Los Feliz cafe, there are no more parking spaces on the lot. As we contemplate street parking, a white coupe pulls up behind us. I don't think my brimming *latte* will survive the gyrations so I climb out, aware that the White male driver is watching. I catch his eyes, don't recognize him and turn away.

While Huz parks the car, I wait at a nearby lamppost, taking sips of my *latte*. The white coupe swerves curbside in front of me, the electronic window lowered. I glance up. The driver's fly is unzipped and he's flapping his circumcision at me. I break into unrestrained laughter. He hits the accelerator and speeds off.

"What's so funny?" Huz asks. I tell him. He wants to kill the guy.

"It was an absurdly pathetic act," I say. He's amazed that I'm so philosophical.

Our favorite Thai eatery is packed, so we take a number, then briefly stroll the grungy Vermont Avenue business strip. We're in an exceptionally romantic mood, holding hands, sneaking a kiss. Suddenly, we're being stared down by a group of Latino men. As they pass, one turns and shouts at my back.

"Puta!"

At a Pacoima gathering, an old acquaintance greets me with a warm hello, then:

"Are you still with that Jewish fellow?"

I look at her thoughtfully, then smile.

"Yesssss."

Polia Stories

I SAY NOTHING, ENTER silently. Polia, in a white gown, reddish-white hair framing her lovely, ancient Polish face, senses a presence and rises in bed, drenched in a flow of golden white sunlight streaming into the hospital room. She is skittishly ethereal as if on the verge of celestial flight. Like she's one of the frail-legged little birds which recur in her paintings. She takes a while to focus, uncertain whether I'm real or dreamt. I hope I haven't frightened her. I know it's all right when she says softly, "Wanda!" her tremolo mixed with wonder and surprise. "I saw Tracey yesterday," I say, "and she told me you were here." Tracey is married to Boris, Polia's composer-son. I proceed to amuse Polia with local gossip. When she laughs, it seems to hurt. "My, my," she says, "it's good you're so busy. I can't quite keep my grasp on time anymore." Then she holds up her hands, flaps them uselessly, drops them into her lap. "I haven't been able to work, you know."

One or two evenings a month, Huz and I join the artists, poets, writers and musicians who gather at the spacious Hollywood-area home of the Pillins, Polia and her husband, William. They left Chicago for Los Angeles in 1948. Bill has authored several books of poetry, but Polia's pottery is the mainstay of the family income. Visitors are welcomed, then guided around back to see Polia's workspace and the kiln. Next comes an offering of cold cuts, assorted crunchies, sweets. Polia rustles back and forth from the kitchen; Bill, at the head of the table, conducts the salon. Over drinks, the works of others are applauded or blasted, political issues gingerly argued, creative theories sounded or ridiculed, music appreciated and stories told.

Often, evenings close with Bill's recitation of a favorite poem or a new one of his own. Occasionally, Boris is persuaded to play the piano. But for me, the singular pleasure of our visits is Polia's extraordinary creations. Polia has a secret glaze that makes her pots unique. She and Bill enjoy tantalizing us with this mystery which has acquired cult status. We're treated to tales of cunning artists and entrepreneurs in pursuit of her formula, which, like Stradivari, she will never divulge. Even her most commercially pretty pieces always betray her deft and dark brilliance.

‡

At times we arrive late to browse through Bill's workroom and "the gallery." If in pocket, we buy items for gifts. When in the neighborhood, I drop in to see Polia. As our friendship deepens, she gives me pots that didn't quite turn out or something for my birthday. Yet, I'm determined to own one of her rarer paintings. When all I can afford is the "Pink Cat," Bill insists it's a good deal. I think it's beneath Polia's Chagall-like standards.

‡

One afternoon, Huz and I happen to catch the Pillin household in disarray. A drunken driver has crashed his car through the front of the house, site of the gallery. The accident reveals the most secret of Polia's secrets—a hidden storage room. In it, Polia had squirreled away decades of masterpieces—her legacy. Many are destroyed. Then later, an earthquake does more damage. While cleaning up, Polia is extremely distraught. She shows us all that's left. "It's just no good!" she cries. I reach into the rubble and pluck out a white-glazed, apple-sized pot ringed by eleven tiny bluebirds. Its neck and a third of the bottom are chipped off.

"Polia, how lovely! This must be what it feels like to find treasure in ancient ruins."

She frowns, astonished, then smiles, throwing up her hands. "Well then, you may have it!"

‡

The salons end with Bill's death in June, 1985. We still manage to see Polia, at home or during a nursing-home stay, but time between visits lengthens as her health declines, then our visits stop altogether. In September, 1992, we learn she'd died that July.

‡

Years later. We're in San Diego, window shopping in Ocean Beach. We wander into a Newport Avenue antique shop. In back, mounted in a drab frame, we discover one of Polia's lovely iconographic plates at five times the cost she'd have asked for it. Caught short, we vow to buy it on our next trip. A month later, we return to the shop. It's been sold.

Six weeks after our recent hectic move, I hang a few paintings to keep the white walls of our new digs from making me stir crazy. One morning, while taking a satisfied look over the living room, I feel eyes at my back. I turn to look. No one's there but the "Pink Cat." I gasp, certain that behind its enigmatic expression, Polia smiles back at me.

Thrown for a Loop

GERRI AND I GABFEST over lunch at a chic pasta hang. A letter from a mutual friend worries us. Like Gerri, she's about to "chuck it all" and try her luck in the U.S.A. Gerri's afraid she's set a discouraging example. I try to dissuade her.

Spurred by best wishes from her daughter and friends, Gerri left Sydney, Australia believing the cultural climate at home gave her little choice or chance. Like thousands of fortune-seekers before her, she took the heart-worn trail to Hollywood.

Gerri was one of a last wave of filmmakers generated by the Australian film industry boom of the 80s. It had taken her one day to raise the money for her acclaimed docudrama about Ned Kelly, a Robin Hood-like legend. But before she could establish her reputation, her career was stunted when the Australian government closed down the system of tax incentives which fueled Australia's golden era of cinema. Deductions of 100% of expenses plus 20% of profits, encouraged private corporate investment in film. But this scandal-ridden windfall for the rich, for whom quality and profits were optional, ultimately hurt small investors. There weren't enough safeguards against rip-offs. When government funding ended, new talents like Gerri floundered.

According to Gerri, the Australian film industry of the 90s is a closed shop where only "the favorites and one or two darlings" make movies. After a frustrating two-year money chase, she put everything she couldn't hock in storage and jumped from the fire Down Under into the palm-handled frying pan. When I ask what advice she'd offer others like her friend, she says, "There's no point coming here if you don't have a list of contacts."

When she talks about her project, a politically incorrect feminist comedy, her eyes widen excitedly, hands sweeping close-cropped red-brown hair. The years and stress lines vanish. But when I ask what's shakin' on the hustle front, the stress lines return. She's been repeatedly told her project reminds "them" of a British film currently a commercial splash. The strongest vetoes come from women execs afraid that her project "will turn off the male audience." About now, she's bouncing off walls, jittery with every Northridge quake aftershock and battered by months of rebuffs, teetering between Prozac and the next plane home.

"There's no logic to these rejections! If my script reminds them of a film that made 80 million but had a budget of 10-to-15 million—well, my film'll only cost about three million!" Gerri moans.

"Hollywood has no humor. There's so much fear and no way to do straight business! 'If we met you socially, then we could accept your script for our clients,' " was the verdict handed down by four major agencies. Exasperated, Gerri approached the Canadians and the English. "The Brits are a lot cheekier. What's most shocking here [in Hollywood] is there's NO RISK-TAKING ALLOWED! And they're not talking about the script—but about *box office*. Creativity is not enough. You have to have a hard business edge. *And how the fuck do you live while following your dream?*"

Lightly, I ask her to make believe in magic and make a wish. She closes her eyes and claps her hands. "Miramax will say, 'Yes, here's the money! Go make your movie.' " Should the impossible come true, Gerri still wants to go home. She enjoys the weather and tooling around in her snazzy little convertible, but ...

"L.A. is like Calcutta! The cardboard houses smash you in the face." Gerri's haunted by the large numbers of homeless, a significantly smaller problem Down Under, and one which doesn't cause Australians the "secret guilt" she finds among well-heeled Angelenos.

Racism is also among Australia's ills, but she's staggered by L.A's version. "I'm allowed to ask questions because I'm White and a foreigner," but she's frequently warned by other Whites to "avoid 'Black areas' and 'greasy Mexicans.' " And she's mystified by the "Alice-in-Wonderland stuff" she hears when people condemn violence while attacking gun control.

"L.A.'s the most intolerant cosmopolitan city I've ever been in. Seems something's going to explode any moment," she says, half-awed, half-terrified. I remind her that L.A. did explode and still grapples with recovery. Then, as an afterthought, I press Gerri to say something different about my hometown. She lowers her chin cagily, raises her brows and twinkles her eyes.

"You give good salad."

Guys, Dolls & Bit Players

SOMEONE, SOMEWHERE, is alone in a dark office, barking out the I-did-it in a raspy, wounded alto, making that ultimate confession, the one that'll send them to The Big House, The Chair, or Eternity.

Or they're out hoofing it in the pitiless night, indirectly lit by the gritty scrim of ominous loneliness. The moon is unwitting witness to their emotional decay. Something is about to happen to a White male anyone.

Our hero/antihero is a private eye, ex-Marine or flyboy, transient good-Joe-gone-bad, prizefighter on the skids, gigolo in vicuña, a mug with a heart of goo. He's a two-bit lone wolf, a coolly offbeat non-conformist. Formerly clean-cut, he's gone craggy, desperately ghost-eyed with terminal five o'clock shadow.

He's got quirky demons. An unsolved slaying, a husband begging cuckoldry, a luscious siren in trouble, a nest of Nazi vipers, a poisonous coincidence—plot complications derived from one or more melodramatic convolutions. Plus there's a secret buried hatchet-deep in his heart—a prison record, a moment of cowardice.

He drinks his straight or on the rocks, occasionally with a chaser—bourbon, scotch, whiskey, or rye—hooch, booze or rotgut. Never touches drugs unless some villainous slime is trying to hot-pop him into next week.

He's existentially alone over his bottle in a sleazy dive, peering at a hostile typewriter, or silently scheming destruction during happy hour in a crowded bar. Or he's hitchhiking along a dangerous curve on an endless road or buying a bus ticket at a scrubby little depot on the edge of nowhere.

She's a blonde, strawberry or platinum, or brunette, raven-haired or auburn. But always a lady—vixen, femme fatale, waif-next-door, heart-stopper. Gowns that shimmer and cling, lamés, silks, satins. Nylons and pumps. Frills and feathered brims. Her doey eyes fill the lens with a dewy tenderness, exotic witchery, or smoldering allure.

They're about to find each other in the shadowy landscape of blue gardenias, white orchids, and black dahlias, igniting the silver screen with fireworks. Of course, he'll be alone when he discovers her betrayal, which can only lead to one thing—the eventual kill-of-passion. Along the way the local gendarmes will inevitably get involved, if only during the sweetly sour denouement.

The weapon is a telephone cord, a low-hung coupe, a smoking gat, enormous, bare psychotic hands. But with unreeling certainty there's a corpse. The body may be discovered in a rapidly jelling pool of blood or grossly cyanotic, stretched out under the expensive illumination of a Tiffany lamp.

Nothing cinematic excites me more than film noir. Five minutes of the grainy black-and-white genre thrills me more than any contemporary first-run flick. *But...*

"Uh-oh," I say, "here comes one of us."

My husband groans and my son laughs. Someone Black has suddenly appeared on-screen. My stomach tightens and I feel the rage start to rise. My psyche is caught behind the metaphorical door, slammed on my temporary exit from reality. It hurts.

At such jarring moments it takes all my strength to resist zapping the TV set. Instead, I reach down deep into my "willing suspension of disbelief." It's only make-believe, my mantra. To enjoy that sentimental journey back to yesteryear, I have to pretend I live in a perfect world. I have to accept the isms that go with film noir turf. I have to force myself back through the door, back into the movie.

He's a Pullman porter, redcap, bandleader or sideman, shoeshine boy, chef, valet, butler, chauffeur, janitor, or humming blues in the next cell over. He then disappears, never to be seen again unless he's resident piano man at a Moroccan cafe or the mulatto son of a fallen horn player. She's a cook, maid, lindy-hopper, finger-popper or nightclub singer.

Theirs is a world of ethnic caricature, bit players always peripheral to the action. They suggest that the progress made by today's Afro-American filmmakers, and others outside the movie business mainstream, is still too painfully little, coming far too late, despite the best efforts of the current generation of filmmakers like Charles Burnette, Spike Lee, John Singleton, Julie Dash, Bill Duke, Mario Van Peebles, et al.

The past can't be undone, and these worn stereotypes are disturbing and important reminders that movies, considered purely entertainment, do, over time, become sociopolitical documents. That, like murder, the racist cultural subtext will out.

Gatherings

I visited the Black part of Cincinnati only briefly a skillion years ago. Local architecture appeared under the spell of Dutch colonial influences. Boxy little homes stood high off the street, wide porches occasionally closed in by elaborate railing, potted plants and mesh-wire screens. It was my first experience of true autumn, to see trees in bursts of flaming reds, golds, oranges and maroons. Everything was foreign except for those stoops. And the dark faces of the men and women who collected around them.

Back in South Central, at 88th and Avalon, I'm struck by double vision. I will always see this scrubby park through my child's eye—that Easter way back when my brother and I discovered our brand-new Buster Browns had been stolen while we played in the giant sandbox. I adjust my sight to take in the five *moreno* men in their 30s. They squat where the old baseball diamond used to be. One is mid-gulp, bottoming-up the brown bag that conceals the short dog.

Off the alley, not far from the old taco stand, near where Central crosses Manchester, is the designated spot. A gathering place. There are no signs except the dilapidated furniture that stays there around the clock, unmoved, untouched, yet clearly used. Sometimes when I drive through it's vacant. At other times, two or three old men sit, gesticulating, laughing. Intermittently women join them, hands to hips, watching the progress of a card game.

The spring day's moist with devolving thunderheads. Cruising south towards Century, I take a right and am struck by the broad expanse of an undeveloped block wild with foxtails and burs we call "cuckabugs." In the middle of this unplanned Wyeth, a collapsible Formica-topped table hosts an ebony-skinned quartet playing dominoes, three men and a woman. As I pass them, one man makes that characteristic waffle of the arm signaling victory, slamming home the winning golden bone.

The Freedom Tree once stood near the tracks, bound by Grandee, Beach Street and 103rd in Watts proper, on an ill-defined lot littered with empty oil drums and piles of wood. I came across it in 1968 when a teenager was killed on the lot in an officer-involved shooting. It was a bad place to die but a good place to congregate, a site of refuge, political debates and "catch action." There was a constant flow of cheap alcohol and drugs, gambling, shooting craps—the kind of business that birthed folk songs like *Stagger Lee*. Nobody knew how long the tree had been there or how it had come by its name. Like the Watts Towers, it symbolized the community. When the police needed informers, they knew where to find them. When no one wanted to talk, there was no one under the tree. It's gone now.

"What's that all about?" I once asked a street-philosopher friend, sharing observations of what I suspected was a kind of communal ritual. It simply happened. People found each other. Swapped stories. Laughed and cried. Then went on. "Is this some kinda holdover from Africa?"

He laughed. "I don't think so. I've seen it too. Not that I've been everywhere. And we aren't the only ones who do it. It seems to be something poor people do all across the United States. Especially in the South. And when they don't have parks, they improvise. It's like having a club without walls."

Three hefty women preside over the ramshackle gray-blue porch on 89th Street, the older obviously the grandmother. Her two little granddaughters play on the patch of lawn behind the chicken wire fence as the younger women chat, brown hair freshly pressed back against their scalps. Everyone's gotten their hair straight-ironed this morning, including the young man. His hair is parted into a perfect gridwork of symmetrical, tightly bound nubbins fanning up from his scalp. With subdued pride, he rises from the stoop to jaw it over with an inquiring film crew. His red polyester shirt hangs to the ragged border of his green pj bottoms, which threaten to drop from his hips.

Yeah. He's a Blood. He fires a cigarette, leans into the fence, and describes how his days are spent. Yeah. Of course, the high unemployment, hours sitting around, smoking marijuana and drinking wine.

And, of course, nothing's changed since the verdicts. It's just the way things are.

Slow Rap for Brandon

tis the season filled with sorrow
pretty manchild no tomorrow
called yourself a rapster a thugsta
another misunderstood youngsta

BRANDON NILES WAS sweet seventeen when he kicked.

The first time I saw him, he was a four-year-old with his mom, Sylvia, my baby brother's ex-girlfriend. For a decade, they shared our family holiday celebrations. Then we lost touch. Until six weeks ago.

"He was scared, Wanda," Sylvia told me then. "He was so scared."

She says that when Brandon gave over to peer pressures, his attitude changed: " 'In order for me to be with them I have to act like them—but that doesn't mean I'm one of them.' "

His homies re-christened him Eyeball. He was always lookin', enormous sad orbs scoping for possibilities—a way out. He took to rhyme in his spare time. He hid his product in a shoe box, wrote rap songs about his struggle to cope, hoping someday to break large and in charge.

Sylvia had tried her best to save him. Three years earlier, after Brandon had been robbed of a brand-new leather jacket at Uzi-point, she got her employers to transfer her to another state. Things did not work out. Within a year she and Brandon returned to South Central. Caught between the law and the lawless, his guilt by association went like this:

"Brandon knew these guys who robbed some people. He tried to stop them, he even told them it wasn't right, but they wouldn't listen," Sylvia says. "He felt so bad he even gave the victims $10 of his own money, all he had.

"When the police car arrived, everybody ran but Brandon. He was innocent, so why run?

"The cops didn't see it that way. Brandon caught the case."

Witnesses and victims alike testified, Sylvia says, that "Brandon was *not* one of the robbers. The judge refused to weigh their testimony. It angered and confused Brandon that the man who decided his future read a newspaper throughout his trial. Brandon was placed under house arrest until his sentencing, which was deliberately set to fall *after* his 18th birthday."

That means Brandon could do more time sentenced as an adult. Brandon believed his rights were being taken for a crime he didn't commit. His life was being put on hold.

"Wanda, they had him trapped like a dog. He was convicted of strong-arm robbery. I told Brandon they were tryin' to strip him of his manhood. That's why they wouldn't listen. He became terrified of the police. Whenever he saw them, when we were out driving, he would ask me, 'Please, Mama, can we get off this street?' "

A month before Brandon died he tried to explain the way he felt to his mother. "You just don't understand," he said when they argued.

"I didn't know how deep it really was," Sylvia says.

" 'Eyeball never rolled with us—never got stopped,' " his homies told her. Whenever Brandon got mad he hung out with the crew, but rarely was he out later than eleven o'clock. Whenever he stayed late they figured, "He musta had it with Mom." The OGs (older gangsters) would escort him, never letting Brandon come home alone. "It was just a way of livin'."

"The court sent him to two Crip schools knowing he was a Blood," Sylvia says. "Wanda, I swear I did not know. I'd wake him up, send him to school and couldn't understand why he didn't have any enthusiasm.

"He was branded a Blood because of the turf he grew up in," she says. "Brandon couldn't ride a city bus, couldn't get out at a certain corner, would say, 'Mama, I can't go into that store,' and I would say, 'Boy, why can't you go into that store? It's a free country!' "

Desperate, Sylvia went back to her employers for help. This time the choice was no choice.

Brandon was shot and killed in a South Central pay phone booth at Jefferson between Wadsworth and Griffith while he talked to his girlfriend, Rosa. No arrests were made.

"The man who killed him lived less than a half block away from my mother. We all grew up in the same neighborhood. It was three of 'em who rolled up on Brandon. The only thing I don't know is who pulled the trigger."

> *your potent youth was wasted*
> *before it was even tasted*
> *of your love her arms were robbed*
> *the future she once had in you*
> *is spent in sobs*

Sylvia takes modest comfort in recalling the times she over-heard Brandon laughing and loud-talking with his friends, fellow Thugstas, the name of their rap group. They were hyped about getting over with their songs, dreaming of the big money, the big time, and someday buying their mothers the big house. She hadn't known they were serious.

Then she found the box.

Sylvia, who hopes to get her son's rap songs published, meets with the mothers of other children who have died violently. Their support group is called Drive-By Agony. It's not enough, but it's a start.

"When goin' through his box, I found this rap song written a few days before Brandon died," her voice trembles. "It tells of his death. He saw himself die, and had risen up—was callin' to his homies but they couldn't hear him.

"And he was rising toward the light."

Library Time

AS I TRAILED PAPA into our neighborhood library, I was awed by the smells of lacquered wood and book leather. A handful of patrons read quietly while we waited at the counter manned by an elderly assistant librarian whose glasses hung at her neck on a silver chain, like extra wattles. Fascinated, I watched her pinched, rouge mouth instruct us on applying for my first library card.

To the annoyance of the head librarian, watching from a discreet distance, Papa, still in work duds, curled up to catnap in an armchair. I happily lost myself in the stacks. Starting at the top of the alphabet, I discovered William Hervey Allen, Earl Derr Biggers, Anton Chekhov, and Mama's favorite, Mary Roberts Rinehart. I roused Papa and we headed for checkout, where I presented my temporary card to the assistant.

"Sorry, young lady! You can't check out *these* books on *this* card!"

"W-w-whattt?" I sputtered.

"These must be checked out by an adult! *Your* card is valid only for the children's sections."

I was ten years old. I looked at Papa. He shrugged. Having overheard, the head librarian steered me to the shelves of thin books covered in glossy pastel paper boards. I settled for the small section for teens, rejecting the girls' books—heroic RNs, female sleuths, waifs coming-of-age—for the boys' section, loaded with delights by Sir Arthur Conan Doyle, Howard Pease, H. Rider Haggard and Robert Louis Stevenson. Again I headed for checkout.

"Sorr-*rry*," crooned the amused assistant, "books in the *girls'* section only."

Papa insisted I obey the rules. Battling angry tears, I plucked randomly from the girls' shelf. I brooded all the way home, refusing defeat. Just before time to return my books, I took Papa aside.

"Daddy—would you do me a favor?"

"What?"

"Get yourself a library card."

"Me? Why?"

"So I can check out adult books under your name." He smiled, game. The next night, armed with his temporary card, he accompanied me through the adult section. During checkout, the assistant eyed us nastily but said nothing.

‡

I've almost outgrown my suspicion of libraries as hostile-if-seductive environs where Western culture guards against us barbarians. The services offered—from bookmobiles to research hotlines—are indispensable. And having one in the neighborhood, accessible to my children, is invaluable. When living on 120th Street, we frequently visited the AC Bilbrew Library after school and on Saturdays.

The site of the Black Resource Center, the Bilbrew houses a significant Black musical collection and the *Los Angeles Sentinel* archives, dating back to 1935. Located on El Segundo Boulevard, it's the only county library designed by an Afro-American, architect Vincent Proby, and named for an Afro-American, AC Bilbrew. Born in 1888, in Washington, Arkansas, she died in Los Angeles in June, 1972, leaving two daughters and, according to granddaughter Bonnie White Mitchell, her treasured grand piano.

AC, her given name (after two nuns who'd befriended her mother), was a film actress (*The Foxes of Harrow, Hearts of Dixie*) and a choir director. Woman of the Year (1958), she was the first Black soloist on radio (1923), and hosted the first Black music radio program, KGFJ's "The Gold Hour" (1940–42). She was an advocate of women's rights and children's literacy ("Don't cry—qualify") and founded the Opportunity Workshops after the Watts Riots.

Worried that the Bilbrew might be among the libraries closed because of recent funding crises, I asked about the impact of cutbacks on South Central. "Whenever there's a state budget crunch, we're always the first to be X-ed out," said Joyce Sumbi, L.A.'s first Black county library administrator, and founding member of the California Librarians Black Caucus. Louise Parsons, the Resource Librarian at Bilbrew, agrees—adding that the closures will directly affect her job, and all Southern California, where the largest number of minority librarians are employed. So far, the Bilbrew has been targeted for shortened hours.

Sumbi complains that circulation figures trotted out to justify the cutbacks inaccurately reflect library use. "Where will our children go?" she asks. "If books aren't checked out they don't show up on the stats," which don't account for businessmen catching up on current affairs during lunch or students doing homework.

ₓ

The poetry fest is ending. As we leave the Felipe de Neve City Library on 6th, I notice a Latino man in his work duds. He sits awkwardly in an armchair near the children's section. I laugh softly. He reminds me of Papa and our long-ago adventure. It looks strangely funny, to see a grown man reading from a thin book covered in glossy pastel paper boards. Then I notice he's slowly, silently mouthing the words. I'm impressed. He's not just reading, *he's teaching himself to speak English.*

Violence, Art & Hustle

MY LIFE IS SO ENTWINED with this city that I can't talk about it without talking about myself—I can't talk about myself without talking about it. This is my art.

I know no other terrain—so intimately.

Its violence is my violence.

A few days ago I received a copy of the text for my listing in a book on contemporary Black authors. As I neared the end of it, I came across a sentence that startled me. It was a direct quote. The interviewer had asked if people were afraid of me. "Oh, God, are they ever, man. And maybe with good reason. Because often …I'm just a moment away from homicide. I'm that kind of angry." I was shocked and dismayed by my own statement—by the truth in it. By its power. By how much it reflected the actuality of South Central's eruption April 30th 1992. It was a statement I'd made four years earlier. It was not the kind of statement I wanted to leave behind. I red-inked it immediately and asked the editor to honor my deletion.

And then I tried not to think about it.

But the violence following the verdict in the Rodney King beating trial, has not gone away. It has been subsumed. I see the evidence everywhere. In the urgent ways people move on the streets. In the increased car chases and accidents. The way local news broadcasts ceaselessly exploit a segment of the city they always ignored. I see it in the ferocity of others, in their eagerness to define and encompass the psyche of Los Angeles—for profit. And I see it in myself.

I was compelled to be involved in this. I called myself being responsible, doing what I saw needed to be done. I saw myself as a medium through which dialogue could take place—the kind of dialogue this city needed. But I learned early on that my sense of dedication would not be appreciated or widely recognized. I have to look at that. To lick my wounds. To be subjective in a way that heals.

What do I want?

What South Central wants.

But what I want is expressed in emotional extremes. I'm paralyzed with rage. With fear of rage, and of acting it out. With the need to strike back against what (and who) has hurt me and mine. Yet, I want to be quiet—to quietly withdraw. To be still—to meditate. To do my work my art my writing. To not pick up the phone and not be up on all the gossip. To not constantly run to this place and that discussing the direction which must be gone in to get where. To not sit on this panel and that panel. To not watch the watchers. I want to work through my grief.

I want to sit at his grave and talk to my father.

I want him to speak to me from his grave.

I want his help.

I want to drive out to the Inglewood cemetery. Dig into the ground. Take out his bones. Resurrect him and say, "Here is your youth. Start over. And this time—succeed."

Here you go, Papa. Here's that sleek new ride you always craved and never divined. Here's that house up on Sugar Hill. Here's those snazzy pinstripe vines. Here's that reeet-street jitterbug heaven. Here's the green, long and deep.

Here's what you could've should've would've done done.

I want to stop being angry about you, Papa.

I want to stop the mourning and the moaning.

He had his life, I keep saying, *now you're having yours.*

And what is mine?

I'm in the little shuttle cart that trucks folks across the motion picture lot. I have an appointment at the office of the hottest young Black Director. My new agent sent my "calling card" or sample script over and they liked it. So now I'm on my way to pitch some story ideas of my own, trying to con myself into believing that this is an opportunity. That these younger Blacks will be more receptive to me than the hoary Hollywood suits I encountered after the Watts Riots. That they'll be more sensitive to who I am. But even as I think these simplistic thoughts I am embarrassed. I am driven here by desperation. The simple need for the money.

I'm struck by the ironies of my trek. They resonate and shimmer.

I keep remembering a friend's words: "They sent your stuff back. You're their worst nightmare. When you show up, everyone gets nervous." I know he's given me the gospel. I'm hoping for a fluke. For amnesia.

𝆩

I drove to the studio in the old struggle buggy—parked it out-of-sight in the garage, praying that my arrival was not witnessed by someone vital to my future. It's leaking oil, threatening to throw a rod. Needs the valve job I can't afford. The Crown Victoria was stolen a few days ago and stripped beyond recovery.

I walked barefoot down the exit ramp to the elevator, my suede pumps in my hand. I've never gotten used to them. And now I'm so overweight the pressure of my step has nearly destroyed them. They'll do for today.

As I get within peeping distance of the guards I slip on my heels. I ask for directions to Mr. Hotshot's office. One guard, also Black, tells me where to wait for the shuttle and which building I'm going to, then hands me a visitor's pass.

The blue and brown shuttle van arrives. Three people have boarded ahead of me. A sistuh, my size, weight and age, is stretched across a rear seat that's wide enough to seat two six-footers. Two muscular White men in work sweats occupy the lounge seat facing the shuttle's panel-door but there's room enough for two more men. There's a small catbird seat opposite the driver, facing the interior. This is the most comfortable seat in the van. I'm anxious about my appointment, like the neat little seat, and take it.

"Excuse me, *Ma'am*. You'll have to sit somewheres else."

I look right into the driver's face. He's an Italian-American, sweaty brown hair beneath his charcoal gray cap. He's got on a khaki shirt and dark gray workman's trousers. He's manning his bus with all 150 pounds of tobacco-laced proletarian machismo. He doesn't like my looks and I don't care for his.

"Why?"

"You'll have to sit somewheres else!"

"I'm fine—right here."

"I want you should move."

Hmmm I think, *Jersey.* "No."

"You don't move this bus don't move."

I fought an impulse to scream on this ignoramus in a modified baseball cap. But I needed any energy I had for my interview. As I argued with my temper for control, he interrupted.

"I can't see through the side mirror there with you sittin' there." He was plaintive.

They do it with mirrors.

I didn't believe him, but since I couldn't see from his angle I didn't know if he spoke the truth. The other passengers were silent but radiated impatience. I decided it was best to be philosophical about it and move. Looking into the pleasant, oval, honey-colored face of the sistuh, I took the seat next to her. Her fried brown hair cupped her head neatly in soft waves ending at her neckline. We said nothing. But she knew and I knew that he'd forced me to move because I was too big and too Black, and it gave him the heebs just looking at me—from the top of my dreads to the tips of my fat toes.

She got off at the next stop and disappeared, her pastel purple print dress hugged to her ample figure in the light afternoon breeze.

$$\sharp$$

Within minutes I was wandering through the building housing Mr. Hotshot's production company. Arriving on time, I'm invited into the office of Mr. Hotshot's assistant. It's shockingly spare—and the mode is temporary. There are no paintings on the walls. The desk is cluttered with reels of film and scripts. I vaguely wonder if mine is in the stack. He's Black preppy fresh, wire-rimmed glasses, long-sleeved shirt, suspenders and bowtie. From D.C.—and doesn't know a thing about me or my city. But he liked my script—it read well—he was curious (but now, disappointed) to meet me.

He gives me the once-over. I'm too big and too black—even for him. I wonder if I remind him uncomfortably of his mother or an aunt. I see that this is going to go nowhere. But I go through the motions.

I watch his bodily movements as we talk, the way he looks down the bridge of his nose at me, then readjusts his glasses with either index finger. He's my height, wiry—a similar build to

Mr. Hotshot's, but about two shades brighter.

As I sit there I recall the morning following the eruption of the violence. I remember seeing Mr. Hotshot interviewed via satellite; how inarticulate Mr. Hotshot was about my city and its troubles; how enraged I was that Hollywood people, the people most removed from the Florence-Normandie flashpoint, were invited to speak but that native-born artists—specifically me—were not.

≠

But wasn't/isn't that the point? They don't want the hard message. They don't want it stated clearly. They want it confused— sweetly confused. They want it coming out the fuzzy-hippy-dippy-Zen-sugary-and-can't-we-all-get-along mouth of someone who doesn't threaten their racist assumptions. They want it mushy and well-intended. Oozing psycho-syrup. Guilt-free and soft, like a suppository.

And now here I am sitting up in the man's office, sipping sparkling mineral water, hoping I can score some much-needed cash. Because he's achieved success in a way that has eluded me. His assistant has a strange smirk—which I interpret as his attempt to imagine what kind of past would inspire the seamy script I wrote. I shine this on and take care of business, reading aloud the ethnic-specific story ideas I've neatly typed on 3x5 cards.

"I like that one, but we've already got something similar to it in the works.

"That one's fine, but I can't visualize your characters.

"I like that one. We'd be glad to take a look at what you do, if you want to develop it further."

He knows and I know that any commitment means cash-on-the-table under the terms of the Guild. To "develop it further" would mean writing on speculation. ("We all do that sort of thing," one scriptwriter-friend once reminded me.) And I see he's not going to give me the go. Then it gets stranger.

"We're having our own troubles—there's just no development money around," he volunteers. "Things were really good a few months ago—now they're tight. We don't know what's going to happen ourselves."

So, as I suspected, Mr. Hotshot's new release is a turkey!

≠

As expected, I leave the office without the proverbial cigar.

Stepping into the return shuttle I realize it's the same one. It's nearly packed. The driver doesn't recognize me (because he didn't see me, just my Blackness) even though our exchange occurred only 70 minutes earlier. To my delight, the same sistuh is also on the shuttle. This time she's sitting on the lounge, squeezed to the rear, in with the male passengers. She smiles when she sees me. I smile back. I take her former seat at the back of the shuttle, diagonal to her, making it easy for us to exchange glances.

At the next stop, an Anglo-Saxon blonde, 5'6", 125 pounds, B-cup, in a pale blue, matches-her-eyes, sleeveless summer dress, climbs on board. We notice the light of approval in the driver's smile. She immediately squeezes into the lounge, directly behind him, and asks for directions. He leers and invites her to sit in the catbird seat so he doesn't risk killing the rest of us in a collision. She complies.

Me and the sistuh glue her down under our eyes. We read her body language, how she semiconsciously flirts with the asshole behind the wheel. How her dress falls open several inches above the knees to reveal well-shaped tanned gams. How she tosses her head, flipping her hair, then primps it into place with birdlike flits. How she engages in inane chatter with the horny idiot, who's clearly trying to score, oblivious to the fact that the rest of us have to endure this drek.

The sistuh and I exchange a look then break into titters. She leans toward me and whispers fiercely, "White girls!"

I notice my stop is coming up. It's also the blonde's stop and she exits first, the sistuh following. I climb out alongside her and whisper in her ear, "More like poor white trash!" We burst into loud, contemptuous sniggers. As I turn to look back, I catch the eyes of the driver. Puzzled, he senses we're laughing at him, but can't figure it. The blonde notices as well, looks at us, then away, heading for the garage elevator.

"Girlfriend—you've got more nerve than I do. Cuz I thought it but I didn't dare say it," the sistuh snorts. "These fools have no idea of what they look like to us."

"You ain't nevah lied."

‡

Then she went her way and I went mine.

I call my agent the next afternoon for the verdict. She tells me that Mr. Hotshot's office has found me insufficient. It's a pass. I'm sentenced to limbo.

Two demeaning strikes and I'm out.

I want to recoup my aborted film school education. I want to shake someone until they tell me that my story is worth the price of the ticket.

It's not gonna happen. Not today.

I decide that somehow I'm gonna make it or break it.

And then I get down in them dumps.

I think about all I'm not doing because.

I tap into the rage I thought I'd vanquished. It raises up and consumes me.

I'm gonna break it.

I'm stung and amazed by my lack of resistance to the powers that minimize my existence. I want them to feel the same pain the same rage the same hopelessness. I want my own private riot. I want to take a baseball bat and crush in somebody's window. Or somebody's skull. I want to loot and burn.

I want to say, "Yeah suckas. You don't want to listen. Except when I get nasty. And even then you don't listen."

On August 4th the sentence comes down. Powell and Koon get 30 months each—2½ years in Club Fed. No fine. No restitution. No justice. Again.

Father.

I want to stop being angry about you. And about the generations of young Black men who've had their heads and hopes beaten in by The Law. I want to stop raging about the lost generations of Black artists aborted by the conspiracy of circumstances. I want to stop being angry about injustice and poverty and the Mississippi goddamned hunger. Father, help me—I don't know how.

And then my father speaks to me.

I hear the slow wisdom of his death.

You know better, he says.

"Yes—Papa," I answer. "I know better."

And the rage gives way to a hurt so deep I feel it to my grave.

Don't think about it. Live it. I know you can do it. I know you have the power. Believe.

Oh, Papa. Would that I could.

Could that I would.

≠ ≠

MANY SONGS ONE CITY
red black brown yellow white, the colors of our hope
together we build our city, paving our streets in stars
desert man ocean woman mountain child river spirit wind
we live this land, plant our faith, harvest its wealth
PSALM FOR THE ANGELS

—poem written to be read in the round, inscribed in wood
at Grand Hope Park, Downtown L.A., dedicated June 1993

The Healing Walls

IT'S A WORKDAY AFTERNOON and except for an occasional docent or security guard, I have the entire Detroit Institute of Arts to myself. I'm alone in the Garden Court, absorbed by the frescoes of Mexican muralist Diego Rivera. I'm overwhelmed by the magnitude of Rivera's angular Amazons. Beyond the elemental symbolism of industry, desire, fertility and creation, what strikes me most is that they look like me and I look like them, the first images of the feminine with which I can identify...

I'm in the seat next to Bobbi as she jumps from the car and dashes across the busy Sydney street. As she hurries into the bank, a fiercely white, squat stucco building, my eyes are drawn along stark, staid corporate walls and captured by a single handprint the color of blood dried to blackening. Four inches below its ruddy base, the insolent palm drizzles to nothing. I suddenly feel it to my bones. As my pulse roars in my ears, I'm flooded by a strange sense of recognition, awed by something aboriginal, metaphorical and insurrectionary...

We're driving east along Sunset Boulevard. "Look," my husband points to the wall of the Echo Park building. "They covered it up! Whatta shame." His favorite stylin'-and-bombin' wall, tagged with the rebellious urban scrawl of graffiti artists, has been painted over with a pedestrian business advertisement. That particular wall always excited his aesthetics, aroused sightings of his bohemian past as if he'd suddenly discovered that a bit of dear ol'

179

Manhattan had broken off and slid west to the cultural waste-lands....

≠

On a diamond-blue spring afternoon, I find myself among the pleased and the preening at the unveiling. In the wake of the verdict in the Rodney King beating trial, and the violence that followed, the staff of the California Employment Development Department (EDD) was inspired to do something to help heal the community. And so the Interactive Arts Team Project was born.

≠

After nearly two years, the 27-foot-long wall inside the department has been completed by six high school students under the guidance of artists Sally Howell Comaire and George Evans. Brought together as an art team by Joyce Silber, I.A.A.R.P. Consulting Facilitator, Comaire and Evans took the project to Cultural Affairs, then canvassed local high school art teachers for student recommendations. Initially funded with EDD money, the project was completed with several small recovery arts grants.

Roses and certificates of merit are presented to Patricia Ayala from Jordan High; Iesha Perkins, from Locke High; De'Shaun Brown also from Locke, but now studying civil engineering at Cal State Long Beach; Reyna Mendez and Horacio Serrano, from Jordan, both awarded Restyle L.A. scholarships to art school; and Milo Pipkins from Inglewood High.

"It made me feel more positive about myself. Not all young people are bad"—Iesha.

"I expected to work with people, but I didn't expect to make friends"—Horacio.

"If I had been in my own country, I would already have babies, and all I would have ahead of me would be many more babies. And now I have in front of me many opportunities... before working on this mural, I would never have dared to dream"—Reyna.

≠

"Ours was a master-apprentice relationship...We gave the students our skills, but it's their concept. It gave me a chance to put something back into my community...something that should've never left"—Evans.

"The qualities you see in the mural are the qualities they expressed with one another: hope, dignity, value, promise, self-discipline, integrity. They would not put their names on something they were not proud of"—Sally Howell Comaire.

≠

Their utopian vision pulls me into an Eden of brightly colored tropical birds and a lush harmony of vines. A child lifts herself heavenward in a swing, her long earthen hair caressed by sighing wind. A young man creates a rolling river of hope from his labor, which feeds and restores Los Angeles—making it paradise renewed. Above, white clouds dot a listening sky....

≠

"Girls used to bother me about being in gangs. They don't bother me any more...All those girls are either pregnant or dead"—Reyna.

"I had never worked with other races outside my own. It helped show me that we can and that we should work together... from the heart"—De'Shaun.

NOTE

Patricia Ayala continues her education at Brooks Fashion Institute in Long Beach, California. De'Shaun Brown is at Morehouse College, Atlanta. Iesha Perkins has graduated from Locke. Horacio Serrano attends a Saturday arts workshop. Milo Pipkins left the arts workshop without notice following, the director surmises, notoriety brought to his family, when an aunt, a juror, was dismissed during the O.J. Simpson trial. Reyna Mendez died of smoke inhalation when her home mysteriously caught fire.

City in Denial: L.A. Diary, 1993

THE CASE WAS TURNED over to the jury at 3:05 on Saturday afternoon, April 10th.

As soon as the jury in the federal civil rights trial of four L.A.P.D. officers was sequestered, a bizarre countdown began. It was my experience that while Blacks went about their business, Whites seemed unable to talk about anything but the next verdict and the next riot.

Determined not to be caught with their lenses down this time, local, national and international media landed on L.A. with the ferocity of swarming locusts. Reporters roared across the urban terrain talking to everyone, from grade school children to Police Chief Willie Williams, from mayoral candidates to the homeless. Not all of the coverage was sympathetic. One Long Beach police officer was embarrassed out of business when a television consumer reporter exposed the cop's 1-900-RIOT survival hotline, a pay-per-dial private-enterprise version of L.A. County's free rumor-control information service.

One station offered "jury watch"—live reports every hour on the hour—reminding viewers that the federal judge had promised he would give only a 15-minute warning or lead time before the verdict was announced. Angelenos were repeatedly informed by KCAL News that this time around the jury would be fairer because it consisted of "two Blacks, two Latinos and nine Anglos" (the jury of twelve had two Blacks, *one* Latino and nine Whites). The night the jury went out a police car had had its windows shot out. Details were few and sketchy.

The media emphasized how important it had been for

Rodney King himself to testify, "to show that he is a human being." As trial coverage progressed, TV viewers were also told that the officers, particularly Laurence Powell, were afraid of King. Viewers were not reminded, however, that King had been surrounded, that twenty-one police officers were present during the beating and that most of them stood around watching. Even if King had single-handedly overcome the L.A.P.D. Four, it would've taken superhuman strength to overcome the other seventeen.

According to a Saturday KCBS newscast, an estimated $2.5 million dollars a day was spent to mobilize 600 extra cops plus another half-million dollars to mobilize National Guard troops in anticipation of violence. Viewers learned that officers had been on twelve-hour rotating shifts since April 8th, costing taxpayers an estimated $170,000 per day in overtime. This in the same city where an initiative to hire an additional 1000 officers went down to defeat during riot curfew last year. The Coliseum parking lot, near the heart of South Central, was the "staging point" for deployment. When the smog cleared, 6,500 officers were on the street, including Highway Patrol officers from Northern California.

Public pleas for calm were echoed throughout the Black churchgoing and business communities. Even the manager of a popular Black-owned chicken-and-waffles chain appeared on TV to preach the gospel of "stay indoors/stay alive." Two Latino members of the Los Angeles Conservation Corps, a job-training organization for teens and young adults, were interviewed on a neighborhood-to-hood news segment in which emphasis was placed on poetry and dance workshops and other cultural pro-grams for teens. Groups like the Conservation Corps and Save Our Youth are still rare and underfunded, in spite of a recent Rebuild L.A. survey showing that residents in the four areas most affected by last year's riots feel that youth and recreational ser-vices are critical to healing the city.

Despite the lack of city services in those areas, tensions seemed to be building everywhere but in South Central. A riot hotline reported the rumor that 200,000 Blacks were going to "invade" Beverly Hills and West Los Angeles. (Ironically, certain side streets providing access to the westside have remained closed since police cordoned them off in May 1992.) Beginning on Easter Sunday, April 11th, the city experienced a calm inspired by dread. Streets were eerily quiet. Traffic was wonderfully, unusually light.

183

Many people either stayed out of the city or left town, like one close White friend who went to Santa Cruz, "to wait for the verdict." The panic-buying of firearms and groceries by well-heeled L.A. Whites and some Koreans received national publicity.

Southern California gun shops and supermarkets did remain open on the religious holiday in order to profit from fear. By contrast, Easter in South Central was fairly quiet: church pews were packed, children hunted for tinted eggs, and the air smelled of barbecue. The only notable violence to erupt was in the San Fernando Valley, miles north, in Balboa Park near the community of Encino. Gunfire claimed two-year-old Ryan Brown, a Black child, when a bullet entered an open car window and struck him in the head. He was one of several innocent bystanders caught in the crossfire of the gang warfare that has continued nonstop since April/May 1992, despite ongoing media hype about a so-called gang truce.

On Monday, April 12th a "law enforcement expert" testified that Powell's baton swings were insufficient because they didn't break any of King's bones or knock King unconscious. Television viewers were repeatedly told, "We'll bring you developments as they occur." Yet several such developments outside the courtroom went unreported. For example, on Tuesday, two bomb threats: one against the fortresslike central Post Office at Florence and Central Avenues, and another against Los Angeles City College.

The media, like local government and law enforcement, seemed to operate on the assumption that Black people are easily incited to violence. These institutions were more interested in superficially managing White fear and Black anger than in questioning or engaging it. Either would pose too great a challenge. News reporters focused on the Black church, replaying image after image of Blacks attending rousing sermons and singing enthusiastically. The images of peace-loving, happy Black people may have been intended to assuage the guilt and dread of White viewers, but many were already, pardon the pun, too spooked. Foot-traffic along trendy business promenades like West Hollywood's Melrose Avenue had dropped to zero, as did attendance at cultural and sports events, especially those taking place after sundown.

On Wednesday, April 14th, Rodney King's appearance at Dodger Stadium ("I want to be a baseball fan today") got twice the coverage of the team's opening home-game loss. Truck driver Reginald Denny appeared on the "Today" show. "I'm willing to give those guys a chance," he said, referring to the trial of his alleged assailants, the L.A. Three (Damian "Football" Williams, Antoine Miller, Henry Watson), now scheduled to start on July 14th. But the unassuming and exceptionally benign Denny admonished the L.A.P.D Four as "trained officers who should know better."

Apparently, L.A.P.D. central was taking heed of the rumor factor, as barriers went up around the federal courthouse on Wednesday. A convenience store chain, notorious for overcharging Black customers, began issuing free red, white and blue peace ribbons. In the meantime, the Panorama City building housing one of L.A. County's thirty underfunded welfare offices was set ablaze by an angry recipient.

That day, KNBC viewers and *Los Angeles Times* readers learned that the city's population would grow at the rate of seventy-six people per hour until the year 2040, the new residents being mainly Latinos and Asians. Increased immigration and birthrates will spur this explosion, and apparently offset the growing numbers of inner-city middle- and working-class Blacks forced out of the inner city in search of better housing and services. To me, the depressing implication of these stories is that with increasing numbers of Asians and Latinos in the L.A. mix, Black demands for social and political parity will become less and less relevant to the political establishment. They won't have to listen to us if we've left.

On Thursday, April 15th, two unsubstantiated rumors of violence circulated on the South Central grapevine. The first was about a young man, purportedly a candidate for the police academy, who was shot and killed by police officers because he witnessed a man being beaten "just like Rodney King." The second rumor was of the shooting of a police officer in South Central, at 92nd and Wall Streets. No witnesses were found in either incident, but some people were taking the rumors very seriously. A journalist friend told me that the Santa Monica office of the *Times* had its employees undergo gas-mask drills. That same day, Parker Center, L.A.P.D headquarters and site of a major post-verdict demonstration a year earlier, was barricaded without explanation. Actions like these lent credence to unfounded rumors and simply heightened the level of fear and expectation in the city.

On Friday morning, the 16th, the anxiety of the entire city was crystallized in the behavior of a young Armenian-American teller where I bank. As I signed my deposit slip, she noticed that I was wearing several rings on both hands and that I also wore earrings. "Aren't you afraid to wear those?" she asked. Puzzled, I looked up to notice that the young woman's multiply-pierced earlobes, usually laden with three or four gold hoops, were bare. Except for a lone ring, so were her fingers. She hastily explained that the one pearl and diamond ring she wore belonged to her mother and she was going to return it that afternoon for safekeeping. She was afraid of being robbed during the violence certain to erupt. I had to laugh.

What wasn't laughable, however, was that the week's hottest information was kept from the public that evening: the jury's verdict. It would not be announced until Saturday at 7 a.m. The city held its breath.

The announcement of two guilty verdicts (out of a possible seven) for Officers Powell and Koon, kicked off a five-hour frenzy of reportage. Media focus was primarily on the relief ("I feel like I'm walking on cotton") and jubilation following the verdicts, the success of law-enforcement mobilization, glad-handing by those who called for peace, victory interviews with Mayor Tom Bradley and L.A.P.D. Chief Willie Williams, and charges of double jeopardy by former Chief Daryl Gates.

That afternoon the streets of Watts were quiet. Attendance was disappointingly low at the opening of the "Memory, Fire, Rebirth" exhibit of African-American historical and cultural artifacts at the Watts Towers Arts Center. Sponsored in part by a Los Angeles Arts Recovery Fund grant, the exhibit was conceived to counteract "lies and misconceptions [about] the African-American ...to set the record straight."

That day, scant few would enjoy the portrait of Huey Newton by Bernard Hayes. An oil on canvas, his work celebrates the symbol of a failed movement: a white-eyed, white-whiskered, white-clawed, snarling black panther.

Few would see the historical reminders of local and national Black heroes, from Biddy Mason and Scott Joplin to Officer Robert W. Stewart, L.A.'s first Afro-American police officer (hired in 1886), or read the tribute to Anna and Henry Laws, a couple jailed in the mid-1950s after buying a home at 92nd and Hoover, in violation of the Housing Covenant Laws, which barred Blacks from buying property in White-only parts of Los Angeles.

The "inflammatory" conceptual construction of a wall of

anger by Greg Pitts would also be underappreciated that afternoon. It was incomplete when I walked over to introduce myself to the artist, careful to avoid stepping on what looked like the makings of several symbolic Molotov cocktails. On the wall he had drilled a neat series of holes, spelling out the phrase made famous by a contrite Rodney G. King: "Can't we all just get along?" Mounted in each hole was an unlit matchstick.

On the Hollywood freeway, headed north, my husband and I marveled at the absence of the Highway Patrol (likely cruising the streets, rousting potential looters, we decided). On the warped blacktop of the parking lot at KPFK, the North Hollywood site of Pacifica Radio, we met fellow volunteer workers and guests for that evening's show. Only three of us were Black. It was still early evening, with plenty of daylight left. As we exchanged greetings, our attention was suddenly diverted as two patrol cars jammed with officers and riot gear drove up on the lot, checked us out, sped past us and disappeared east along Cahuenga Boulevard. Three hours later, as my husband and I shot pool in the funky digs of Fais Do Do, a Crenshaw-area nightspot, six uniformed officers strolled in and spent a full twenty minutes establishing their presence. As we tried to ignore them, I couldn't help but recall the caption I'd seen, while at the Watts Tower exhibit, in a photocopy of the Black Panthers' newspaper. It read, "Let the Pigs Oink for Themselves Till Their Last Oink."

Meanwhile the rest of the city celebrated.

There was a party held at the site of last year's flashpoint, the intersection of Florence and Normandie in South Central.

"We must move forward," is the battle cry of city fathers and politicians. But there's a nasty undercurrent that's almost palpable. There's a new Black rage in South Central, the anger that comes from still being misjudged in spite of all the talk and hype. Many are dissatisfied and bewildered at those outside the war zone who seem to have no way of fully comprehending the siege mentality that has dominated life in Southern California, before and since August 1965.

There are those who feel justice has not been served, and may never be served. They are inclined to point out that Koon and Powell plan to appeal their cases and may be successful. They voice expectations of minimal sentencing, "slaps on the wrist."

They express relief over the verdict and say the hailing of Chief Willie Williams as a hero ultimately demeans the residents of South Central. They know the prevailing assumption, nearly impossible to dispel, is that it was the Simi Valley verdict in the original King beating trial which caused the Spring 1992 violence rather than a twenty-seven-year accumulation of tensions and frustrations.

The tensions were merely *ignited*, not created, by the decision in the Rodney King beating trial. The media have played down the failure to establish a citizens' police review board; the impact of hate crimes (736 in L.A. in 1992, the largest number against Blacks); the episodes of police brutality and racism, particularly the shooting-death of 50-year-old Eulia Love, on January 3rd 1979, over an unpaid utility bill; and the dismantling of property tax funding for public schools. Also played down are the deficits in decent low and median income housing: skyrises reporting a 52 percent vacancy rate (rumor sets the figure at 72 percent), while a highly visible predominantly Black homeless and jobless population congests downtown sidewalks surrounding the law-enforcement headquarters at Parker Center and the palm-lined promenades of Santa Monica. These factors contributed directly to the anger that propelled the riot, and they continue to pose untenable challenges to political and civic leaders. It is no coincidence that race is at the core of each.

There are those Angelenos who are thoroughly cynical about the fact that the politicians are already buzzing about the impending "long hot summer." There are those who believe the future looks very grim for African-Americans in South Central L.A. There are those who are struck by the irony that the sentencing date for Powell and Koon is August 4th, 1993, days shy of the twenty-eighth anniversary of the Watts Riots.

NOTE

As of June 13th 1994, all talk of "recovery" has been eclipsed by the region's preoccupation with the slayings of Nicole Brown Simpson, Ronald Goldman, the trial of O.J. Simpson and the media storm in the aftermath of his acquittal. South Central remains a community troubled by gang warfare and economic disparity.

Apartheid Local

YOU BARELY MAINTAIN sanity when your survival behind the Orange Curtain is dictated by the cruelties of denial and oppression camouflaged by the sunny sumptuous palm-lined veneer of swimming pools, private stables, tennis courts and smiling tawny-skinned maids. You're weary of the cumulative negatives of day-to-day insults and slights generated by your blackness. The disbelievers are the first to accuse you of whining, bitterness, or paranoia. The Freud you can live without.

As you pull up at the checkpoint, the surfer-buff armed guard in his charcoal uniform rises from his perch and glowers. You can feel his steely-gray assessment. He asks to see your driver's license. Dutifully, he reaches for his vinyl clipboard and asks where you're going, runs his pencil down the roster, scrawls something, then releases the crossing gate. It rises slowly. When you glance into the rearview, he's jotting down your license plate number.

You enjoy the peaceful drive along winding, shady avenues. You enjoy your business luncheon. But hours later, when you return to your car parked off the crescent driveway, you discover someone has scrawled "maggot" all over your paint job, bumper-to-bumper.

≠

Inside the warmly-lit, high-ceilinged, oceanside trattoria, a maroon-haired beauty steps into the aisle clutching two large menus. You feel her chestnut eyes scorch your dreadlocks. "Yipes!" those eyes say, but she gracefully escorts you to a table. You have a ringside view of the busy chefs. As you sit, Feldman sees you frown and asks what's wrong.

"Did you notice," you smirk, "that they sat us in the *kitchen*."

Her eyes get big. "*Where* would you rather sit?" She follows your glance to the adjoining half-vacant area of cozy booths and blushes with indignation.

"That's okay," you demur. You remember the time you were denied seating at a popular Hollywood diner. Some day, you promise yourself, you're going to get in on a class-action suit.

"No, goddamn it!" Her dander is up. You smile as Feldman marches across the room and demands another table. The reluctant young hostess seats you in one of the cozy booths. Savoring victory, you order drinks and appetizers. Then you notice she's put you right next to the exit.

≠

It's been 15 years since Inga was in Los Angeles. You're touring her old stomping grounds, from Westwood to South Central. She can't believe how eerie everything's become. She senses the fear. The Village is virtually deserted. You walk past the site where a visiting female athlete was killed during the 1984 Olympics when a crazed young Black man drove his car down the sidewalk, knocking over pedestrians. After that, you say, they closed off The Village, beefed up patrols and made parking expensive and exclusive.

As you drive, you pass the husks of burned-out buildings and mini-malls. "There's so much graffiti," she says, "and why are the houses so dark?" You explain how the city has gotten meaner. Everyone's into their own little ethnocosms, behind razor wire, bars, floodlights and double deadbolts. Rather than solve the city's difficult problems, they've retreated from them. You give her the crash course on gangs and drive-bys—how the late-night glow from a TV screen can make the viewer a target.

At that precise moment, a passing car backfires. Inga ducks down, shudders against the floor, her back to the dashboard. When she recovers, I tell her about the night my Buick caught a sniper's bullet high in the right rear fender, while I was on my way to get barbecue for dinner. And how my sister-in-law's new coupe picked up a stray bullet, evenings before, as she backed out of my mother's driveway.

≠

Cliff sits on the passenger's side, shoulders hunched. He stayed late for the Santa Monica performance art show and the buses back to The Jungle have quit running. He needs a ride. You're sitting in the back seat, next to your son. Your husband is behind the wheel. After a brief discussion, you decide to take the shortcut through Beverly Hills.

"Uh-oh," your husband disrupts the chitchat. "It's the cops!" He grips the steering wheel.

"Oh, shittt!" hisses Cliff.

"But we didn't *do* anything," my son says, turning to look as a bright light hits the rear window and illuminates his face. You don't know how to tell him that this is only the beginning of life under surveillance and demeaning suspicion. You don't want his spirit crushed. Not yet.

"Well *I* haven't done anything, baby." Your husband tries to reassure you. Now they're on the driver's side of the car, flashing the light on him. "Don't look at them," you caution.

Now the black and white patrol car falls back, then speeds up to flank the passenger's side. Cliff's dark complexion reddens in the light as the officers study his face. You all sit silent, waiting for the blast of sirens. At the intersection ahead, the light turns green. You pray.

Suddenly the patrol car veers sharply to the right, turns south and disappears. You've crossed the border. Everyone starts breathing again.

Saving Our Youth

POLICE OFFICERS CAME to my son's Los Feliz area junior high recently to break up warfare between the KP and the LP. "KP is Korean Power!" he explains excitedly, hipping Mom and Dad to the new dynamics of gang activity, "LP is Latin Power. AP is Armenian Power." We learn the difference between "taggers" (graffiti artists) and "saggers" (who wear their baggies low off the backbone). We listen quietly, fear motivating our questions. We want to know what's going on. For all our sakes.

Our children are killing our children.

There's no such place as safe. Not anymore. Not the suburbs or gated communities. Not at home, even if watching TV in the dark or asleep in bed. Not the backyard, the park, or the beach. Not the bus stop. Not even a hospital room. Not the school ground or the classroom.

"It hurts when you hear about what's goin' on," says Ron Mokwena. Misha McK of Orange, New Jersey, nods. The two actors and cultural activists who founded Save Our Youth Arts & Education Organization (S.O.Y.) met in London in 1979. On their 1986 arrival in Los Angeles, Ron discovered confusion, apathy and a brewing uneasiness. "There was something about to happen," he recalls. One evening two brothers were shot in a local drive-by while taking out the garbage. That incident and his deep discontent inspired Ron to start the group in early 1991. A veteran of the 1976 Soweto youth uprising, Ron's been in exile since age 13, forced out of South Africa, "where children have no voice, no future."

I ask Ron and Misha what the hundred or so young people they work with say about the increase in violence on L.A. campuses. "Protection against gangs," Ron says, "that's the big thing that comes up. The educational system has provided a false sense of security. The kids are dumped at school by their parents. The teachers, glorified babysitters, just want to get paid. The kids have lost their sense of self. And they need something they can carry with them constantly, something to give them a sense of security and of self—a gun."

Ron (*A Different World, Sarafina!*) and Misha (*Mrs. C. and Me*) believe celebrity status is a valuable tool when making an impression on today's teens. Building self-esteem—without guns—is pivotal to Save Our Youth's success. Misha was especially motivated by the numerous letters she received from youngsters across the U.S. during her appearance on the NBC program. "They wanted my character to reflect their issues, their realities—like teen pregnancy." Family values are important, but when the family *and* the system fail, Ron and Misha believe artists should redirect and reeducate.

"Mindless work keeps 'em dumb deaf and blind," says Ron. "We get them the *right* kinds of jobs," Misha adds. "They're too young and tender to be flipping hamburgers and stacking flower pots. Those jobs feed the desire to gangbang, to think about material things. We hire them to rap for terminally ill kids, to do chores for the sick and dying, to get *involved*. They have to work with their elders to respect their elders. When you value life you can't waste life!"

When I arrive at the couple's Pasadena address, three clean-cut, earringed 15-year-olds, in plaid shirts and baggies, are studying the flyers and articles in the windows. The kids are hungry for this, so hungry that several of them have joined the 32-member cast of "Graffiti Blues." The rap opera was performed before President and First Lady Clinton during his inauguration. Ron and Misha have hopes for a film version.

Save Our Youth is not just for impoverished teens because "…self-esteem is not an economic issue," Ron asserts. "Millionaires may be worse off emotionally than poor South Central youth," Ron asserts. "We don't care how much money your parents have." They urge teens to share their new social responsibility with others. As the key to positive development, Ron and Misha believe it must be shared.

Good enough. But I'm thoroughly cynical about past malignant neglect of the nation's youth. I despise the current media exploitation of gangsta glam, the kind expressed in this anonymous street rhyme:

Call me Terminator
Call me Robocop
I jes pull dah triggah
Watch dah bodies drop

Having turned down roles they feel create harmful or demeaning images, Ron and Misha are emphatic. "These cartoons teach the kids bang-bang-you're dead," Misha laughs at the ugly irony, "but the people always get back up."

Among the innocent dead who won't be getting up again are 11-year-old David Polion, 13-year-old Tanya Cadle, 13-year-old Adrian Ferrusca, 16-year-old Demetrius Rice, 17-year-old Alfred Clark, 17-year-old Michael Shean Ensley, 18-year-old Salmon Paul Daniels, to name a few. The list is frighteningly long and growing. Ron and Misha are devoted to stunting that growth.

But so are the ranks of Save Our Youth. Twenty-one-year-old Nadari is optimistic: "We're gonna get the message through that youth are our future." And 15-year-old Mike is determined: "We got some funky rhymes to open your eyes...to stomp this...."

Letter to Jamal

DEAR JAMAL,

I'm blue in the face. Exasperated, disgusted, disillusioned. I'm suffering the fatigue endemic to prolonged entrenchment on the battlefront in the relentless cultural war against racism. I am ill with psychic pain. And it's become so difficult to articulate my pain to the living I'd rather talk to the more sympathetic dead. I'd rather talk to you.

Exacerbating my illness is the recent sudden onset of a severe case of double vision. Suddenly I find myself at two different points in time simultaneously: August 1965 and April/May 1992. How can that be? I reside here in this future yet I have been hurled backwards into the ghost city of a Los Angeles past. And I find you were still living there.

You were one of my first mentors. Also known as Allan Donaldson, you went by Hakim A. Jamal. Together with Ron Karenga, you headed US, an organization that rose out of the ashes of the Watts Rebellion of August 1965. One morning my then-husband attended a political rally at Los Angeles City College. When he came home he brought you and Ron Karenga with him. I was on the couch, an old portable typewriter in my lap, typing out my fledgling poems. The two of you sat down, read some of the fresh revisions and decided my talent could best be used drafting propaganda for The Cause. I was immediately hooked.

Within months antagonisms between you and Mr. Karenga split US in half. Malcolm X was your patron saint. You lived by his words and shared them with us. You preached the gospel of self-determination. "The chickens have come home to roost," you'd say, mimicking Malcolm, savoring each retelling of his rhetorical militant response to JFK's assassination. We followed your faction as two of the first card-carrying members of the Malcolm X Organization of Afro-American Unity, a Black nationalist organization. You loved the ideologic irony contained in its acronym "MOAAU," pronounced the same as China's Chairman Mao or, if said twice, it evoked the legendary Mau-Mau freedom fighters of the 50s who were instrumental in liberating Kenya from the British. You also started the Malcolm X Foundation which operated a Montessori school. We followed you to meetings, rallies, and fund-raisers. You introduced us to Sister Betty Shabazz, Macolm's widow. We watched your evolution as spokesman for Black Los Angeles, as you became a newspaper correspondent, author (*From the Dead Level*) and television personality. We watched, listened and *believed* until it became clear that The Cause, however defined, was failing. That the issues we'd naively invested our lives in were being eclipsed by the war in Vietnam.

Within less than a decade of the Watts riot, the ensuing economic and cultural rush gave way to the oil crisis and apathy. My husband and I were divorced. Sunday morning pow-wows at your home, with your wife (Malcolm's cousin) and six children, ended. I abandoned The Revolution for The Literary Life.

Remember the last time I saw you?

One night, around ten o'clock, there was a knock at my door. There you stood, clad in brown leather, that black lamb's wool hat glued to your head. It was just like Malcolm's. I never saw you without it. You even wore it in your own living room. Slung across your right shoulder was your favorite sawed-off shotgun. You were in a hurry so we talked over the threshold. Things had gotten too hot for you in L.A. Death threats had become attempts. You were on your way out of town. You had received my letter, written-in-hurt, bemoaning an article about you published in the local Black fishwrap. It viciously impugned your integrity as husband, father and community leader. My opinion of you still mattered so you came by to set things straight. The article was a lie. You were "still real" and wanted me to remember you that way. Your last words to me, "Keep the faith, Little Sistuh," followed by a quick kiss to my forehead.

Later, I heard through the grapevine you left your family, were run out of Trinidad, and fathered another child by a famous

English actress. Your obituary appeared May 3rd 1973. I sent word out on the grapevine asking who "put paper" on you. Word came back, "You don't want to know." Newspaper details surrounding your death were scanty, but your obit reported that you were ignominiously blown away by four members of De Mau Mau in Roxbury, Massachusetts, while seated in an armchair—you who always despised those you called "armchair revolutionaries."

I sorely wish you could see me today, Jamal. I've made it as a poet. Everything good I've written has been published. Not that that means much. If I really wanted to make it Big-Time, it would be as a dramatic scriptwriter. But there's little ongoing business in The Business for Black female producers, directors or any of that, of any age or any degree of accomplishment. Unless you're into comedy or pornography. My Emmy is rusting in the basement. The White male has not ceded one micron of his control over Black images. There are no Black distribution networks. We do have a Black-owned cable television channel now, but it's unapologetically imitative and offers little serious programming worthy of viewing. Even in terms of what the dominant culture embraces, Black is allowed only as long as it gives good Box Office. As always, censorship is a way of life. Quality is of little value, except to a few critics. Experimentation is an utter joke. In order to get over we either have to be safe/nonthreatening to Whites or be dangerous enough to appeal to a certain sadomasochistic constituency. Therefore, everything Black is continually reduced to fad value. When the fad passes we're out of work.

But let me get off the self-righteous soap box. Nothing in present day America counts if it isn't translatable into cold hard cash. And poetry ain't.

It's really a trip, Jamal. Poetry is the most marginalized of all the arts, yet equally subject to the whims of regional prejudice. Approximately ninety percent of the private and public sector grant money doled out to artists and writers, in these United States, goes to New York. And that wouldn't be so bad, but in Southern California our institutions barely and rarely support the local White artists, so you know what we Blacks "and multi-ethnic others" can expect. When I began my grantsmanship chase in the early 80s I was repeatedly advised that a New York City P.O. Box address would considerably increase the odds in my favor. I hate to sound parochial, man, but whenever a major position opens up mainstream or alternative (as you know, the underground was dead by the mid-70s), invariably someone from the East Coast is flown in to fill the chair.

It's the same old same old, Jamal. I can't get the experience because I can't get the chance. I can't get the chance because I don't have the experience. Get the experience by hook, crook, luck or fluke and I can't get the recognition. Get the chance and I have to prove I'm a saint to stay long enough to make it count. These days the process of dehumanization, like the bullet, does not discriminate. I never thought I'd live to see the day that a White male would cry "discrimination," but that's just what increased foreign business investment in the U.S. brought about in the late 80s. For Blacks-of-slave-origin who've never been free of the onus of dark skin and kinky hair (like me), it's a killer. What happens is: the only time you work is when THEY come looking for you. And when THEY come THEY are almost always motivated by some hidden political and/or financial agenda. It's rare that it's about raised consciousness. And altruism is even rarer.

A few months ago I was among local Afro-Americans invited to sit down at a Hacienda Heights conference table to discuss Black participation in the 1993–95 Los Angeles Festival (now defunct). Famous Black poets, arts curators and spokespersons were brought in from across the country for collateral input. I was like the proverbial kid in the candy store, pleased to meet these famous East Coast people. My excitement hinged around the opportunity to finally discourse with Black intellectuals who could-and-would effectively listen to and *understand* the plight of Black Los Angeles artists. I zeroed in on three individuals whose written works suggested their sensibilities and concerns were virtually identical to mine. They wore their labels proudly: A Black womanist sociologist, a Black homosexual male poet, a Black female poet. And I was flattered to discover each knew my work.

I effusively began my explication over dinner: it was rumored that a recent poll showed former Ku Klux Klan Grand Wizard and neo-Nazi sympathizer David Duke, a 1988 presidential contender, would get seventy-seven percent of the vote if he were running in Southern Cal, blahzeh blahzeh, when mid-sentence the sociologist and the homosexual male poet turned their backs on me *in unison*, got up, took their plates and left my table. Talk about struck dumb? Perhaps my roll-on deodorant had failed. During a later break in the conference, I asked the Black female poet which press had published her latest book. She crassly replied, "I have to go take a piss," turned and bee-lined for the exit.

That's how nasty it gets "on the Black hand side."

You see my point, Jamal? If we can't talk to each other how do we talk to Whites, Jews, Arab-Americans, Latinos, Koreans or anyone else? We all seem to be too busy breaking for the crossover door, trying to be Niggah-of-the-Minute.

Now this Rodney King Madness has busted loose. The Verdict was rendered by The Jury and by The Mob. If the police officers were innocent then The System was guilty. Payback had to be issued not only for Rodney King but for Jonestown, Eulia Love, Yusef Hawkins, Latasha Harlins, Michael A. Donald, the Philadelphia razing of MOVE, Willie Horton, the Anita Hill vs. Judge Thomas mini-series, the dethroning and media-lynching of Mike Tyson, and on and on.

In my recent work Hollywood has become a metaphor for all of Southern California. Disneyland started here and went global. McDonald's proliferated here and went global. Location in this heartless "Entertainment capital of the World" absolutely has its advantages when it comes to corporate expansion. Our April 1992 insurrection was a well-made sequel to the August 1965 revolt, except it appeared via satellite. The Watts Riot was done on a shoestring, but The South Central Uprising had a megabuck budget and was fueled and enhanced by developments in video technology. Yes—a *rerun*. And while the first played only to local houses, this one not only went nationwide, it got international distribution.

I am struck by the uncanny similarity between what happened after Watts and what's happening now, after the burning of Los Angeles. Both were sparked by the maltreatment of Black males by police: Marquette Frye and Rodney King. There was alcohol consumption on the part of both men. Frye wasn't beaten but he was arrested. Within hours of the insurrection The Clowns began descending out of the clouds, preaching and speechifying, throwing money and sniffing the wind for opportunities. But this time everyone's got their "pimp-macks" down. The same platitudes about rebuilding, recovery and solutions are spewing forth.

I was present the day the leaders of Watts Village and Slauson Village, two of the most notorious L.A. street gangs of the 60s, embraced as brothers in the office of the Malcolm X Foundation and swore off violence at your behest. Likewise, the

Crips and the Bloods have knotted blue and red do-rags in a show of unity. They, too, have sworn off the senseless violence. Driving through South Central the other day I saw a Black gangster and Latino gangster slap palms. I commend the young bloods, Jamal, so pardon my cynicism. I don't mean to sound so flip. But, as before, ignorance reigned. THEY got the idea ass-backwards. Once more, shops and stores were the primary targets of the insurgence instead of the courtrooms, the insurance companies, the Department of Education, the State Board of Equalization, Parker Center, City Hall, the Bureau of Immigration and Naturalization, and every office of the Department of Human Resources and Social Services in the county—testament to the efficacy of The Power Structure. Someone in Long Beach did get the idea and took out a Department of Motor Vehicles building. Again the violence was spontaneous and leaderless. Again greed superseded genuine outrage. Further testament.

When, if ever, is it gonna get serious?

Jamal, I've kept my 1965 copy of the McCone Commission Report near my desk for ages, right next to my 1966 copy of the first issue of *WATTS–from Riot to Festival*, along with my "Protect Black Images" and "I-Love-Watts" bumper stickers. The magazine was published by the long-defunct Watts Festival Publishing Company. I've often speculated if these relics from the 60s would ever have any worth beyond sentiment. There's a picture in the upper left-hand corner of the second page which shows smoke billowing up into the sky off Anzac Avenue. In the lower right corner there's a picture of a float sporting a bevy of smoking young women, Black and White. The caption is staggered right to left along the page and reads: "Out of the Chaos...A New Brighter Hope."

We know too well what happened to that hope, don't we Jamal?

I cried when I heard The Verdict. I was deeply depressed. But the second I heard The Violence had started my spirits vaulted. I was high off adrenaline for days after. My phone started ringing the afternoon of April 29th and the calls, locally, from across the nation, and from overseas kept coming in. I spent so much time talking about The Verdict and The Violence which followed I didn't have time to write one single poem. I was too busy taking my bows as a visionary before the curtain dropped with the relentlessness of a guillotine.

But sincerely, Jamal—I'm sick of White Folk dogging Black Folk for solutions to *our* problems. Blacks have been offering solutions to Whites, here at home, in South Africa, and Europe since Denmark Vesey, since Nat Turner, since Sojourner Truth, since Frederick Douglass, since W. E. B. DuBois, since Ida B. Wells, and on and on. I'm sick of this syndrome that blames the slave for slavery, and which places the burden of justice and equality on the back of said slave.

Excuse my rancor. Perhaps I've also got a touch of what's called "the victimization syndrome" on top of my battle fatigue.

I'm trying to do my part, Jamal. As far as I'm concerned, the McCone Commission Report came up with the correct solutions the first time. It was dismissed. Those solutions are still equitable. I'm not a sociologist or an urban planner so I don't have any grand rebuilding schemes to offer. I do have a good fix on the mistakes of the past. That past we briefly shared. I will do my part to keep reminding those who have forgotten the lessons of that past. I will teach those who want to learn. And while I may or may not do that from a podium, I will do it in my work as poet. I will factor-in feeling. I will do my level best to clothe those bone-cold statistics in human flesh.

Truth is, I'm afraid THEY have won, Jamal. I'm afraid the "capitalist pig oppressors" did their jobs too splendidly. I'm afraid the pathological wedges have been driven too deep and that the sociological divisions are too wide to bridge. I'm afraid that over these twenty-seven years the sharks, gamesters, tricksters, shysters and pseudo-intellectuals, of all colors and creeds, have become too deeply entrenched to be rooted out. I'm afraid the conspiracy of greed and racism has become a noose around the necks of the American disenfranchised; from the dependent old and disabled, to children-of-color trapped in urban hell-holes or on bipartisan cultural reservations, to the victims of AIDS. And the only option I can offer is a play on that tired age-old adage: those who have The Faith must persist as keepers.

I have kept The Faith, Jamal, but it hasn't kept me.

Angels with Rap Sheets

REFLECTING ON L.A.'s lackluster "recovery" after the '92 uprising, I envision my home turf as Das Gangsta Kapitol with no one left but Fierce Young Perpetrators—a death camp culled from rock-hard unemployment, run by prison-calloused low-lifers—not 10 Righteous Men or Women in sight. After hearing comparisons of riot/fire/quake/flood-torn L.A. to beplagued Egypt of Old and wondering if there's a Lot, Moses or Messiah among us, I took my questions to someone whose social activism was underscored by faith.

Can one man of God curb violent social trends?

"Probably not." Harold A. Jackson Jr., Ph.D., a 64-year-old United Church of Christ ordained minister and Pepperdine University graduate, is as firm-jawed as any cinema classic Irish priest, except he's Black as well as Protestant. He speaks with the not-quite-relaxed expertise of twenty years and nine months as the state correctional system's first African-American chaplain of the Youth Authority hired, in his words, "for content not pigment." It was 1974, Vietnam had wound down, and Jackson, then forty-three, and ex-dean of students at Claremont Seminary was dubious. "What can a Black parson say to young Black men? Would they say I was just part of the system?"

Now it's 1995. What have you seen?

"The System is as hostile now for African-Americans as it was then, reflecting the racism outside. Generally speaking, the institution understood my role as chaplain, if critical about it. I made it my business to establish a good rapport with Chino staff persons as well as wards. There was respect and appreciation of my integrity."

Reverend Jackson saw an overwhelming rise in the Black

gang population in prison and a corresponding increase in Black-on-Black crime among the men, who were largely between ages seventeen and twenty-five. This put others at risk even in church. The gangsters "wanted the chapel to be their place and tried to claim it by coming to Mass in overwhelming numbers. No deal. It took a few years—but to the day I retired, it was understood: refuge was the chapel."

Do other changes echo those in our broader community?

"Yes. For example, the Vietnamese now compose the largest Asian prison group. There's lots of Hispanic versus Black tensions from outside. Black power inside prison culture has diminished. Latinos are the larger group…from Guatemala, El Salvador, not only Chicanos. Hispanics wouldn't come to Protestant service but would come see me during the week. I developed ethnic-based Bible study groups. Forget being Home Boyz even at the price of threats and beatings. By embracing faith, guys could draw strength from each other."

On the streets, are the gangs winning?

"The Gang has won! And I don't mean poor Black and Brown teenagers. THE CRIMINAL JUSTICE SYSTEM IS CRIMINAL, especially to African-Americans and people of color. Excuse my shout, but the only way to improve the penal system is to fire everybody and start from scratch."

But didn't "the uprising" have positive impact?

"Nothing came out of the riot. It proved inarticulate because of disunity among and within groups."

But what about that truce?

"If you're honest, you don't call a truce but declare THE END by calling it what it is—an END. No hostilities implied. Riot said: there is no leadership. The community is so fragmented it's difficult for anyone to take the role of leader—MLK, Malcolm X. We've got to look to many leaders. Otherwise, how do we establish community again? The person who is true to the community must lead without recognition."

Rumor says the Black leadership crisis is planned.

"In California, more of our young men are in prison than college. We're creating a prison economy that taxes people to maintain itself. Yet 90% of those incarcerated will get out someday. We must be more creative. Warehousing must stop."

Any solutions, Dr. Reverend Harold?

"Take gangbangers out of the streets and into settings that

stress worthwhile values—in school—with adults, male and female, willing to provide strict but loving discipline. Require them to be responsible without demanding perfection. Our community must be willing to forgive and start over again when someone fails. It is incumbent upon the system to guarantee that it succeeds in helping us succeed."

<u>*Days of Lang Syne*</u>

CERTAIN FOLK OCCASIONALLY surface during conversation, or are remembered warmly at chilly moments, extra-special someones briefly embraced during one of life's trepidations, who, at a critical moment, made the going a lot less tough. Time passes, and good things said about them echo across the communal grapevine. One might expect to find a foundation stone laid in their honor, an unobtrusive plaque in some park or museum, a small street or branch library rechristened in their name, maybe a walk-of-fame accolade. At minimum, it's assumed they've somehow earned a lucrative retirement along with a hefty chapter in the ledger of good souls. But to suddenly find them old, fragile, disillusioned, virtually abandoned, emotionally and/or financially needy, even if with a certain dignified grace, is altogether unsettling.

"So it's come to this—having to fight the old battles all over again." The activist elder statesman and I are standing outside the Santa Monica bookstore, spontaneously chewing the gristle of current events.

"I thought we'd really done something! That when I got this old I'd be able to rest on my laurels." He's a self-assured, soft-spoken White man who was once flamboyantly active in the glory days of the civil rights movement, witnessed the emergence of Martin Luther King, Jr., knew Langston Hughes. We take a headcount: JFK, RFK, the thousands dead in Southeast Asia, the long ugly death of a naive American 60s idealism capped off by Abbie Hoffman's suicide. "I keep asking myself," he whispers, "how could we have been so wrong?"

The quiet Malibu salon is held to honor the ancestor, an African-American poet who was bused in from artistic self-exile in Europe to inform us younger acolytes of beatitudinal history, with a little tut-tut, "make it positive" on the side. None of his peers are present, but then there were only two, sad to say, and one of those gents long ago upped the ghost, while the other's rooted elsewhere.

After a brief ritual of gourmet crackers, brie and white wine, the gathering unfolds. The sprightly graybeard, dapper in dress and hip in demeanor, assumes the muted spotlight and begins to blow. As a means of self-definition, as well as protection, he summons up, among a multitude of spirits, Monk, Miles and Mingus. Then, soaking in the appreciative applause, he hustles microprinted missals hastily assembled by a descendant of Gutenberg, at X-times-the-cost American, several generations removed. We buy them, politely, dutifully, if not effusively.

The "Friends of" envelope is made of cheap white stock, my address printed legibly by hand in wispy blue ink. I rip it open, expecting to read an obituary, then am relieved to learn that an old acquaintance isn't quite on his deathbed. He is, in fact, about to celebrate another birthday. More troubling and heartbreaking is that the announced celebration doubles as fund-raiser. I feel confused and embarrassed for the oldster. I had assumed that life had provided him with substantial rewards, last I heard, anyway. This public plea for support, on-going or onetime, contains a biographical sketch composed of illustrious quotes, a pledge sheet and a wrenching call to arms in the name of this pioneer of California's gay and lesbian community.

"The younger women at the office treat me like somebody's aunt. I've paid my dues. When it came to feminism, I was on the front line, baby, but they can't see that. I have to keep proving myself." We met while she was still "on a roll." Hard times have kept us apart, but recently, we've made it a point to meet over dinner. Lack of recognition, loneliness, the constant pressure to justify her existence has worn her thin. Haunted eyes hold mine over sparkling water and Continental cuisine. She's in her 50s, Jewish, formerly of New York City. She's spent more than fifteen years trying to adjust to Southern California. But... "I don't have boyfriends here. Only friends who happen to be men. When I step out of a cab in Manhattan, I get noticed. I'm alive! I'm sexxxy! Men *flirt* with me. Here?—They don't even look anymore. L.A.'s not a town you can grow old gracefully in...."

Classified Scam

"GOD," MY FRIEND Pamala cried, "I've sent out a hundred resumes! And nobody calls back." She was ripe for the con and there was one waiting for her in the want ads.

On the promise that she'd be groomed as an assistant director, Pam was suckered into working the phones for a film company on Melrose. She labored happily, content with her sub-minimum wage because her renegade bosses weren't bothering with unemployment insurance or "all that official crap." And she had no qualms about running a little con herself. She could cover her household overhead by "double dipping," collecting her stipend from the state while not reporting earnings.

In less than three months, Pamala was out of work again, deeper in debt, owed money but afraid to collect it, afraid the state might find out she'd been naughty.

During recessions, those desperately seeking work are easy targets for those desperately seeking a fast buck. Occasionally, the bait is a top-dollar offer for entry-level, white- or pink-collar positions. There's always a number to call for an interview. None of that anonymous "send-in-your-resume" business. You'll always get the chance to sell yourself. Or be sold.

Once in the office, you'll be hired, though the salary and the hours aren't quite what you expected. You've been discovered by a new and/or *growing* opportunity to get in on the ground floor. Lucky you.

Another friend, Ralph, also fell victim to a want-ads scam.

"She's so sincere!" he said, describing his new boss as a hard-working and dedicated Black woman. He nearly cried as he repeated her tragic tale of losing two brothers to AIDS, devoting her life to finding a cure. When she offered Ralph his choice between telephone soliciting or working out in the field to raise money for the cause, he chose the latter.

"Forget it," I said. "It's bogus."

"How do you know?"

"I smell it. Instinct."

But Ralph couldn't wait to start fund-raising for the American Society for AIDS Prevention (A.S.A.P.). Ralph loved the acronym and thought it was clever. Plus the society was located in the same Hollywood building as a glitzy AIDS group noted for its celebrity supporters. A.S.A.P. promised business cards ASAP, his name embossed in bold.

Ralph showed off the group's brochure, impressive right down to the Social Service Department information card with the seal of the City of Los Angeles in the upper right-hand corner.

"Dear Donor," went the pitch, "We are a national organization dedicated to AIDS awareness...day-to-day care to patients who otherwise could not maintain themselves. The epidemic has spread so rapidly throughout the world that A.S.A.P. has accepted the awesome task of creating a strong, preventative environment ... the American public must take a stand."

Ralph was hooked for six dollars an hour, plus commission. Amazingly, his territory was the whole of L.A. Instead of being suspicious, Ralph was ecstatic.

Within ten days, Ralph's first paycheck bounced. Ralph confronted his boss lady, but she convinced him she'd been victimized by another employee who'd stolen from the account. Ralph called the bank, and it confirmed that there was a problem. When he redeposited the check a few days later, it cleared.

Despite strong doubts, Ralph continued with A.S.A.P., believing someone dying of AIDS would benefit from his efforts. He worked from 10 to 6 until the day his distraught White male supervisor confided that he, himself, had not been paid for weeks and was being consumed by debt.

Ralph immediately checked with the state to see if the A.S.A.P. corporation number was legitimate. It was. He went down the list of directors and governors, locating as many as he could. He asked them about A.S.A.P. They'd never heard of it. A further check revealed that there were only two directors listed, his boss and her assistant. Ralph immediately called his supervisor and gave him the bad news.

Ralph quit that day. He fumed for a couple of weeks, then

decided that he should "get these guys" by going to the authorities. By then, it was too late. A.S.A.P. had closed its doors and relocated, setting up another scam, for college scholarships, charging for a service that can be had elsewhere for free, in a new office on another floor in the same Hollywood building.

Job hunters, beware. Somewhere their ads are running.

Sistuhs in Arms

WHO IN THE HOOD *do you ask about breast cancer?*

When National Breast Cancer Month arrives each October, ethnic women are left out of the media play. As usual, the health issue discussion revolves around middle and upper class White women. What's prevention and treatment for the larger population is prescribed for all. How does this affect the lives of Black women? Does malignant neglect by media reflect deeper societal problems? I took these and other questions to an afternoon session of Women of Color Breast Cancer Survivors (WOCBCS) support project for African-American women sponsored by Daniel Freeman Hospital and the National Black Leadership Initiative on Cancer. I got my ears blistered but came away inspired:

Black women get it earlier. Its effects are more devastating because it occurs during our most productive and sexually active years. ◊ *We're almost totally ignored by every major newspaper and organization.* ◊ *To talk about us is felt to be too morbid. But we're positive—we're about living.*

Doctors are insensitive. They are the issue that started this group. ◊ *We face discrimination and neglect. You must insist on information. These doctors don't like it when they have to explain and get real surly when you ask questions.* ◊ *I told my oncologist, "I can feel it!" He said nothing.* ◊ *They never gave me any educational materials.* ◊ *My doctor said my examination was* IN-CON-CLUSIVE *although my tumor had doubled in size at 2.5 centimeters, which is second stage. He told me to GO HOME, WAIT and WATCH IT!* ◊ *I was very down, depressed. I didn't need a psychiatrist. I needed a support group.*

Our women are diagnosed in the later stages and have a higher death rate. ◊ *My OB-GYN saw it and remained silent.* ◊ *Don't trust general practitioners, no matter what color they are.* ◊ *My tumor had*

211

got so large it had burst and was running. I lost a breast and a lung. Get a second opinion, a third if necessary.

We tend to be given the strongest medicines without necessarily needing them. Without any consideration as to what they might do to us. ◊ Treatment modalities lack a database as to the effects on our bodies. The statistics don't indicate ethnicity.

‡

Our cultural background has put us in the background. ◊ We have children and landlords to feed. If all I had to cope with was breast cancer, I would be fine. ◊ What you do is you put it on the list and you deal. ◊ THEY don't understand the stress, how we're carrying 3 to 4 loads. ◊ It's hard for US–we're working- and professional-class women. So you can imagine how tough it is for sistuhs in the hardcore ghetto–too busy worrying about food which comes before *health. Usually she hasn't been to the doctor since having her last child–which may've been 25 years ago. ◊ When you go to a group that's not ethnically sensitive, in their neighborhoods, you find them dominated by Whites who do not understand "waiting on the check."*

Little old White ladies are nice but can't relate to how I responded. I was angry, real emotional when I found out "They're gonna mutilate me!" ◊ There was this 72-year-old, 35-year survivor who looked at my short hair and said, "That's okay, you don't have much to lose anyway." ◊ After speaking to an American Cancer Society rep, most of the support groups they refer you to, "wellness clinics," are located some place way out.

‡

We're so busy taking care of everybody else, we neglect ourselves. ◊ Your life and diet must change–more vitamins, fresh fruit, cut out animal protein. ◊ Your body tells you when something's wrong. Trust your body. I experienced recurrence in spite of all the tests. ◊ I couldn't stand to look at my body taking a shower ... Gotta get them tears out ... gotta cry.

Most of us are abandoned by our men. They're so self-centered. ◊ My boyfriend, a cancer doctor, didn't contact me anymore. ◊ Going home to an empty house–it's very scary to be so alone. ◊ My family didn't make me feel isolated. ◊ You are still a woman even if both breasts are cut off. *◊ My life turned around when I found this group.*

Committed to Memory

BLUE CLOUD-SWEPT SKY and brilliant October sun betrayed our expectations as we somberly walked the Melrose border of the Pacific Design Center that Sunday morning. We were on our way to see the NAMES Project AIDS Memorial Quilt.

Climbing the steps, I heard a shout. A white sedan pulled up, passenger window lowered, and a brown-haired, starry-eyed woman barely twenty waved me over. My husband and son waited while I skittered curbside.

"Where's that apartment building they feature on 'Melrose Place'?" Her chipper mid-Western politeness was edgy. "We've been driving up and down here for hours and can't find it." Sitting behind the steering wheel, an older man shvitzed in his shirt-sleeves, maps strewn across the seat. "Welcome to Hollywood," I smirked. "But it's *all* an illusion. Sorry, darlin'."

She blanched. He shot her a sweaty leer, hit the accelerator, spun the car into a U-turn and sped east. This incident was an ironic preface—reminder of how make-believe and denial shape our geographical and emotional terrain.

Two days earlier I had visited the Wall, the Vietnam War Memorial in Washington D.C. The elongated black granite wing rose regally from the earth. Young women and children mounted the patient shoulders of men, boys, and determined older women to make frottages (rubbings) of names onto paper. Along the base there were dried, dying, and fresh bouquets, along with poems, letters and diaries laid open. Public contemplation and private introspection were accentuated by repeated sighs, muted weeping, or an excited "I found him!"

Now, barely 32 hours later, we wandered toward the Pacific Design Center information desk. At site center lay a canvas of signatures reading "People Do Care." Encouraged to view the new panels to be added to the quilt in an afternoon dedication ceremony, we hurried over to glance at them. Giddy with jet lag, I tripped over my own feet and stepped on one. I looked down and into a familiar face.

An ex-colleague smiled up from his modest panel, graced by a few elegiac lines by poet Gwendolyn Brooks. Twenty years had passed since we'd last met over lunch at The Old World, a defunct 70s Hollywood hang.

"There's Rico! I know Rico!"

During the escalator ride to the main exhibit, I looked over my shoulder into a large room housing the panel-making workshop. Workers busily selected fabrics, laid out patterns and stencils, fashioned decorations, ornaments and trim, leaned over sewing machines. We stepped through an improvised rest area and into a dazzling maze of approximately 1,600 panels, a fraction of the total of more than 24,000. Volunteer readers intoned a melancholy litany of names.

Some panels were painfully humble; others, works of art. In between were the homespun, the kitschy, the outrageous. Some gave only a first name, others provided histories. A few were nameless.

By midafternoon we were drunk on grief expressed in a multicolored blaze of styles, textures, icons, military emblems, flags and themes from the comically irreverent to the sacred. Quilt flora included the tree of life, century plants, long-stemmed red, white and yellow roses, lilacs, lilies and daisies. Among the fauna were favorite pets, butterflies and spiders, owls and eagles, lions and tigers, elephants and giraffes, rattlers and asps, koala and teddy bears, unicorns and griffins. There were lighthouses, the Eiffel Tower, Ms. Statue of Liberty, pianos, guitars, musical notes, the Starship Enterprise, champagne glasses, dancing silhouettes, sequined dress shirts, high heels, pjs and zippers.

Some were unforgettable, like the one for a Black dentist who grinned toothily out at us from the inside of a giant molar. The panel for one single mother was signed by each orphaned child. Some bristled with rage, screamed "murdered by AIDS" or declared "I have done nothing wrong. I am not worthless. I do mean something."

After experiencing the abstract, stony, dignified permanence of the tribute to the dead and missing in Southeast Asia, the AIDS Memorial Quilt is an eerily fluid and soul-wrenching testament. It is a living thing. And it continues its relentless growth fed by the fear and denial of those who'd rather make-believe it doesn't exist.

Catalina Reverie

WHILE MY HUSBAND'S employers were moving from their mid-Wilshire business location to Downtown, some of the staff celebrated with a midweek excursion to Santa Catalina Island. I agreed to go, but when the alarm went off at 7 a.m., it was a struggle to haul my less-than-enthusiastic self out of bed.

"Ever been there?" Huz asked. "No. Maybe. I'm not sure!" I muttered. Sea and surf have never been my style. I prepared lethargically, Huz prodding me at intervals with reminders that the company rendezvous was set for 8:30. Racing from the house at 8:20, we beat morning traffic, arriving seconds shy of missing the Catalina express. The upper deck was packed, so we sat in the forward compartment. The mood turned romantic when we went outside to stand at the prow, arm-in-arm, enjoying wind and spray, watching the coastline recede. The sky was overcast and gray—my kind of weather. The water was aquamarine and choppy. The cabin cruiser clipped rockily along at 25 miles per hour.

After ten minutes, my landlubber's legs tired of the pitching and yawing, so we went inside. While Huz read a book, I went to the front of the cabin. Kneeling on a leeward seat, watching the ocean, I got the full effects without being buffeted by the wind. The grumble of the engine conjured up the adventure novels of my youth: Sinbad's hapless crew on his fifth *Arabian Nights* voyage, his doomed ship meeting the rocks; aboard the Hispaniola, avoiding the peg-legged wrath of *Treasure Island*'s mutinous John Silver; or aboard Ahab's Pequod, hunting *Moby Dick*.

Minutes off Avalon Bay, sunny Catalina Island emerged on the horizon. I switched media—imagining awe-struck Ann Darrow, John Driscoll, and Carl Denham on the deck of Captain

Englehorn's sea-weary tanker on its filmic approach to Skull Island, home of "Kong Rama Kong."

Onetime retreat for Laurel and Hardy, the 21-mile-long island was a sometime movie set. Former colony of Spain, pirate's hold, gold rush bonanza, and splashground for the wealthy, Catalina has been a familiar tourist flock since the Jazz Age. Today you can jet ski, play miniature golf, ride horses and go parasailing. But in our state of citified ennui, sports seemed too much like work. We opted for a tour package. Eager to see some buffalo, I picked Skyline Drive. Huz preferred the Glass Bottom Boat.

As we boarded the M.V. Moonstone, I had a sudden *déjà vu*. As a petulant teenager, I once visited the island with my mother's church youth group. I had enjoyed the boat ride but thought Catalina dull stuff. Now I stared, mesmerized, through the window to the underworld, blinking only to compare the creatures below with those illustrated on the flyer. The calico bass, Day-Glo orange garibaldi, opaleye and halfmoon fish were abundant, but few of the more exotic denizens came up to play. What passed for a couple of eels wiggled near the ocean floor. A spiny lobster crawled between rocks. The high point was the unexpected sighting of a large, shadowy bat ray.

Under a hot blue sky, we walked toward Descanso Beach, studied the Art Deco murals over the Avalon Theatre entrance, then visited the adjacent tiny history museum. After lunch, we skittered back along the boardwalk to catch the tour bus and were soon navigating interior roads so dangerous, mirrors were placed at intervals to help drivers make safe turns. From the two-hour narration, we garnered that the buffalo were actually bison, the world's only saltwater toilets had once been installed here to conserve fresh water and all surviving Gabrielino Indians had been forced off the island before the turn of the century.

Back in town, our trip nearly over, we enjoyed root beer floats, feeling like slightly overbaked truants. Sure, it was corny, but it busted our routine nicely. We talked about returning, someday soon. On the way back to Long Beach Harbor, Huz read quietly, then fell asleep against my shoulder. Miles from shore a daredevil skyrider dangled from his parachute. Then I noticed a flock of gulls. Fins appeared and arcing dolphins broke water level. I watched until they disappeared. Then I shut my eyes and imagined having that kind of freedom.

The Saga of Darren Stroh

'Twas mid-late afternoon on Melrose
as the story goes—when our path was first
crossed by one Darren Stroh. Just twenty-and-two,
he was about to die and only he and God
know the reasons why.

LATELY, LOCAL LIVE-ACTION news telecasts have featured the high-speed car chases of distraught motorists by law enforcement, with the frequency and melodrama of soap opera episodes, climaxing with arrests or deaths. But on January 3rd, 1992, one such chase took a personal turn when my husband and I found ourselves in the midst of what looked like another typical Hollywood movie stunt.

We were driving south, down Vermont Avenue toward the entrance to the 101, hurrying to beat closing time at the bank. Crossing Melrose Boulevard, we heard sirens scream. A little red VW Cabriolet with a white top sped toward us, followed by a dozen California Highway Patrol and L.A.P.D. cars. Six helicopters buzzed overhead. We thought we'd inadvertently driven into the midst of a staged chase scene. But after hasty discussion, we decided this was real.

As traffic stopped, we pulled over to the right. The VW cut through a corner gas station, zipped alongside us, passed us, then zagged in front of us. The sandy-haired young driver gripped the wheel, coolly smoking a cigarette as he monitored the side mirror, the rear-view, then the road ahead. He drove with such *authority* he seemed to be leading the officers instead of running from them. He raced east on Clinton Street, enforcement vehicles in his exhaust.

During our 10-minute crawl on the freeway, we speculated on the demons driving that VW. Exiting north on Mission Road, we heard screaming sirens.

"Not again," Huz groaned.

The red and white bug weaved through a gas station lot, zagged into the intersection, passed in front of us, swerved due north and around a large triangular island, zooming east, The Law and news choppers dead on his tail.

"What are the odds of his crossing our path twice in one day?" we marveled, as the light changed thrice and we fought the urge to join the hunt. We heard the *pop-pop* of gunshots. We opted for the bank. Within the hour, Stroh was a footnote to local folklore.

‡

On that winter morning, unemployed electrician and murder suspect, Darren Stroh started his 300-mile Los Baños run with two rifles and a double-barreled shotgun taken from his granddad's home in Foots Creek, Oregon, cruisin' I-5 south for San Diego. He picked up Michael Graham for a 12-mile hitch till Stroh's '78 Toyota sputtered and died. Responding to Stroh's help sign, David Baker offered him a jump. When the car wouldn't start, an impatient Stroh killed Baker with two shotgun blasts, then took his Nissan. Graham stayed behind.

Around Coalinga, Stroh commandeered a Volkswagen Cabriolet (KRUL FA8), and continued south through Bakersfield, where the CHP spotted and trailed him all the way into Los Angeles, off the 101 exit and into our lives.

‡

Suspecting the media frenzy caused by Stroh's run spawned copycat chases, I contacted CHP Information Officer Christine Rogers, public affairs field coordinator in Sacramento, who generously provided scads of statistics.

I divided the state at 37° latitude, roughly at the Los Baños-Merced area. Predictably, from January through July, 1993, car chases in Southern California outnumbered those further north two-to-one. Stats from 1988 to July of this year show that no CHP officers have been killed. Figures for innocent parties killed or injured don't exceed 1.1%. The highest figure for suspects killed was 7% (1989) and the highest figure for suspects who escaped was 24.7% (1991). CHP stats indicate a steady yearly increase, with jumps to 1,199 in 1990 and 1,341 in 1992.

But what makes motorists run?

All of this may be scant evidence, but I suspect the live broadcast of Stroh's run inspired other motorists, especially some of the twenty-odd who wound up dead in 1992, to try to outrun the police. But what does make them run? Statewide figures for all law enforcement agencies in 1992, CHP included, reveal that only 29.4% were motivated by felonies and only 15.3% by misdemeanors like DUIs (driving under the influence). Surprisingly, 54% of all chases started with minor infractions.

> 'Twas nobody's guess Stroh's
> story would end southbound on
> the 405, where he played possum
> behind the wheel, then called out
> the action going for his steel.
>
> In olden days, they'd have
> said he was mighty slow on the draw
> and that's suicide, going down
> against The Law. Shots were fired.
> One man expired. All of twenty-and-
> two, and he chose to die. But
> only God and Darren Stroh
> know the reasons why.

NOTE

This piece appeared nine months before O.J. Simpson's low-speed chase in June, 1994.

Jah in Packaging

Children get your culture
And don't stay there and gesture
Oh the battle will be hotter
And you won't get no supper
Natty dread, natty dread now

–Bob Marley

WE WERE SITTING ON a post-riot panel, a public forum at Beyond Baroque Literary Center. Under discussion were the little-known divisions between an African immigrant community in America and Black Americans of slave descent. The topic of hair was raised. Just how African in origin were the dreadlocks popularized by the Rastafarians?

"In our country," the man from Ghana said, embarrassed into frankness at my insistence, "it is a sign of insanity. Only the mad wear their hair the way you are wearing yours."

Well, I thought, at least that's apropos for a late-20th-Century poet. Madness has become a standard part of the mystique, Sylvia Plath and Delmore Schwartz most notably. Both infamous self-destructs. How much of their equilibrium was consumed by "bad hair days"? While it is universally within normal limits for women to fret and primp over their hair, Blacks-of-Slave-Origin have elevated this art to pathology. At that time, I wasn't that mortified. But I knew that keeping my wild and woolly tresses would be construed by many Blacks as economic suicide.

I was going to have to find some way to earn my living outside the non-glare phosphorescent heights of the corporate or civil service boardrooms. Nobody but entertainment people were going to hire a woman with a Brillo pad gone berserk on top of her head.

"Amen," Dee said, when I voiced this concern to her.

"That means," I said balefully, "I'm going to have to finally really support myself as a writer."

These days, I straddle the chasm between the commercial and literary worlds, hoping to escape falling into the void. I go on lots of interviews to sell my script ideas for large money. The industry people I pitch to express few pretensions of intellectual superiority even if they have them. Doing it for money in the real world, whatever the dope, is free of the snobbery found in the literary life because often the score is dirty. Even when it's clean, all eyes all hues have that same money chase gleam—praying for a score big enough to put poverty in the past tense. But before I sell I've got to get my front office appearance together. Talent isn't enough. Looks still matter.

‡

Following my father's death in January 1991, I neglected my hair care for several days, giving in to grief and tears. My already thick ebony naps, worn in an afro, began to tangle, twist and dread. Days later I stood in the mirror and attempted to fork it out. It would not cooperate. It had wadded into large clumps that could not be worked apart. Combing it meant cutting it first. I would have to go to a barber shop. And I'd have to get a *quo vadis*, the haircut favored for Black boys when I was in high school and currently sported under do-rags and duck-billed caps by many gangster rappers. The image of myself as bald rankled.

So be it, I thought. I'll let it dread. I've always wanted to do it. Ever since that time I first met Bob Marley and the Wailers, I had always had the nerve. But in the early 70s it was tough enough finding a good job when I wore my hair *au naturel*. Dreadlocks, new at the time, were associated with renegade Jamaicans and evil weed.

But now was the time. At last. Young White ska aficionados had made it trendy for Whites to adopt the hairstyle. More than a decade had passed since Bo Derek aroused the ire of Black women by wearing her blonde hair braided in *10*, her name momentarily attached to *our* locks. So I figured the do had to be safe, at minimum, if never quite fully sanctioned by the corporate establishment.

222

And if I tire of it, I can always shave it off and start growing a fresh thatch.

Several years ago, I dropped out of the nine-to-five work force to make ends meet as scriptwriter and part-time journalist. No longer having to punch the clock contributed to my decision to "let my hair go." I work at home and don't have to bend to the grooming standards of White middle management or bourgeois Black peers. The paychecks are irregular but there's loads of self-esteem.

One week I came home from an interview ripped on adrenaline. I pitched ideas A, B, C and D to the assistant producer. A and D made it to first base. A was an action-adventure plot. D was action-adventure with a family values subtext. Both gritty but heartwarming.

The assistant producer was effusive. "I'm going to make notes on these and take them to The Chief." I accepted her enthusiastic handshake. Piece of cake.

Otherwise, I was struck by this pleasant White woman, ten years my junior, because she had more crowsfeet and wrinkles than I'll have by the time I'm seventy. Agelessness, I surmised, is damned near the only advantage to being dark-skinned in our society. Certainly the dreads help.

I crossed my fingers, clicked my heels, and waited for the callback. It came but it didn't come. The message from my agent was terse: "They want to talk to you about packaging."

I was disappointed. Isn't that the production company's job? Since when does the writer have to provide the star in order to sell the script?

"The networks are nervous about taking on more Black product," the assistant producer explained. "Especially anything dramatic. We feel we can sell this with the right lead, some star who could carry the picture."

"Sorry, I'm a writer's writer. I don't hang with the celebrities. Especially the current generation."

Oops. There I went betraying my true age, the assumption that I must be running with the Hollywood Black brat pack. I could "do a Jack Benny," stay on the high side of thirtysomething for another decade. Dreadlocks are associated with youthfulness. Until I really go granny I can avoid being shelved among the dust-ridden with the adept application of a good pair of tweezers. And once the tweezers fail, my complexion, broken only by an occasional mole, will only make me seem prematurely gray. I won't need serious cosmetics until I'm sixty, if lucky enough to live so long.

Plus, I need my kinky crowning glory to balance my weight. It makes me look slightly more streamlined. A trim of fifty pounds would put me on the low end of voluptuous. Have to get that excess under control, as my friend Dee (not her real name) keeps not-so-subtly saying. If I ever decide to lop off my dreads, I'll look better as a skinhead, and my earrings will stand out, if my weight's down.

> *And that's a long way*
> *for natty to be from home,*
> *Don't care what the world seh*
> *I and I couldn't never go astray*
> *just like a bright and sunny day*
> *Oh we're gonna have things our way*
> *Natty dread, natty dreadlock*

> —Bob Marley

Dee is many years a vegetarian and has learned that giving up red meat and animal products, and steady exercise are not enough. The steatopygia that characterizes most women of our race is stubbornly diet-resistant. At forty-three, Dee's been skinny for nearly two years. More class, status and fad conscious than me, she's hooked into a Culver City fat doctor who melts the flab off overnight via some mystery concoction. She's offered his number, anytime I'm ready for the cure.

Dee once cut an eye-popping, traffic-stopping figure at size twelve. But, in her case, economic considerations outweighed sexiness, with a mortgage, a college diploma, and an upscale sports car to support. She found her answer in the combination of drug treatments and a yoga class.

"Mama's down to a size seven. My babygirl and I can wear the same clothes—blows her mind."

"I'm selling my words, not my body," I insisted.

"You're not only selling your writing ability, you're selling how young, hip and Black you are," she argued. "Media White boys don't like butter and they don't like dust."

Faith in her talent keeps Dee going. Yet, for all her gyrations she remains an industry fringe-dweller. For emphasis, Dee told me her price paid was the loss of some righteous steady dick-whipping. Her twenty-something Black love-interest complained, "Where'd those hips, thighs and ass go?" then made his exit.

As broad as I am, my "catch action" remains strong. Heads still turn. Should granny get angry or enjoy the compliments while she's still hot? Short of having to revamp my wardrobe, how would skinny benefit me, since I'm married and not in the market for male companionship? It might lengthen my planetary staying power. But I'm not anxious to live another thirty years in poverty. But if I must, why not live it as a dread-head?

The most immediate effect of going dread is a deep and instantaneous rush of relief and inner well-being. Dee's having none of that. In order to maintain the appearance of being politically correct, Dee has gone as far as having her hair woven and plaited into intricately attractive styles. She has spent as many as 48 hours and as much as five hundred smackers having her hair braided. But what I respect Dee for most is that she has, thus far, resisted the temptation to go blonde.

Whenever I get homesick, I leave Hollywood to crawl into a funked-up little ghetto bar somewhere and sit among down-home Black folk. Getting my blues fix has become one of my few luxuries. It's not the alcohol or the cigarette smoke. It's the flesh that gives me the high. It's the chorus of so many Black voices passing the minutes. It's the darkness inside the darkness. The way nappy brown black hair waves under the pressure of social pomade. It's the sawdust politics that sprout out of the understanding that we are who we are because we've had no choice but to be who we are.

But the good feeling of group belonging is instantly spoiled when an unnatural blondie sashays through the room, fair-skinned mama in wig hat or ebony queen with dye job. Sistuhs with fair skin are often born with flaxen hair or reddish hair which blondes easily when exposed to sun. But only dark-toned bimbos who've succumbed to self-hate go phony ash, platinum or gold. And the effect they have on the crowd is always the same. An atmospheric bristling takes place. Racism has intruded.

But not all of the bristling is unfavorable.

"A blonde will always draw," a brutha once informed me as I pouted, wondering why there was almost always a light-skinned or blonde-haired woman behind the counter in working class Black joints (tony Black places can afford *real* White women). My inability to strongly argue his point made me even angrier.

"You brown-eyed girls are common," he said acidly, "and what's common don't make for excitement. Or didn't you ever see *King Kong*?"

‡

The record promoter had set it up for me to meet this guy Bob Marley and his group, The Wailers, at the Tropicana Motel, since demolished for a shopping plaza, used to be up on Sunset. They sent me the *Catch A Fire* LP. I liked the sound. When I got there, Marley was sleeping. I waited outside about twenty minutes before they finally invited me in, nervously clutching my tape recorder.

In those days I enjoyed celebrity interviews. Almost all of the stars I talked to were Black men and women. The usta-wases, the justabouts and the wannabes. Among them were Smokey Robinson, Jerry Butler and Martha Reeves, long without the Vandellas. Most were into blues, soul or rock. But this Marley guy was something new. He was on his second tour of the U.S. and on the verge of igniting the reggae rage.

A petulant, gorgeous mahogany Peter Tosh (Mackintosh) opened the door when I knocked. He had on cutoffs, a denim shirt open at the chest and this large yellow, red, green and black cap. There was an odd electricity in the air, and I immediately suspected an argument had just taken place. The Barrett brothers were standing around. Brown-skinned Bunny "Wailer" Livingstone was sitting in a lounge chair, his massive dreads draped in a partial snood. He rose and went to the bathroom to check on Bob Marley, a big funnel-like thing held in his fingers. He was taking puffs from it. I'd never seen any such dingus before.

"What's that?"

"A spliff," Tosh answered.

"A what?"

"Yonno, mahn. Kinda like a joint. Much bettah."

"Oh."

I got it. But I didn't smoke marijuana on my own and, at that point, had never been high. Peter Tosh was darkly edgy. Bob Marley trailed Bunny Wailer into the room, yawning sleepily.

Peter Tosh gestured, and they went off into a corner of the room, the three exchanging words in rapid-fire shantytown patois, too quickly for me to understand, then Tosh about-faced and hit the door. The Barretts stood silently for a moment, then followed Tosh outside.

Bunny Wailer opened a leather pouch and busied himself rolling another spliff, stuffing it with a rich red-brown weed as tangled as his dreads. Marley sat down on the bed. I looked around for a comfortable squat. One of the Barretts appeared with a chair. I set the tape recorder on the bed next to Marley, and scooted up to the edge of it so that I was close to the microphone. He was handsome, with small features and honey-colored skin, and radiated magnanimity. His finely braided dreads were slightly flattened in the back where he'd lain in bed. He was bare-chested, modestly buff, in denims and bare feet.

I tried not to stare, said there was no hurry and he could put on a shirt if he wanted. Bunny snorted, went into the closet, came back with a light blue, long-sleeved shirt and tossed it to Marley. He put the shirt on but left it hanging loosely open.

As I did a brief sound check, I looked over at Bunny Wailer. He had fired up the dingus and was pointing it at me. I looked around. The door was standing wide open, failing to close behind the hasty exit of the two Barrett brothers. Marley reached for the spliff, took a draw and inhaled deeply. He handed it to me, amused. I looked at it.

Shit–what if I we get busted?

The seconds were stretching out and I figured that if I wanted a good interview I'd better go along with the ritual. I took the spliff and imitated Marley, drawing deeply, inhaling and letting the smoke exhale through my mouth and nose. They watched me closely.

"Youlikedatganja, eh?"

"What?"

"Ganja. We grow it in Jamaica."

"Oh. Sure. Yeah. It's great," I lied. I was afraid I'd end up too punchy to do a decent interview. But I was so numb with fear I couldn't feel anything except the sweat rising in my scalp.

In those days I usually wore studded denim slims, black leotards, stacked-heel boots and a black leather jacket. I wore my hair in a packed trim little 3-inch afro, always accented with monster earrings. I fancied myself a cultural outlaw, but wasn't looking forward to cooling my butt in Sybil Brand for possession. During the Marley interview I kept glancing towards the door. No irate police officers appeared. Later, I learned that the motel management discreetly looked the other way, and that the gendarmes tacitly avoided the Tropicana, infamous for housing music business banditos, unless violence occurred.

Swallowing fear with the smoke, I proceeded with the interview. Marley was laid-back, open and made a major effort to communicate. It took about twenty minutes for us to get into each other's idiomatic rhythms. Reggae/dub/ska was such a fresh cultural phenomenon I had few linguistic reference points. That night and into the next day, I spent 16 hours pouring over the tapes, doing my best to "translate" our awkward exchange. I was very proud when my Marley interview made the front page of the *L.A. Free Press*, Art Kunkin's underground counterculture rag of local note, months away from folding. When I read that interview now, I blanch at my naiveté.

As strong an impression as the Wailers' music left on me, their hair left the strongest impression of all. For months afterwards I thought about Marley, the Wailers and their wonderful Rastaman dreadlocks. I envied them their hair freedom. I fought the temptation to go nappy, reminding myself that I had two children to support. I was experiencing enough hostility towards my afro, from both Blacks and Whites. My now-classic hairdo was still regarded as a sign of political militancy even into the late 70s. Dreading my hair would make me virtually unemployable, to my family's detriment.

By the end of the 80s fellow Blacks frequently chided me about the bush I sported. When was I going to get a Jeri-curl or a braid? My 'fro was horribly passé. Once, while I was guest-speaking before her mixed-race class, a Black English teacher pointed to my afro as an example of the old-time hairdo discussed after reading a chapter from *The Autobiography of Malcolm X* that previous week. She then thanked me for being such a staunch individualist.

‡

It's not only blonde hair that makes a Black woman sexually preferable, it's long hair of any color. Another remarkable thing I learned from Rastas is that dreaded Black hair may grow as long as any colleen's or geisha's—right down to the toes. Male or female. Something I always suspected but never accepted as probable until seen with my own eyes.

Dee informs me that human hair is the best for a weave or extensions. Italian is the first choice, Chinese second. But not all Blacks can dread their hair. Or wear the hair extensions. Dandruff may become manic. Extensions, woven into natural Black hair in order to lengthen it, often cause permanent damage if not removed every few weeks so the scalp can "breathe." Permanent hair loss can occur. And it takes forever to put in fake hair extensions. But the results can be wonderful.

The price I paid for the two times I had extensions woven into my hair included brain-deadening conversation, and having to endure endless soap operas and schlock talk shows. The most beneficial aspect of this torture was that the braids, when done correctly, promoted rapid growth of my natural hair. Ideally, over time, one can abandon the extensions and let one's own hair take over, a boon to sistuhs with short or chem-damaged coifs.

My second braid experience resulted in an eight-inch bush once I tore out the extensions, removing them after a maddening itch-fest. Another drawback of hair extensions is it's difficult to get the scalp squeaky clean. In order for the dreads to "take" you have to go three to six weeks without washing the hair.

It's probably a myth, but when I expressed concern about contracting lice, one girlfriend told me that lice did not like hair as kinky as mine. That figured, since, apparently, nobody else liked my hair either. I did the dare and got away lice-free.

ǂ

Aunt Enid nearly died of shock in front of us when she saw my head. Hooked up to a respirator, she was barely able to breathe. I'd driven a hundred miles to bring mother for that final visit. But Aunt Enid seemed more concerned about my dreads than impending death. It floored me when she asked her sister what (on Earth!) had happened to my head?

"It—it's a new style, Aunt Enid. It's called, uh, dreadlocks," I stammered softly. She didn't seem to hear. She could only stare, raise a frail entubated arm and point at my head. Attempting to explain Rastafarian culture to this devout Methodist would be useless. Obviously a distraction, I discreetly left my elders to visit alone.

Children get your culture
and don't stay there and gesture
Oh the battle will be hotter
and you won't get no supper

—Bob Marley

Mine are not the neat, acceptable plaits of artificial or store-bought hair. My twists are straight out of *Jungle Jim*. It gets mother's goat when we're in public and I get compliments on my dreads. Good words come largely from Whites of all ages, but when it comes from Blacks at all, it's from those under fifty.

Once, one young sistuh leaned over the restaurant stall that separated her table from ours to ask my advice on how she should start dreading. My mother stared at me with a rueful little smirk, no doubt envisioning Chinese bangs and Greek curls.

"Your head makes me itch!" Mama frowned and offered to take me into the kitchen, wash and straight-iron my hair the first time she saw my stubby little nubbins. She hadn't voluntarily touched my head since puberty.

"You'll get used to it."

"No I won't."

And she hasn't. *But the longer my dreads become, the less she complains.*

The incredulous stares I drew at one family picnic didn't unsettle me. Instead, I felt a vague pity for my dyed and fried bloodfolk. They had little choice but to buy into the mainstream's lie about self-image. I felt liberated from such mental tyranny, freed of looking-glass slavery. Just like the Rastafarians.

Ignoring the occasional double take, transfixed stare, or Tracy Chapman joke, I wear my dreads everywhere. They've grown out to nearly shoulder-length. When preparing to go out, I sometimes cradle my dreadlocks in a bandanna or scarf, or wear a hat to match my outfit. I'm acutely aware of just how dreadful they are to the uninitiated. Especially to colored folk who haven't embraced the Black new age aesthetic. This is the notion, as explained by one hair stylist, that Blacks who do not have their hair "in coils" when the millennium arrives will face eternal damnation. That's one worry off my chest—er—mind.

The longer my knots become, the wilder. They snake and fork like The Medusa, the name my son christened my do when I first revealed that I was "going dread." I knew it embarrassed my kids to see Mom's tresses in such a severe state of kinkiness. But I knew they'd adjust. They have. And they know that the only possible influence on how I wear my hair is the job market.

An Interview with Bob Marley
December 1973

BOB MARLEY WAS STAYING at the Vagabond Motel in Hollywood. I wondered if it would look like that flea bag he was staying in the last time I interviewed him. Things had really been uncool that day. Not only did the tape cartridge in the recorder louse up, but the Wailers had an abundance of ganja on hand and were busy tuning in. I was so uptight about being busted—the doors were wide open—that I could barely concentrate on the interview.

I had been told Marley had to stay where there was a kitchen available since food for vegetarians on the road is a major problem. When I arrived I checked out the joint. Hmmmm. Not bad at all. It wasn't the Beverly Wilshire, but....

Marley was in bed when I got there. He was dressed, lying across the bed napping. The Wailers were in and about, and there was still an abundance of ganja. While he got himself together, I set up the tape recorder, cursing it silently, daring it to cross me this time. I looked around for a place to sit, put the tape recorder next to Marley on the bed, and sat down on the floor beside it so the microphone could pick up my questions.

Marley is fair skinned: about 5'9", not so much a thin build as a small one. His eyes appear hazel, flecks of gray. His hair is medium brown, styled in the massive dreadlocks worn by Jamaica's Rastafarians. I wanted to touch them, but resisted temptation. Periodically, as we talk, Marley habitually ran his hands through, rather, over his locks. Between my Black slang and his Jamaican patois, we had difficulty understanding each other. Getting this from the tape onto paper was murder.

ME: When did you get to bed last night?

BOB: We wake up about five o'clock this morning.

ME: How has the tour been going so far?

BOB: Good and bad. But mostly good...I think some canceling must be going on because Sly have a group that wanted to do this gig—you know—exposure.

ME: Oh, you kind of got pushed out, shoved into the background, huh?

(*He nodded and we both laughed.*)

ME: What are some good things about the tour? I mean, where did you go and how were the audiences?

BOB: The audience's great! Go some city where—like Los Angeles —they got juke boxes. They got juke box city...You know, this place is out in the country, the desert. It's big place, pure gambling.

ME: Oh! Las Vegas! Slot machines!

BOB: Juke boxes—haha—where they gamble a lot.

ME: What was it like, playing there? What did you think of Las Vegas?

BOB: I did not like it. It so much—it a type of experience—

(*We both laugh.*)

BOB: I didn't like that much there.

ME: You composed just about all of the songs [on the *Catch A Fire album*] didn't you?

BOB: Yeah. When I really compose—I played plenty sounds you know. But right now other members of the group dem start writing songs. It's all got mixed. First time we write, most of my songs used to be the ones more attractive to the people. With this mixed thing, everybody start writing now. So, you know, more's strength.

ME: You and Sly are so different—sort of opposites. Did you get a lot of Black people in your audience?

BOB: You mean with the Sly tour? Yeah. Plenty Black people... Sometimes I don't know if really Sly dig it that much because all our lyrics are so heavy. Our dress, all of that. Still, we opposite of Sly, like maybe Sly really can't believe what we tell people. But otherwise—mahn, Sly a genius, yeah.

ME: What are some of the problems in Jamaica?

BOB: Sometimes the real problem is our Queen still run Jamaica. After we have independence everybody pretend, like say Jamaica run itself. Underneath they take order from the Queen.

ME: Really?

BOB: Yeah. That is one of the big nasty thing, why Jamaica riot, and much violence and otherwise, because people just don't care again. You can really feel the pressure coming in. And when you Rasta, you fight against the Queen—you no serve the Queen. This brainwashing business and all of this "God Save the Queen," you know what I mean? Because the police, the whole police force deal with the Queen, what the Queen tell them from that time. Then for after a while them have independence—you go to this big police place—it's the Queen's portrait still hanging there.

ME: Her photo's still up in the police station?

BOB: Yeah. And so now we don't respect that authority so you know me no respect as Rasta. We curse the Queen. We curse the Queen.

ME: Do you have a family or are you by yourself—outside of your mother? I mean, do you have an ol' lady? Kids?

BOB: I don't know where my kids at. My kids are by different girls, you know?

ME: Huh?

BOB: No really a one lady yet.

ME: Anyone special?

BOB: No—I don't really settle down. No, I not ready settle down with lady.

ME: You're not ready?

(*I laugh.*)

BOB: No—me not ready.

(*He laughs.*)

ME: [*An unrecorded question about what kind of music Bob likes to listen to when relaxing.*]

BOB: I really no listen to White music now... The only thing I want to hear is some sweet music, like easy-listening music.

ME: What about jazz?

BOB: We have jazz down there plenty... Me, I couldn't even

understand jazz. I see all my friends listen to jazz. It took me a long time before I could dig it...you know, Sun Ra, Coltrane, whatever. Jamaican musicians was interested in nothing but jazz.

ME: You yourselves are Rastafarians—have a message. But you're not representing any specific group. You're not a representative of anyone, you're just bringing the truth and carrying the message?

BOB: Yeah. We don't represent nobody. Us free...the free earth great...The world rightfully His, His Imperial Majesty. The Bible said that. So the White guy no really accept Imperial Majesty as God 'cause we don't really come from the inner prejudice world, 'cause if you're prejudiced you can't come free. I cannot talk to White mahn and I talk to my Black people same way. I can't just witness a truth and then shut my eyes like I don't know what's going on, because it's easy for the Black mahn to look upon Imperial Majesty and say yes, because dem Black. It's very hard for White mahn to say dem Black and Him God. But it's very easy for the Black mahn to say he's Black and He's God and it's true, you know. Black mahn have to realize that He the greatest, He the King of Kings.

ME: Say, last time I was here you were smoking, um...

(*We laugh.*)

ME: It ain't cool here, it's illegal here. Is it illegal in Jamaica?

BOB: You can get hassled for it down there, but if you know police you can send big guy—big with police. Some guys just leave you alone 'cause you can tell a bigger mahn and big mahn may even push dem off the force. It legal but it not legal...Sometimes you have police who wouldn't carry you to jail for herb and then you maybe one out of 100 really carry you to jail for herb if he catch us smoke herb. But it's irregular, 'cause you know when I go Jamaica, I go out into the country. And you stop people who plant corn and yam in big field and when I check the people, dem don't plant that again, you know? The people dem plant pure herb.

(*I laugh.*)

BOB: I look and I see the whole lot is weed....People no plant food again. It's pure herb dem plant.

ME: What kind of significance does it have? Does grass have that kind of religious significance?

BOB: Yeah, mahn. But, you know, herb.

ME: Okay. Herb.

BOB: It's the healing of the nation. You know, herb the thing what build up your feelings toward human beings. Like you get sensitive to the things that hurt people, you know? And you get real sensitive, and you want to live in commune if you can—if you can get the chance to do it. Herb make you live with people good, you know? You just have to live with people good because it tell you when you smoke it, it directly show you. It's love. It's love in me. So like directly it's like a mahn who tell you, "Well, when I smoke this is love." You must deal in love, love all people 'cause sometime you have guys who smoke and dem smoke to have fun. Like a guy who smoke and get high and that's it. We have a mahn who been smokin' since a child. Him say, "Blessed the God Rastafari, Him ever faithful, ever sure." Him pray before him start smoke. So meditation is upon God, you know. So him smoke and him meditating on God, him get plenty inspiration towards God. It's like people use herb for any direction they want to go...I mean, if a guy smoke herb, him could be a bad guy, him meditate on how to be bad and if it's bad. And if you smoke it to be good, it show you how it is to be good. It's not really herb still when it's reached by a pusher mahn.

ME: You got a room here to cook your own food because you're a vegetarian. It gets to be a hassle, it gets to be difficult eating on the road, I would imagine.

BOB: Well, yeah. Because we don't eat pork or meat or anything.

ME: Tell me why you don't eat meat.

BOB: Well—meat. I personally do not believe in eating it while devils still in it. Now you check the cow and say "beef." Everybody eat beef. You can have more tender meaning toward a cow. The cow give milk. I mean, should not really kill a cow to eat the cow. Because I feel dem can drink the milk and then you have other things wha' you can get to eat to get the same things like meat protein. Well, you can eat other things that is the same thing. I don't exactly like big dead flesh in front of me.

ME: Dead flesh—not any kind?

BOB: Well, we eat fish. Meat—used to eat meat plenty. Then all stop eat meat. You know, the Bible tell you the type of meat you cannot eat, like the cow. You can eat the goat; him foot split.

ME: Oh, cloven hooves?

BOB: And chew cud. Like the pig, now. The pig have the cloven feet but him not chew him cud. The donkey chew the cud but him don't have cloven foot. So dem both have to have cloven foot and chew the cud.

ME: You shouldn't eat—?

BOB: The one that have cloven foot and don't chew cud; or chew the cud but don't have cloven foot. See?

ME: Oh, you can get away with eating the cow, but you can't eat the pig and you can't eat the donkey.

BOB: People eat it, but it's sickness. It's like the meat different, it really sickens people.

ME: I'm just an old meat-eater. I tried. I managed to give up pork. I don't eat pork—any pork. Well, no. This is something about Black Americans. We just can't give up barbecued spare ribs, mahn.

BOB: Is it pork?

ME: I don't eat any bacon or ham or nothin'—but barbecue spare ribs! Here it's kind of a joke—you can eat every part of the pig but his oink and you can put his oink on radio for a commercial.

(*Bob laughs.*)

BOB: What you want the pig for? Pig have touch of devil inside him. You know, pig, there was such a thing where dem have seven devils inside. This is not White talk—this is Black talk, you know?

ME: How many devils inside? Seven?

BOB: Yeah. Seven devils inside the pig, but otherwise they grunt like inside the pen. I tell you, mahn, me stop eat meat, me can feel different—it feels different.

ME: Do you think you could live here in the United States now that you've seen some of it?

BOB: No. I wouldn't really want to live here. Soon as the people realize Rasta, dem go to Africa.

ME: You'd go to Africa?

BOB: Yeah, because even in Africa dem people live with His Imperial Majesty and do not know His greatness because family too near to Him. But Bible say that people from far off shall see it and know it, you know? And we take it Rasta. I-mahn is right, 'cause we in Jamaica—Marcus Garvey said it, you know. They kill Marcus Garvey, I mean. Some people say dem and me go along with people say dem doing that. Well you can then really try and put dem on some crucifixion. It's time to go home. It's time for the Black man really go home.

<u>*Imagining Disaster*</u>

I JUMP UP FROM BED and listen, alert. I hear the hisses and yowls of terrified cats. Fierce sun shimmers in a cloudless morning sky. A continuous rumble deepens to a churning. As the house pitches and yaws, I rush out to the patio. The concrete has buckled in some places, shattered into jagged fragments in others. I stumble back to the bedroom, grope for my street clothes, rouse my snoring husband.

"Sweetheart, quick! It's an earthquake!"

I've said these words before but this time I add, "It's been going on for two minutes. This must be The Big One!" He grabs his slacks, dressing hastily. I go to my son's room and shake him into consciousness. "Earthquake!" I caution. He scrambles into his clothes as books bounce randomly from shelves.

Oddly, I hear loud, annoying sitcom theme music. I wake up. It's late afternoon. Succumbing to the ninety degree heat, I've fallen asleep in front of the TV. Coincidentally, my guys are out walking, discussing the day's school lesson on quake preparedness. When they return, I amuse them with my daymare.

Eagerly, my son shares his survival savvy: we need an emergency kit, dehydrated food, flashlights, several twenty-gallon containers of water, portable toilet, battery-operated radio and/or TV, sleeping bags, tent, twenty-year shelf-life battery pack, etc. He instructs us to secure the water heater, not to burn matches—in case of gas-leak, and to eat the stuff in the freezer.

Whenever calamity looms, my priority is family—even above personal survival. The idea of spending my last moments with loved ones is comforting. I don't mind dying, but I'm choosy about whom I die with. The thought of going to eternity in the company of strangers unsettles me. I'd much rather face brimstone with friends. I had similar thoughts when I went AWOL on the morning of July 13th, 1986. I arrived on the job at 6:30 a.m. and had barely put my purse away, made the coffee and warmed up the computer when the Oceanside temblor hit at 6:47, notching 5.3 on the Richter scale. My Hollywood office was located on the 3rd floor. Tons of steel and concrete suddenly turned to jelly. Semi-dark hallways were pierced by screams and shouts. The floor supervisor vanished. I resumed my duties.

When the second jolt struck, I got my purse and, dead calm, headed for the stairs. As I exited to the streets, others ahead of and behind me fled the building, structured on rollers and purportedly one of the most quakeproof in Los Angeles. I spent the next 48 hours at home watching local coverage on the damage and aftershocks, hubby and son cozily nearby. I managed to break through the overloaded phone circuits to make sure other family members were safe.

Two years later, I was forced to take the employee's course in quake preparedness and learned, among other facts, that they came in swarms. I spoke privately to the fireman lecturer—a downright frightened man who complained the public was being deceived. He believed The Big One was imminent. He planned to leave California ASAP, family in tow. No amount of preparation could help him sleep nights.

I respected but couldn't share his fear. Perhaps my pragmatism comes from growing up in quake country, or reflects the stubbornness of folk who rebuild once the shock of catastrophe wanes. Maybe the disaster you know is better than the one you don't.

My Oklahoma kin seemed similarly blasé, one recent trip "down home" during tornado season. Fascinated, I watched a dozen dark gray funnels twist across the horizon. Unperturbed, Uncle Lesile and Cousin Ossie battened down farm equipment and sealed off the barn, while I gawked at a good-sized bird forced into backward flight by the wind. Inside the sprawling Hennessey ranch, we helped Aunt Kathryn close specially designed storm shutters, then enjoyed lunch while the weather raged outside.

I can't begin to imagine the kind of devastation that seasonally ravages Bangladesh—7 killer cyclones since '63. Or even Hurricane Andrew, which roared through the Bahamas, Florida and the Gulf Coast in August '92 at 165 miles per hour—to date the worst natural disaster in U.S. history. Or maybe it goes deeper. Or perhaps, you become unfazed by Mother Earth—whose most destructive tantrums still manage to leave the bulk of humanity intact—when you grow up under the everpresent threat of *man-made* doomsday.

♯

"Drop!" our high school chemistry teacher yelled.

Instantly heads ducked down, bodies scrambled under desks for cover. I sat motionless, drolly watching the spectacle as the campus was transformed into the make-believe epicenter of atomic Armageddon. The teacher rolled his eyes at me and smirked.

"Class, I'm sorry to report we have one casualty."

Everyone laughed—even me.

Day of the Bargains Mall

NOONTIME PARKING IS fairly accessible, but we can tell by the number of vehicles in the multileveled, aboveground lot that the hordes are already ahead of us. Dozens more are queuing up behind. There's a predominance of RVs, vans and station wagons. Clusters of parents and children shuttle to and from this mecca for families. Our destination: one of a corporate chain of retail warehouses where, in theory, the shopper is beneficiary.

I have the dining table, but I've spent months looking for a matched set of chairs, occasionally stopping to quick-browse thrift and antique shops from Sherman Oaks to San Diego. But even the most marginally functional assemblages of splinters command woefully spectacular prices. I've decided I might as well splurge on new ones.

The store's interior is designed in blond wood, stainless steel and concrete painted a semi-gloss off-white. Glazed-eyed patrons tote large primary-colored baskets or push enormous shopping carts that accommodate heavy items. We notice the easy-to-read signs in simple English with well-defined arrows pointing the way. I thrill to the smell of bargains.

Grabbing a cart, we fall in step and begin oohing and awwwing along, following the primary-colored line on the floor that will, according to our sign, lead us to the wonderful world of dining rooms where countless specimens of chair await our inspection. In and around we merrily wind, stopping when something catches our eyes—the glint of brass, the shimmer of crystal, the muted gloss of finished wicker. Normally we *hate* shopping, yet we begin to dreamily refurnish our modest digs—pausing to linger and speculate, salivating over new things—this and that to go there and there.

Arriving at our destination, we're delighted to find *beaucoup* chairs of metal, plastic and expensive woods suited to every function and taste, down-home to opulent. We've noticed several strategically placed stations manned by smiling, tag-wearing clerks and a number of tagged individuals assisting customers. We motion one young man aside, and he respectfully tells us that we will find membership forms at each station, that all we need do is fill one out, select our purchases—noting each serial and lot number—then follow the arrows to the storage areas with matching numbers where we'll find the very items we've selected. All we need do is place those items on the cart, make our way to checkout, present our membership form and—*voilà!*

Serious fun begins as I relax into browsing. Huz is antsy at first, but gradually grooves to my mood as I compare patterns, styles and quality. Once I make my deliciously difficult first, second and third choices, carefully noting serial and lot numbers, we're surprised to discover more than an hour has zipped by. Smilingly, we cart off to meander through display after display until we find ourselves in the designated storage area.

Yipes! It's a drab rat's nightmare, a dim-lit mile-high maze of endless aisles of unfathomable stuff. We break into flight-or-fight sweats. Huz is ready to chuck it and split. I want those chairs! Doggedly we push forward, our cart intermittently colliding with the rudely competitive carts of other shoppers.

Quicker than you can recite the Bill of Rights, we're lost! But how can that be? We were careful to note the correct lot number. I anchor myself and the cart to a cul-de-sac while my better half hurries for help. When he finally returns, his shirt is soaked, his hair disarranged, his face flushed with rage.

"These idiots use a double-digit system!"

Identical series of numbers in massive clusters are demarcated only by different primary-colored lines. We're at the wrong end. We now have to go forward through check-out and *start over at the beginning.*

We bristle, turn around and jostle our way backward through the maze. We quickly realize that the Mall God has provided no exit except checkout. The lines are twenty-deep. Exasperated, we ditch the cart and begin again only to discover the store's population has doubled. Defying jangled nerves, we scramble through the sea of bodies, savoring a small victory as we finally stand before the proper lot.

"Uh-oh! Oh, no!" we chorus as we discover none of our choices are available. Crushed, I admit defeat.

Making our late-afternoon escape, we marvel at the happy faces carrying giant boxes to and fro, people who actually enjoy shopping according to crowd control. We're desperate to relieve ourselves of the icky anxiety. I recommend a nearby watering hole where the munchies are savory and the drinks run deep. He gets us there as fast as our wheels will drive us.

The Ultimate L.A. Litmus Test

LOS ANGELES NATIVES are presumed rare and virtually indistinguishable from newcomers and out-of-towners. But we always manage to make our oversensitive presence felt the minute anyone from elsewhere dares bash our turf. There's an undeniable undercurrent of territorial pride that accompanies our righteous regional indignation. After all, no one can trash our beloved city better than we home folk. While we natives may be the last to deny the absurdities that characterize our daily existence, we are the first to insist on the darkly sublime beauty of a landscape that seems to hold us forever spellbound. Chauvinism aside, anyone bold enough to pass the following test may consider themselves an honorary native Angeleno. Pencils ready!

You're a newcomer to L.A. when you think:
> a) LAX is a description of airport security.
> b) You can reach someone by dialing direct.
> c) Lasorda is an opera house.
> d) The grunion run is a charity marathon.
> e) "The blue crew" is a rap group.

You're officially welcomed to L.A. when you get up in the morning and your car:
> a) Is covered with bird droppings.
> b) Has a window broken out.
> c) Has new dents.
> d) Is booted.
> e) Is not there.

You know L.A. is in your blood when:
>   a) You figure out "later" doesn't mean "I'll be in touch soon."
>   b) You can eat your burrito with chopsticks.
>   c) You get the hot gossip six months ahead of the talk shows.
>   d) You have your most stimulating philosophical conversations while waiting at the bus stop.
>   e) You're self-conscious because no one is staring at you.

You've got L.A. down when in the space of 30 minutes:
>   a) You just miss ten accidents.
>   b) You dodge ten panhandlers.
>   c) You get ten parking tickets.
>   d) You meet ten people you're no longer on speaking terms with.
>   e) You experience ten aftershocks.

L.A.'s got you down when:
>   a) Your mom asks you for the name of your agent.
>   b) Your internist is writing a screenplay.
>   c) Your babysitter auditions for a soap and gets the part.
>   d) You need a translator to read the billboards.
>   e) The latest find at the La Brea tar pits turns out to be a relative.

You've earned your first I-love-L.A. bumper sticker when:
>   a) At night you find the whirrr from low-flying helicopters soporific.
>   b) The student you flunked last term signs a $15-million record deal.
>   c) The people the next table over are flossing their teeth.
>   d) When your masseuse asks you for the name of your agent.
>   e) Your gynecologist says, "Don't worry. I'm a vegetarian."

You know L.A.'s recession isn't over when:
   a) All your favorite restaurants keep going under.
   b) All your favorite bookstores keep going under.
   c) You hear ice cream trucks making rounds at
      11:00 p.m.
   d) The 60-year-old woman in front of you is buying cat
      food and bagels.
   e) The neighborhood panhandler asks for the name of
      your agent.

You know you've finally settled into L.A. when you:
   a) Buy all your produce off the freeway on-ramps.
   b) Stamp "copyrighted" on all your shopping lists.
   c) Purchase a starter set of designer burglar bars.
   d) Notice the smog has turned your nose ring green.
   e) Drive instead of walk to the corner store.

You know you'll survive L.A. when:
   a) You sleep through 6.2s.
   b) You stop counting the new cracks in your walls.
   c) You can leave home without consulting your Tarot
      deck.
   d) The house shakes and you ask, "Was that a sonic
      boom or a truck rolling past?"
   e) You develop an immunity to Hepatitis B and E. coli.

You know it's too late to leave L.A. when:
   a) Your roaches ask for references.
   b) Your dog's haircut costs more than yours and looks
      better.
   c) Your parakeet is taking Prozac.
   d) Your cat is an informant for the tabloids.
   e) The shark that bites off your leg refuses to give it
      back unless you grant him a percentage of the movie
      rights.

Surprise! There are no incorrect answers. Therefore you've
passed and are now a citizen of The City of Angels, if you weren't
one already.

<u>*Of Fatness and Fitness*</u>

IN GOES THE GOOD shape, out goes the bad.

Yesterday's aerobics craze may have cooled, but today's budding market for smart-drink cabarets, rivaling coffee bars, is evidence that physical fitness (a.k.a. cyberpower) is still actively pursued by flesh-conscious westerners. Joining the current generation of body-building Angelenos, I like to think I'm finally on the right track to conquering stress, high blood pressure and that old nemesis, fat.

Wrapped in contemplation as tight as my stretch-alls, wrists gripped by one-kilogram weights, surrounded by health-seeking walkers, trotters, runners. We're all moving forward, in twenty-minute to one-hour spates, on treadmills, bicycles and stair-steppers. Each keeps to an individual regimen, yet together we strive for mind-body perfection.

As I go about my timid pumpings of iron, anticipating the renewed me, I lapse into reverie. Worries suspended, eyes focused on digital calibrations of calories burned, I drift across time to relive Mama's traumas as she waged her tireless War-on-Obesity, makeover spas and European hormone treatments being far beyond her reach.

Lovingly, I return to that South Central living room of the 60s. The cobalt-blue mirror-topped coffee table is pushed back against the sofa, and the gray shag rug is rolled up by the mantelpiece. Mama is exercising with determined vigor in front of our black & white TV and high-fidelity console, the one Pop bought at Sears over on Olympic and Soto last Christmas. Onscreen, Jack La

Lanne, in bodysuit and headband, guides her through hamstring stretches and jumping jacks.

A Lane Bryant teen, I was frequently drafted into Mama's low-calorie causes, like the one, the fanzine swore, that kept all Hollywood starlets amazingly celluloid-thin. For an entire summer, enormous green heads of iceberg lettuce, severed into wedges, dominated our plates. They were accompanied by revolting piles of small-curd cottage cheese, alfalfa sprouts and wheat germ, all consumed without dressing.

Once, having violated the forbidden candy box Mama kept hidden under her bed, I stealthily liberated a golden nugget from its clear cellophane wrapper and plopped it into my mouth. Ugghhh! DIET CANDY bitter as horehound and about as tasty as a tin can.

I will forever be nauseated by the memory of before-meal chug-a-lugs of gelatin blended into giant highball glasses brimming with salty red vegetable juice. When the gelatin didn't dissolve properly, I was forced to swallow the slimy lumps rising from the bottom. Ours were the days of hushed rumors about bee pollen, royal jelly and something called ginseng the Chinese kept quiet. Not to mention endless bouts with waist-cinchers and corsets in J. C. Penney dressing rooms. Or mail-order deluders like those steam-it-off-in-the-shower coveralls of garish blue plastic. And a weighted Hula Hoop, spun diligently, promised inches off the most recalcitrant middle.

Mama's battle was valiant but, ditching gimmicks and fads, she eventually lost the war to a blitz of late-night candy bar binges, half-pints of pistachio-nut ice cream and an endless stream of holiday gift boxes of See's chocolates.

♯

Predictably, my sampling of today's diet fads proved them as ineffective as those of the past. Weight loss is disappointingly little even with at-home exercise. But the regular gym workout has me taking in my slacks at the waistline and, overall, my clothes hang better. Lately, I've noticed I'm "startin' to get some leg on my leg," no longer winded after climbing stairs or running across parking lots. But squeezing quality fitness time from my caffeine-ridden schedule remains problematic. Battling the clock and a sleep deficit, admonished by my conscience to give up junk food, I scurry gymward for a workout whenever possible—thirty minutes here, forty there. Feeling like the slightly-below-average L.A. health hamster, I push myself to the guilt-inspired limit.

Out goes the bad fat, redistributed is the good.

Jungle of City

MAGENTA INFLORESCENCE rains briskly from above, clings to my hair. I'm caught in a light shower of bougainvillea.

For years now, I have observed this growth. Languid at first, now it extends with an insatiable appetite for space. Almost surprising are the bursts of blush erupting from sturdy, thorny, yet elegant tendrils. In our neighborhood, on long walks, I've spotted several variations—white, orange, red-orange, red, purple.

Knowing nothing of its origin, I'd always thought of it as exotic, of another tropical place, listened to it as if it were music—a fado guitar strummed in the back rooms of a smoky consciousness. Rhythm in the snap of leaflike bracts clammed like hands clasping, clapping, cupping. I heard rubber soles and boot heels hissing and rapping along finished mahogany. I've seen the ambitious legs of dancers expressing the hunger of torsos; weighty vines swaying like hips, a heaving, seductive, movement to the windsong castings of a spell.

The jungle come to the city.

On certain mornings—the metacognitive kind, when dust and sunshine join in a way that epitomizes the season—I turn to see them scratching and peeking in against the window, divinely rose-colored eyes at the panes. Life seeing life and feeling so much more alive in that shared instance of seeing.

Or when drenched and bleeding afternoon sun....

Approaching home, we can see it, from half a block away, arching skyward, blanketing the aged roof. Pulling curbside to park, I can't resist looking once more to discover which virgin corner of our tiny lot has been violated. There now hangs a drape of magenta where a gardener-for-hire pruned back the small rose bushes that once annually banked the white wood fence in a blaze of bright yellow blooms. In spots, this renegade liana has become heavy and violently threatening, attempting to strangle all lesser bushes, having long ago overwhelmed our bird of paradise.

The slim, olive-skinned young Latino stands outside our house and looks up. We called and asked him to come by and give us an estimate on the job. His partner watches us from the truck. We're all looking up, necks craned. The bougainvillea is half as tall as the telephone poles. One hand on my hip, the other waving and pointing, I indicate how many feet I want trimmed from there, there and there. I want more sun coming in through the windows. My husband wants the assurance of privacy. When we finish telling him what we want, he stands back and takes another unenthusiastic look. Of course, he'll have to use a ladder.

"I'll call you with the estimate on Monday." Then he and his partner drive away.

He never calls.

Plowing through reference books, I discover the name is French, the plant christened after the 18th-century explorer, Louis Louis de Bougainville, who found the species growing somewhere outside Rio de Janeiro.

Brazilian and beautifully deadly—it's the double-barbed hex of a *curandera*. Beneath a verdant surface, the vines thicken into the dense brittle cording of self-strangulation. Dead yellowy-orange and magenta leaves litter our yard and the sidewalk outside. This may be a fire hazard, we think, every now and then attacking them with the rake, bagging them for discard. We have purchased a special knife, its serrated blade perfect for hacking the overgrowth obscuring doors and windows, woven in and around the burglar bars.

Passers-by have to abandon the sidewalk to get around our little house, which promises to collapse one day soon, smashed to smithereens not by an earthquake but under the weight of *bougainvillea spectabilis.*

It has become a popular atmospheric component in the works of writers describing this region, a strong contender with the palm and the Joshua tree. Bougainvillea seems symbolic, metaphor for an unstoppable migration, an irreversible change introduced into our social topography.

Death off Barham

LADY, YOU NEARLY MADE a royal mess of what was left of my morning.

If you rate a mention on the 6 o'clock news this evening, I'll be too busy to know. But I expect that within 24 hours I will know as much about you as will any halfway decent member of the news-reading public. An article is bound to appear someplace with all your vital statistics and perhaps a few quotes from a grieving loved one speculating about why you took that forenoon dive from the Barham Boulevard overpass onto the northbound lanes of the Hollywood Freeway.

For now, I'd rather not know the details. My shocked imagination is writing and revising your death scenario, opting for the more pragmatic possibility that ultimately made me witness to the bloody aftermath of your irrevocable decision.

My personal scenario is much more mundane. Day began with the transgression of oversleep. The alarm went off at 6:30, but it was 9:30 when I jumped up, groggy but alerted that certain terribly important things were going to be left undone. I had barely enough time to bathe, dress and tend to vital correspondence before leaving to make my usual run on the P.O. box and then an 11:20 appointment with my favorite dentist in Reseda.

In spite of a loving warning from my husband, as he hurried off to work, I forgot to mind the clock. When I looked up again, I realized I was even more off-schedule than before. I did a frantic leaving dance, double-checking to see if I'd turned off all the lights and the Mr. Coffee, followed by a two-minute scramble for my eternally mislaid keys. If I'd been on time, I might've been behind the wheel of one of the six vehicles that struck you and kept going.

In minutes, I was racing up Wilton toward the Hollywood Boulevard on-ramp. I figured it would take a mere 15 minutes to make Reseda, speeding ticket notwithstanding. But instead of merging with a light *stream of traffic, I waded into a bumper-to-bumper jam. I made a quick exit at Cahuenga. Finding a pay phone (I haven't gone cellular yet), I got the receptionist. She green-lighted the hasty rescheduling of my appointment, giving me another 20 minutes.*

Zipping back up Cahuenga, parallel to the freeway, I was dismayed to discover even worse gridlock before the entrance ramp. It was closed. A small white hatchback weaved boldly through Day-Glo orange cones, violating the Caltrans dictate. Equally brazen, I followed, forcing my way into the slightly faster-moving left lanes. Relaxed into the incremental flow, I hit the AM dial. All-News 1070 was in the midst of its broadcast about an unknown woman who had fallen to her death at the Barham overpass, barely a half mile ahead. An apparent suicide. Her body was still on the freeway, an investigation under way.

Well, no wonder!

Creeping toward Barham, I inched toward the right to see what I could see. Several emergency vehicles and cars, most likely those of witnesses, were parked on the shoulder. A small crowd stared down at your body from the overpass. A man in a sky-blue shirt held a camera at his neck. There you lay, under the yellow tarp, guarded by police and highway patrolmen, the area marked off with yellow tape. In spots there were soft mounds of flesh, some flattened and scattered in a trail of skid marks. A few yards from your body lay a single brown loafer, as if you'd been knocked right out of your shoes.

There are no clues to your race, size or hair color. But that well-worn shoe punctuates my scenario for you—the one about a woman's failed struggle in a metropolis gone mad, where the only politics is survival and success is measured in multiples of zero. She finds facing yet another sunshiny day intolerable, knowing she hasn't got the quarter it takes to call for help. I feel what I imagine to be her pain. Then I imagine the pain of flight that must be gnawing through the guts of those who hit and ran. Would I have stopped? I don't know. Life on fast forward has negative side effects—a certain hardening that starts in the wallet and works its way to the heart.

As I exit the Ventura Freeway at Reseda, I hit the FM button. A blast from 106.7 clears my neurons. Suddenly I'm struck ironic by the hard-driving rhythmic lyric of Ziggy (David Bowie) Stardust and the spiders from Mars cranking "Suffragette City":

"There's only room for one and here she comes, here she comes…. Ahhhh wham, bam, thank you, ma'am…."

When Jury Duty Calls

IN MY DISTANT PAST, I'd immediately toss the officious-looking envelope into the trash, mistaking it for cheap advertising or a dun for a previously paid bill. But after a friend pointed out that the addressor was the Superior Court, I began regarding the letter seriously, opening it carefully, reading it over slowly, working myself into a snit, worrying that I wouldn't get out of serving jury duty and resentfully answering the questions correctly in capital letters and bold type.

When steadily employed, I'd smugly take the form into the office for my supervisor or employer to fill out. By that time, I'd lost my fear of jury duty and was curious to learn what it was all about, but at the nominal rate the county was paying, I couldn't afford the blessing. For a hard-working mother of three, in a city where survival demands two adult incomes, answering the civic call seemed a liability. But thangs've changed. Radically.

A few weeks ago, yet another pesky letter from Superior Court arrived. As I fished it from the mailbox, I immediately recognized the quail's-egg-blue envelope. I felt the warm flush one feels at that precise moment when one suspects Destiny has tapped one on the shoulder. This time, I carefully opened the envelope along its perforated top, then studied the familiar form printed inside. I took a few days to think it over. Had it escaped *anyone's* attention that Los Angeles, home of Hollywood, had also become the world's hotbed of legal-eagle celebrity?

I recalled the controversy, the accolades and threats that seemed to overwhelm Simi Valley jurors following the Rodney King beating trial. Several of them appeared in the tabloids, on radio and TV talk shows. I remembered a couple of the jurors following the Menendez brothers' trial as they, too, made their rounds of public forums. The Heidi Fleiss trial also paid shooting-star dividends—not to mention the *enormous* international brouha-ha that surrounded Michael Jackson, who not only never went to trial, but was never officially accused of wrong-doing. Mere publi-cized allegation was trial enough and generated more than its share of media hustlers who occupied hour after hour of pander-ing to insatiable appetites for speculation.

But nothing has produced more notoriety than the O.J. Simpson trial—a veritable factory of tinsel celebs. Anyone even vaguely connected to the slayings of Nicole Brown Simpson and Ronald Goldman, or to the trial (even the most discredited wit-ness) can boast limitless *money potential*—speaking fees and book deals ad nauseum.

‡

For the first time I hesitated, studying the return envelope addressed, "Office of the Jury Commission." Returning it took on ramifications as never before. It was no longer a simple summons to join the pool of citizens who were potential members of the grand jury. It was AN OPPORTUNITY! My imagination ran wild. "I Was a Juror in the (fill in name of celebrated defendant) Trial— A Day-to-Day Account," was the title I envisioned for my book, written and published instantly, of course. I imagined Mama hap-pily clipping articles in which I'm prominently featured and which double, of course, as book plugs on gabshows like "Larry King Live," "Oprah" and "Geraldo." Sure, I might only make peanuts initially, but movie rights and guest appearances would be more than adequate compensation. This was no longer an issue of civic duty. Sequestration aside, jury duty in the 90s is a money-making proposition—a chance for the ordinary citizen to score the megabucks that come with being a celebrity juror.

Grudgingly, I filled out my form, answering the questions in large, bold type. NO, I HAVE TO FEED THE KIDS AND THE LAND-LORD AND HELP MAINTAIN THE HEAD-BARELY-ABOVE-WATER LIFE-STYLE TO WHICH WE'VE BECOME ACCUSTOMED.

Ruefully, I dropped it in the mail.

Courtroom celebrity will have to wait.

Night of the Living Verdict

AN EERIE SMOG-LADEN boulevard on a sultry evening at sundown. A stretch limo careens into an estate driveway. A young White woman, 30ish, leaps out and runs toward the main house. She beats frantically at the door. It's opened by a tall, handsome Black man in bathrobe and slippers. She rushes inside.

O.J.: Heidi! What's the panic? Jes stepped out the shower.

HEIDI: (*screams*) Lock the door! They're coming!

O.J.: (*sighs*) No peace, no justice. I haven't even had time to restock the bar, fill the pool or heat the jacuzzi.

HEIDI: We've got to get out of this celebrity-trial-crazed town!

O.J. goes to a window. On tippy-toes, Heidi tries to peek over his shoulder. O.J.'s POV: Hoards of ghoul-driven cameras with probing lenses surround the house and grounds.

O.J.: Whoa!

HEIDI: Notice anything else strange?

O.J.: All media hounds look alike to me.

HEIDI: The White ones are all coming from the right, the Black ones are coming from the left and the perverts are coming right down the middle. Listen!

They hear repeated chantlike moans, "Innocent!" "Guilty!"

O.J.: Holy Darden, it's a war zone!

HEIDI: Are they after us or each other?

O.J.: Looks like summa both. Don't be afraid. We're safe here. The alarm system is a mutha. Hustle on into the kitchen. I've got some Haagen Dazs defrosting. Vanilla.

Dazed, Heidi trails O.J. through the immaculate mansion. Distant moans follow them.

HEIDI: S'pose they break in?

O.J.: Better find some weapons!

O.J. searches the cutlery drawers, flashes several single-blade knives, tosses them back.

O.J.: (*to himself*) Too dull.

Suddenly a camera-wielding zombie smashes through a window. Heidi screams. O.J. picks up the quart of Haagen Dazs and smears the telephoto lens. The zombie shrieks and retreats as the obscenely dripping lens thuds to the floor. Heidi half-swoons to her knees.

O.J.: For Cochran's sake, don't look at it!

He drop-kicks it through the broken window.

O.J.: We've got to keep cool till our attorneys get here.

HEIDI: You really think they'll save us?

O.J.: I'm absolutely one-hundred-percent sure.

More moans of "Innocent!" "Guilty!"–louder, closer. Heidi squeals, tears at her hair. O.J. starts barricading the room, glides the refrigerator in front of the shattered window. Heidi turns on the radio. O.J. plunks a heavy oak table against the door.

HEIDI: I thought you had arthritis?

O.J.: This is one of my good days.

Sound: A loud fhhupp-fhhhuppp. They look toward the roof.

HEIDI: What's that?

O.J.: Telecopters! Head for the basement!

HEIDI: A basement? In L.A.?

O.J.: The last owner was eccentric.

HEIDI: What about Erik and Lyle? They're still out there!

O.J.: Who?

HEIDI: The Menendez Brothers!

O.J.: Too late. They're retrial meat.

HEIDI: What about me? Is it too late for me?

O.J.: When the book and movie deals kick in, you'll be fine.

RADIO: …developing crisis over the verdict…sudden epidemic of civil disgruntlement…

HEIDI: Why are we standing here talking? The phone!

O.J. plucks a cellular phone from his robe pocket, hits the tabs, listens.

O.J.: That's funny. It's dead!

Heidi, hysterical, laughs and cries. O.J. shakes her by the shoulders. She won't calm down. He slaps her. She collapses in his arms. He props her up in a chair then fiddles with the cell phone.

RADIO:…a nation polarized by the verdict! No one is safe from this wave of hysteria! Stay tuned.…

O.J. goes to a closet and plows through racks of old clothes.

HEIDI: (*groans*) You hit me! If we were dating, I'd sue for abuse of a significant other.

O.J.: (*distracted*) We need disguises to escape.

HEIDI: Wool ski outfits in 80° weather?

RADIO:…devoured by media coverage…with lynch-mob glee.…

Suddenly the basement door slams inward, startling the pair. Heidi lets out blood-curdling yells. Two men, one White and one Black, emerge from the depths, smiling broadly.

O.J.: Hey, what are you guys doing in my basement? We're expecting our attorneys!

MAN A: You have our sympathies.

HEIDI: O.J., they look dangerous. How's the old arthritis?

MAN B: Don't be scared. We're as normal as you are.

O.J.: Look, whoever you are, the media's got the place surrounded.

MAN A and B: (*simultaneously*) What! Not again!

O.J.: So what's the score, friend or foe?

MAN A: Allow me to introduce myself, I'm Reginald Denny, Reg to my friends.

MAN B: King, here. Rodney G. And I do hope we can all get the ef along.

After the Fallout

LESS THAN 48 HOURS after the acquittal of O.J. Simpson, I stepped through the Magscanner metal detector, snatched my purse and carry-on off the conveyor belt and hurried through the usual LAX crowd of travelers, well-wishers, airport personnel and others, half-trotting toward the boarding gate. My mind was on the four-day weekend business trip ahead—repeatedly going over my mental checklist to be sure I hadn't forgotten anything vital, wondering about the weather, worrying about the car rental reservation and hotel accommodations—hoping everything would go smoothly.

But as swiftly as I walked, the turn of heads, snaking as if to strike, and the distinct snatches of heated conversation disrupted my self-absorption. The confluence of talk-bytes from clusters of people flowed together to create an uncanny and spontaneous chorus of whispers:

Ojojojojojojojojojojooo.

I felt chills. I was being watched and so, probably, was every Black person on the premises. This was a new phenomenon tinged with an all-too-familiar ring. It was as though I had stepped out of the Los Angeles of October 1995 and into the city of my childhood, thirty-odd years earlier. The architecture, clothes and hairstyles had changed, but *the atmosphere* was the same. Hostile eyes were all over me, searching and sizing me up, those mean, measured stares that pointedly reminded me that I'm Black and that I'd best watch how I behave in public if I wanted to remain unmolested.

Shrugging this off, I made my way to the counter at the gate, was greeted by a smiling attendant and given my boarding pass. Thirsty for something sparkling, and noting a ten minute wait before boarding call, I headed for the nearest airport watering hole.

A woman left her spot near the end of the crowded bar. I stepped in behind her, leaned against the stool and plunked my bag on the empty stool next to it. A young brown-haired White male, thirtysomething, occupied the last stool over, directly adjacent to the TV monitor.

A local station was airing its final segment of what I had dubbed "The O.J. Show." Between the opinions expressed by the program moderator and designated pundits, the young man made cryptic, double-edged remarks. His strong voice was flatly ironic, directed at no one specifically, yet his tone was calculated to unsettle and provoke anger in certain African-Americans or O.J. sympathizers. I ordered a club soda from the bartender of Asian extraction, paid for and drank it while half-listening to the O.J. wrap-up, half listening for the call to board. When it came, I hoisted bag and purse and headed for the gate.

As I approached the exit, a sudden movement to my left caught my attention. My amused glance was momentarily held by an extremely handsome White man with silver-gray hair, wearing whitewashed denims. His spectacularly clear, deep-blue eyes radiated the most animated and virulent race hatred I had seen in decades. It was the kind of stare-down I had grown impervious to on L.A. school grounds, encountered rarely since the civil rights movement, except when passing through small California towns or suburban enclaves of bigotry.

On board, as the plane readied for takeoff, I heard another faint "O.J." above typical passenger jostlings and grumblings. As I watched other takeoffs and landings, I thought of the events that define my postwar generation: the assassination of President Kennedy; the burst of militant Black pride after Watts burned; the night of Martin Luther King's assassination; the Charles Manson slayings; the shootings at Kent State; the day the Vietnam war ended; the mass suicide at Jonestown and its eerie replay at Waco; the Challenger explosion; our Rodney King-inspired blitzkrieg; the federal building explosion in Oklahoma City. Wearily, I assigned the Simpson verdict its place among these all-American milestones and speculated on the next.

Because the next is inevitable.

Where the Heart Is

OKLAHOMA CITY—We click our heels and descend into Oz, driving Interstate 35 north. The gray-brown panorama gives brief kisses of sunwashed rain. Rich green plains occasionally segue into subtleties of wheat and rye broken by splashes of wild purple. Brick-red soil is revealed in layers and muddies ponds and lakes. The farms are manicured, windmills whirling, oil wells pumping. We stop at Stuckey's for burgers and shakes, then traverse the limitless horizon at 80 m.p.h. Ahead Howard Johnson's, Wichita, Kansas.

Not all of the family could come, but we gather Friday evening, Memorial Day weekend, for the sixth reunion of Dunbar and Hall high schools (Hennessey, Oklahoma), closed forty years ago because of integration. Hands over hearts, we pledge allegiance to our flag. Bleats of rainfall penetrate the garden room roof like the beatings of angel wings, and the eerie sound lends a somber undertone to songs from the Phillips Singers. Everyone joins in for the Black national anthem. *Have not our weary feet come to the place for which our fathers sighed?* Names become faces—a roomful of people who look like me. We are here because I'm the oldest child of the secretary of The Hennessey Old-Timers Club of Southern California, my mother, graduate, Dunbar class of 1938. Plaques and anecdotes are presented, emphasis on the Last Class of Dunbar, 1955, but when full roll is called, we honor the lone surviving 1920s graduate with applause.

Saturday morning, my sons, husband and I join aunts, uncles and cousins for breakfast, family news updates, sharing photos and tales of an American farm life where racism was muted by strong common decency. That windy afternoon, we visit the Omnisphere and Science Center on Main Street, then reflect

263

on the disappearance of the buffalo and White King laundry powder at the Wichita-Sedgwick County Historical Museum two doors up. Saturday night's gathering begins with The Serenity Prayer, commemoration by Uncle John Scott, Dunbar Class of 1941, then more memories à la chicken *cordon bleu*, followed by dancing to the sassy downbeats of the Ninth Street Blues & Jazz Band.

Let me remember things I don't know. Sunday morning, we don't quite know where we're going but get there, trailing the busload of nostalgic schoolmates across the Kansas state line, returning to Oklahoma for the Hennessey picnic. After the two-hour drive, hungry and thirsty, we pull up and idle behind the bus, which has stopped outside a tiny graveyard off an unpaved road. The elders pile out and roam among headstones decorated with flags and flowers. My roots are here, great grandfather, grandfather, grandmother. Hawks circle overhead and red ants dominate the Mount Zion Baptist church grounds. We gather over country fried chicken, roast beef and coleslaw. Afterward, we wade through wild, shoulder-high wheat and rye to visit the ruins of granddad's farm. I've been here before. This time, I own the memories of baby chicks, the old outhouse and grandmother's tears.

‡

Oklahoma City—On Monday morning, Memorial Day. After biscuits and gravy, we drive the 81 south, pass through Kingfisher, Okarche and other small towns. Flags are everywhere, on stoops and rooftops. Outside El Reno, we head east into Oklahoma City along the new business strip. We notice all flags are at half staff. We have three hours before our flight and are anxious to see the federal building bombing site. We ramble toward downtown, then make our way to 5th and Broadway. Many buildings are boarded up, including one auto repair shop called "The Dent Authority." Overcast skies exaggerate the devastation.

We park and walk to the fenced-off site. Work crews and cranes search for remaining victims. Police keep tourists like us outside the corridor where onlookers gather for autographs of rescuers. On the fence in front of the YMCA, mourners have hung a wreath from which an angel dangles, along with flags, flowers and poems. We take snapshots, buy souvenirs, collect autographs, move on....

‡

Images of Oz buzz my head as we jockey through LAX. I'm not Dorothy and my story has no Wizard. Cruising Century Boulevard east to the 405 north, we slip back into the rhythms of honking horns and cursing drivers. There's no place like L.A. for me. *Amen, I'm a city gal.* And though this is so, I'm haunted by the feeling that I've left home to return home.

Sorry, Wrong Wanda

"OH, THERE YOU ARE!" Grinning, Huz did an exaggerated double take as he exited the post office and greeted me with a handful of mail. While he'd checked the P.O. box, I'd dashed across Vermont Boulevard for a pound of coffee. "I thought I was talking to you, but this other young woman turned around. Quick, I'll show you." But when we got back inside she'd vanished. Rushing through the same post office a day later, my friend Donna saw the same young African-American woman. "G-r-r-r-lll! She looked *just* like you, 'specially from the back."

Once again, there was a tear in the space-time curtain. But this doppelgänger and I would never meet. Relieved, I assumed I had once again avoided impending cosmic doom or displacement by an alien. Besides, it wasn't the first time I'd been mistaken for someone else.

Frequently, I'm cast as celebrity look-alike. In the late 60s, though still a teenager, I was pegged for folk singer Odetta because, I speculated, we sported similar 'fro hairstyles. In the mid-70s, I was a ringer for Maya Angelou or Tamara (*Cleopatra Jones*) Dobson, all of us tall, dark-skinned. In the late 80s, it was writer Alice Walker (outspoken), and lately, it's either Whoopi Goldberg (shared birthday) or Oprah (shared tendency toward "heavyset").

But being big, Black and misidentified in L.A. can also be scary. Early on, I learned to carry a tome-sized book when traveling by bus after sundown. Vice officers, looking to roust prostitutes, would pull curbside to the bus stop, spot my book, then speed off. Far worse were those times when I was mistaken for a Black male. My giant earrings didn't always save me the outrage of being stopped and frisked.

More amusing are those moments when my nationality is

mistaken, like on one return from Mexico.

"Where'd you come from—Honduras?" a border guard once shouted, eyeing my yellow head-wrap suspiciously.

"I was borrrn in East L.A!" I sang out.

He laughed and waved us on our way.

Strangest of all was my twenty-year head-bump with another Wanda Coleman. When I enrolled in one arts workshop, she joined the rival one at Mafundi Institute. After my director and two associates accused me of betrayal, I maintained that it wasn't me. But attitudes were cool. There had to be another Wanda Coleman. I drove over to Mafundi to confront her. She wasn't there, but our name appeared on actor William (*Blacula*) Marshall's workshop roster.

Later, after moving into my first Hollywood apartment, our "double starring" increased, and I received her calls from feminist groups and old boyfriends. Once my phone rang at 3 a.m.

"Where you livin' now!? Still livin' in the Valley? You always were so bourgeoisie," the man blurted without name or hello.

"Huh?"

"This is loverboy, Deacon."

"Sorry, I don't know you."

"Don't bullshit me, baby!"

"Oh! You want the other Wanda!"

He apologized and hung up.

At a late-80s poetry reading, another old flame looked me over and gingerly stated he'd expected to meet the other Wanda, we looked nothing alike and that she was "more modest."

A year later, I deplaned in Sacramento on a business jaunt. I was puzzled by the unusual royal treatment. My host explained he'd expected the other Wanda, having worked with her before.

Months later I was selected Poet of the Year by Pasadena City College and performed at the award assembly. An unfamiliar white-haired lady kept drawing my eyes, moved nearly to tears. Afterwards I was disconcerted by her big familiar hug. I asked if she knew me. She said she was my 12th grade English composition teacher.

"Oh," I said, "you mean the other Wanda Coleman!"

I explained the mix-up. Disappointed, she said I'd probably been a wonderful student too.

One Friday, I received a gift from a friend in Oregon, *Pages of My Mind*, a 1968 student yearbook featuring work by high school seniors. His note said he thought I'd treasure it. In it was "Virgil," a story by—guess who—a senior at San Fernando High, a school I'd never attended.

That very next day, at a public forum, a tall, brown-skinned woman approached me and said flatly: "Hello. My name is Wanda Coleman." Beside myself, I babbled, "I've so much to tell you!" I scribbled my home number on a card and pressed it into her palm. "Please call me!" That was six years ago. She never called. And, oddly, we haven't crossed wires since.

Days ago, at my favorite Larchmont coffee hang, I again felt that familiar starstruck gaze. Ignoring it, I placed my order. The countergirl hesitated, then asked "Are you Angela Davis?"

"*That*," I sputtered, "is a new one!"

Rides of Spring

WE'RE NIGHT CREATURES, trapped in the searing eternity of day. We cope, but secretly we believe our behaviors have been modified to fit the demands of contemporary living. Craving the rewards of work, we rise just before or with the sun. Our morning newspaper is ever on the porch and we retrieve it while the coffee precipitates. Half-conscious, we shower to the Muzak of newscasts, then pore over the daily calendar and account books we maintain with religious ague. There's the endless flow of breakfasts, lunches and dinners, departmental meetings, guild affairs, business pow-wows. And having to parent, we are as married to the rhythms and dictates of the Los Angeles school district as we are to each other.

There's the ceaseless scramble to improve our TRW, belt-tightening for the IRS, weighing the advantages of the latest high-tech gizmo from AT&T, or cost-saving offer from GTE, working out at the YMCA, keeping abreast of the latest NIMBY scuttlebutt and, of course, the juice on O.J.

Then there are private obsessions, get-rich schemes and easy-living dreams that cause us to frequent late-night photocopy, fax and coffee shops, seek out galleries, museums and poetry hangs at every odd moment, squeeze out precious spare seconds to explore the musty-dusty shelves of vintage bookstores and collectors' racks. We chew over our frustrations in low-rent Chinese or Thai restaurants or sweat them off in upscale westside billiard hangs. We do it yet feel simultaneously cursed and blessed, living within the speed limit as we carve out our spot on the cutting edge of the 21st century.

Then something hits, like a psychic temblor. The evening desert—blackened heads of raffia stark against the gold glow tinged with red violet lingering on the blue western horizon—

ignites the fires behind our eyes and under our soles. And that gibbous moonrise awakens the night owls. Suddenly, there's no such thing as sleep. *Time to ride.* As fast and as far as we think we can afford, rambling the 101 east to the 5 to the 710 south to Long Beach at 3 a.m., surfing the AM dial until James Brown screams, "Gimme mah thang—what you got, what I need. What you need, what I got," as we count the off-ramps still closed for quake reconstruction.

Now the sky is steel-gray and silver smoke billows against the purple haze dotted with amber and white glistenings, the lights of refineries where the earth is pumped for the slick spoils fueling our universe of nonstop consumption.

Bell Gardens ahead.

There's the draw of The Bicycle Club, for another type of bird, mini-Vegas around-the-clock. We swoop and dive. It's too nice a night to be inside. Marvin Gaye and the road call for nostalgic healing. We circle around and head down San Pedro way to the cliffs. I point out the ghosts of romantic places where lovers used to come to neck, parked shoreside, watching the tide, the rhythms of golden oldies and sweet somethings accompanied by the rush of waves.

We find our way to a viewpoint, park and pick our favorites among the constellations. We share recollections until a ribbon of sunrise threatens the basin, announcing it's time to go. We hurry back to the car and reluctantly head homeward. A brief jam near the 105 breaks the spell, with traffic backed up from where they're still working on the people mover, then the lanes open again. We're surprised so many other drivers are caught in the early rush. Perhaps a few like us, with just enough night left to catch a few winks.

Meanwhile, back in our neighborhood, someone's slouched at a bus stop, picking through the change in his palm. Someone's crouched at a pay phone, talking urgently, slapping at the air. Someone's switching hurriedly up the pavement in institutional work shoes, tugging at the wrinkles in her uniform. Spring has come to Los Angeles. Time to get ready for summer.

The Short Goodbye

REINFORCING THE IMAGE of trendy Los Angeles as domain of impermanence, mirage, a shallow past and the fluid address book, Chasen's follows Perino's and the Brown Derby onto the list of disappearing landmarks. Nothing here stands still for long or, once adjusted to, remains as it was. Ever again, our terrain, actual and psychological, proves whimsical by nature, fickle by design—a fluctuating gridwork. Los Angeles demands ongoing renewal, mobility and flexibility—demanding the stressful dance we do to stay with it:

The merlot is flat and has a tinny aftertaste. When Huz and I ask what happened, the waiter says the proprietor has opted for a cheaper house brand. We still frequent the Franklin Strip bistro, but now, when we're in the mood for wine, it's strictly Zinfandel. On local *trattoria* chain has the habit of dropping our favorite appetizers when making "seasonal changes"; I still hanker for that *pancetta* and pesto salad, while Huz eulogizes the fig and *prosciutto* starter. And I haven't been back to our fave Hancock Park Thai hang since it dropped its killer drunken chicken.

Gone's our little 3rd Street mom-and-pop *yakisoba* shop. The Vine Street Bar & Grill, always good for an impromptu jazz fix, is defunct, as is the Columbia B&G. Now X-ed, Bullocks Wilshire was the only department store left in the city that looked and smelled like downtown during Christmas when I was knee-high. Strolling the lush grounds at the Ambassador Hotel once provided an occasional after-dinner respite. The kids always enjoyed winding in and out of hotel shops, buying foreign magazines, touristy kitsch, or sweets for dessert. After arguments, me and Huz sometimes kissed and made up over drinks, cozied up in the red plush bar. Being romantic was easy over veal Marsala at that family-owned Italian place on 6th near Berendo, a disco the last time I looked. Neighborhood stores no longer carry the carob milk Huz loves to drink by the half-gallon.

Barely surviving being sacked during the '92 riots, one of the only two Southland outlets that carried ribbons for my electronic thingamabob, once only five minutes away, has relocated to the Valley. After appearing and disappearing, then reopening again, my stompin' ground rib-and-sweet-tater stop at Manchester and Broadway is boarded over like the Russian auto repair shop that was around the corner whenever the struggle buggy refused to start. Driving up to purchase some new sounds, we find our music hot spot has been torched, as was our Santa Monica family barbecue habitat.

Suddenly we're chasing around town to find my favorite ice cream, Haagen Dazs Honey Vanilla, which transforms the most tepid torte or cookie into temptation feast, going from store to store—finally found only at Mayfair, then *zap*, poof! Huz calls the main office to discover it's discontinued in the U.S. and available only in Canada. Likewise, our favorite Pepperidge Farm cookie assemblage disappears not only from shelves nationwide, but forever. Getting my best over-the-counter sinus-flu drug now requires a special call to the local supermarket manager, who then contacts the distributor. Huz complains they've discontinued his preferred cat litter. After a traumatic afternoon's drive through Glendale, having followed it from site to site for a decade, I discover my tall girl's shop vanished. Not to mention whatever befell that glossy little Armenian store where I usta buy stuffed grape leaves for Huz.

Reliable David no longer manages the counter at the Sunset car-rental place. "Joe on Thursdays" went back to Mexico when the Larchmont fish shop changed hands. Chattertons' Los Feliz bookhang is a ghostly ruin since Koki died. We haven't had a decent mechanic since Long Tall Charles retired from Hollywood service-station duty. And at our place on the Vermont Strip, since the chef's wife went back to Thailand, we live without the best fried won ton and crispy catfish under this smoggy corner of heaven.

♯

So on and so forth we cope, buffeted by chronic transience and social shifts, grateful to be among the lucky who are mildly inconvenienced by natural and man-made upheavals. Taking a breath to speculate, we agree L.A. might be better with a touch of the rigidity that comes with long-established institutions and communities anchored in a common history. But on the flip side, where the only tradition is no tradition, life is everything but dull.

Future Perfect

Huh?

It's all been a blur. Did someone say Christmas?

I can't believe the holidays are here—again. Already! It seems that just a January ago I was surveying the months ahead, savoring all the zillion things I was finally going to do, especially those nagging holdovers from last year and the year before. Now this year's end is imminent, the beginning of next year impending. In spite of living my life at full hamster, few of my urgent missions were accomplished.

Never lost those 40 pounds.

Never made that trip to Laughlin.

Hardly a dent in that mounting stack of hundred-odd best-sellers I was going to read, cover to cover. "I'll get to these later" is my self-hypnotic chant whenever my ill-balanced, dust-ridden stack of neglected correspondence, 3½-feet high, is periodically knocked over, spewing motes. Unfiled clippings, manuscripts and low-calorie recipes wither and yellow in the dark crevice under the deskside table.

Light stuff is easy burden, but I bend under the weight of the heavies—friends, relations, beloved ones not seen enough of... the unwritten, the unsaid, the undelivered... the wonderful moments that never happened except in my well-intentioned, over-committed imagination.

My mood becomes pensive and introspective as I zombie through the shopping, phone calls, dinner dates and other seasonal rituals and obligations, trapped between confusion and dismay. An acute awareness sets in. I feel the axial spin of Earth as it moves relentlessly forward. It's winter and my thoughts are preoccupied with the days to come.

The future is a place of endless comfort at the terminal of sacrifice and hard work. There must be a time when everything will be better, well organized, and spanking. Or is it simply that what's possible makes the inevitable palatable? Funny—there are no mysteries in the future. Everything is known there. Cures will have been found for the incurable. Wars will cease and doomsday weapons will be shelved.

There will be plenty of time to revel in the arts and travel the world. Urban homelessness will be a sociological curiosity of the late 20th century. There will be enough of everything for everyone—the cultural-economic cornucopia will vanquish the poverty of heart, mind and spirit.

There are no civil evils in the future. There will be no traffic jams and no traffic accidents. The criminal justice system will be eradicated because there will be no crime. Society will embrace and nourish the different, the disabled, the dissident. The cantankerous old and the rebellious young will bury their contentiousness in mutual respect.

‡

Believing in the future requires an almost relentless optimism, an idealistic outlook, an agenda of hopes and dreams. All forecasts are ever-fresh and blossom with potential.

The future is the great motivator. It inspires the faithful and fuels the determined. Sometimes the future is so dense it seems to crush the present, suffocating the psyche. At other times, it's buoyant, uplifting, and makes the here-and-now tolerable. The future is the smile of a child, the kiss of a lover, the hand taken in a brief parting or a lasting one. Too frequently it's the only thing lived for. It's the domain of fancy and fantasy, where the memories of those who have remained in the past are cherished.

It's hard not to look forward to the future even if it never comes, despite meticulous planning. The present confirms and the past guarantees that every living thing will somehow in some way contribute to it.

Tomorrow, nothing goes to waste.

Tomorrow, the pains of the present are past. It is where the truth lives revealed, untarnished and celebrated.

The future is a home built of memory, the one to grow up and grow old in—where lives are rich in unblemished love, perfect expectations are reared and death is an openness to all that is possible. It is, and always will be, the only place that's absolutely safe. In it, everything and everyone continues. And it will get me through these holidays, as it usually does.

Nails Nails Nails

IN THE SOUTH CENTRAL beauty parlors of my childhood, hairdressers were divas whose business savvy usually came smothered in loads of maternal warmth. Customers were often part of an extended family of children and spouses, shoeshine and delivery boys, ministers and salesmen, bookies and hustlers whose interactions generated excitement—buying Irish Sweepstakes tickets, ordering shrimp fried rice, raising funds for local politicians or "sick and shut-ins." Folk went to the same churches and nightclubs, and shared intimacies, gossip, and aspirations for success in a world that did not want them. But the manicurists fascinated me most.

While my hair was being washed, dried and fried, I studied their high-gloss spatulate talons, pointy spikes, and semicurled wands, which were so long that the ladies had to hold and manipulated objects, like hair clips and spoons, with the fleshy tips of fingers, and used a pencil, knitting needle, hair spike, or chopstick to push buttons, turn dials and flip the pages of fanzines, datebooks and trashy novels.

Like hairstylists, nail stylists required appointments, often sharing customers, even men for whom the lye-permanent "conk" and clear-polish nail job meant status. The ladies talked and smoked cigarettes as fast as they worked, discussing the dynamics of nail growth from cornstarch to gelatin, and putting on nylons without causing runs. They had the best-looking hands in the joint and usually did their co-workers' nails.

Cosmetologists who doubled as manicurists seemed to find the latter role more glamorous. Manicurists always had the biggest hair, best figures, and tightest-fitting uniforms. They had the handsomest boyfriends and the sweetest husbands. In that ethnocosm, they were celebrities.

After I left home, poverty and social awareness convinced me that the beauty shop clashed with my new self-image. Manicures were too bourgeois and too expensive. But by the mid-70s I was back, *for the nails*, the one girl-girl luxury I guiltily allowed myself. By then, the old shops had closed and I found myself in the hands of strangers, still mainly Black women, and trends had changed. One no longer needed an appointment. Business in beauty parlors had declined because a new kind of nail shop had sprung up all over L.A., offering an artificial high-fashion nail cement that could be shaped, styled and studded out-rageously with rhinestones, beads and spangles.

On my small, fragile nails the pricey fakes looked fab. But as busy hours passed, I noticed that despite the agile use of pencils and chopsticks, and typing with the balls of my fingers, I was becoming increasingly clumsy, and the tips were starting to throb. I bore the discomfort, to the point of restless sleep, but when the nail on my left ring finger snapped while I was vacuuming, wrenching away half my natural nail with it, I wrapped my bleed-ing hand in a towel, rushed to the shop, and had the remaining nails buffed to the quick, repeating the process until the natural nails grew out. Nearly twenty years would pass before my next manicure.

On a recent San Francisco trip, I was seized by the urge to have a manicure—nothing fancy—clipped short, clear polish. I cruised the avenues for a beauty salon, found several but, oddly, no manicurists. Finally, given the address of a nail shop, I rushed over and stepped into a sweatshop. Ten tiny Asian women, heads lowered, labored at stations resembling sewing tables. There was the familiar stink of the overworked and underpaid. More unset-tling, every customer was an Afro-American.

The prices were far cheaper than I recalled. The French manicure was most expensive, followed by the full set of artificial nails, airbrush, silkwrap, waxing, etc. I could now afford weekly manicures if I wanted; however, communication proved a draw-back. But with the aid of one regular, I made myself understood and, within fifteen minutes, had my manicure.

Back in L.A., I noticed a nail business boom. Along Man-chester, down La Brea and up Crenshaw, I've counted more than thirty shops identical to the one in San Francisco, their clientele predominantly Black and Latin women. Reluctantly, I give them my business but sumpthin's gone out of the experience.

Gone are the aromas of fried chicken and fish mingled with Dixie Peach and pine tar; the bouts of braggadocio, handclasps and struts, between high-signers and signifiers; crooner-inspired swoons and whoops, low-down stomps of high and heavy hips; the inspired spontaneous cries of "Amen!" and "Honey hush!" Gone is that strong sense of *community*, a transformative ritual which, in my child's eye, will ever seem as beautiful as it was uniquely Black.

Exit Hollywood

"I CAN'T BELIEVE IT! No bums begging for handouts and no one following me around the store, looking to see if I'm gonna steal a cart." Huz, a bag of groceries in each hand, grins broadly as he marvels at another advantage of living in our new, quiet, freeway-close, residential neighborhood. Our move was traumatic, as we wrenched ourselves from a lifestyle of nearly a decade, our routine timed to the precious second—always in a functional circle that took us from post office to photocopy shop to cleaners to supermarket to carwash to work and back without waste or worry. But as the days pass, our years lived in and about Hollywood take on bad-dream qualities.

From now on, there'll be no more of those restless nights, when we'd fall asleep, only to be jolted awake by a chorus of rude car alarms, the *whirrr-whirrr* of surveillance helicopters, the grating metallic shriek of some motor unable to turn over, the sirens of emergency vehicles roaring to the rescue, or the *rattle-clap* of shopping carts pushed by late-night ramblers foraging for recyclables in trash bins.

Our new neighborhood is lightly traveled. We haven't seen one single accident, unlike the continual gum-bumpers we witnessed at our old corner, in spite of the posted 25-m.p.h. school zone speed. The screeching of brakes, the crunch of metal kissing metal and quarrels between drivers were a daily affair. For a couple of years, Huz and other concerned residents lobbied for a traffic light. As we loaded the U-Haul, we noticed an intersection being painted onto the asphalt, and four-way stop signs being installed that day, our last.

On our new street, parking's plentiful. We not only have a real garage but can actually get the car into it. In the old 'hood, parking was a challenge, with barely enough garage space to accommodate the 10-speed. Not long after we moved into our little Hollywood house, zoning changed, meters went up and unrestricted parking vanished. Despite additional parking structures for employees of the local film companies, congestion increased for the entire area. All our attempts to get residential parking permits failed. To avoid parking tickets, we moved the car two or three times a day, parked in the neighbor's driveway and, occasionally, on the sidewalk. As a last resort, we competed for the few metered spots with hundreds of audience or audition hopefuls queued up for the local TV sitcoms.

Gone are the unpredictable episodes of window-smashing, when every car lining the avenue was vandalized.

Gone is the tagger graffiti and our local one-man vigilance squad who always painted it out.

Gone are the placards designed to look like parking tickets, stuck under the windshield wiper, soliciting cheap labor or cheap sex.

Gone are the dreaded marathons! Their causes were worthy, but more than once we left home to discover ourselves trapped in a maze of runners, orange tape and gesticulating officers, unable to get back to our door mere blocks away.

And gone are the peeping-Tom neighbors, the drunks who left beers on the stoop, dog owners who left pet poop under the palm, picky garbage men who didn't like olive-green trash bags, whacked-out street fighters, junky muggers, the bag woman with legs of steel and the barf sisters.

We miss our favorite schmooze spots, malls and service hangs, of course, but the new neighborhood promises all of that and more. We've already scoped out the shopping centers and spot-checked for the new post office. We'll get to the clubs and restaurants later, after we finish unpacking.

Strange. After so many years in Hollywood, we had begun to feel part of the insanity. But now, that feeling is lifting. We're starting to breathe fresh air again, fingers crossed, hoping the welcome wagon won't be burned on our lawn.

Late Night Callers

HE GETS BOTHERED by the sound. I try not to be.

Sometimes it's a sharp, piercing *zzzinging* that disrupts a delicious sleep. Other times it's a *brrrinng* that resonates. Whatever the tone, these kinds of phone calls always come around, at or after midnight. Instantly, he jumps up to answer it. Invariably, I'm the one doomed to miss the end of the movie we're watching.

"Why don't you tell 'em not to call after ten o'clock?"

I shrug. "Suppose it's an emergency?"

I used to make these kinds of calls myself.

Most come from the emotional brink, from those about to fall and crack. Someone, somewhere is in need. Abandoning them to the answering machine is not my style. Could be it's friend or blood kin. Sometimes the caller is drunk, doped or both—whether off booze or adrenaline, and is in a fit of despair. Two out of five calls are long-distance. Rarely do they come collect, but when they do, I accept the charges. Always. Seldom are they wrong numbers.

Often these calls come with a side dish of adventure, and I throw on clothes, go out into an ever-chilly morning, feeling mildly like a schnook, waiting as the windshield too-slowly defrosts, checking the fuel gauge to be sure there's enough gas for the trek to who-knows-where. Could be I'm delivering an urgent message from a frantic attorney to her incommunicado client, bagging bail money to liberate an indigent jazz musician, rescuing a night-riding girlfriend from a seedy downtown bus depot or depositing a manic-depressive guyfriend at a Skid Row shelter.

Occasionally there's the deep-ghetto foray to help move an angry friend who's stealthily vacating a hellhole by dark to avoid the indignities of paying back rent to some rapacious manager fronting for an absentee landlord.

My favorites are the calls from ex-Angelenos who miss this city and won't admit it. Some swear they're never coming back. Some wish they could but can't. So I curl up on the living room couch for a little homespun therapy, stifle my yawns and give up some ear.

"How's the old Fox Venice? Is it still there?" His voice drips nostalgia.

"No, Jeff—it went swap meet a couple of years back."

"Whatta shame."

Then there are the night howls from new arrivals suffering culture shock. Like Joyce. A mutual friend gave her my number.

"I don't understand the Black men out here. The Black people, period. They *look* Black but after that, the resemblance ends."

"Well, you understand the difference between hot jazz and cool jazz. After all, cool jazz was born here in the west."

We resolved her consternation with an hour's discussion of the differences in region, East coast vs. West.

Joyce called me a second time, during regular waking hours, to thank me for taking time to listen to a stranger, late one night so many years ago. She has settled in Los Angeles and is doing very well.

Being receptive has its hazards, including the occasional crank. Once, as I sweated over my typewriter in the wee hours, wondering how I was going to meet a steadily advancing editorial deadline, the voice box screamed. I answered. A chatty young *brutha* announced that he had written a poem especially for me.

"Yeah?"

"Would you like to hear it?"

"Might as well," I sighed. After six hours of typing I needed a break.

"Here it is!" He sucked in his breath for a pregnant moment then began to enunciate: "Slow down...slow down... slow down...slow down...slow down...slow down...," he droned in mid-range alto. I slammed the receiver onto its cradle. Dizzy with rage, I went back to my typewriter. I envisioned his head beneath my fists as I spent my fury banging on the keys.

With increasing rarity come calls from old flames. My spouse barely tolerates such holdovers from my previous life. When answering the phone, he rudely douses any still-smoldering embers. Otherwise, he begrudgingly accepts these brief, intermittent intrusions. As do I, but—one never knows who might be calling, who may require some sympathy, some understanding.

Once in a while, it's his mother.

Once in a while it's mine.

Dollar and a Dime

HE IS ALMOST HANDSOME. But he has that look. I've seen it before. I've worn it on my own dark face. His mouth, an amber slash drawn tightly against his teeth—intermittent flashes of yellowed white as he soundlessly talks to himself, jerkily, to match his anxious walk. I've seen that walk before. I've walked it.

He sees me. I see him. And when he sits down on my neighbor's stoop, I know he waits for me.

The air is brisk and clear, and the sky is clouded. It's a Sunday and summer is near. Damn, I think, just what I need, and I was in such a good mood. The day had started with breakfast with old friends at a cozy cabaret to the lilt of a troubadour on acoustical guitar. The man played old folk favorites, crooned "...parsley, sage, rosemary and thyme...."

Now here comes one of *them* to spoil it.

I am usually filled with anguish at the sight of such men. And such women. But especially the men. They crowd the sidewalks outside post offices and supermarkets, their palms up, carrying rags, squeegees, spray guns. They sit with inverted pockets on crates outside restaurants and nightclubs or stationed at freeway on-ramps or mid-traffic, signs, cups, caps or buckets held waist-high, eyes radiating everything from madness to threadbare dignity.

But sometimes these street encounters offer adventure or surprise.

Once, while driving east on 6th towards Highland, I approached the intersection, about to turn left, kids in the back seat. I waited as an emaciated White man in his late thirties, with pockmarked skin and long, stringy blond hair, crossed the street. He was very poorly dressed, brogans worn down to sandals. He walked as though he was overly medicated.

Suddenly, a westbound lime-green Mercedes-Benz rounded the corner. Behind the wheel was a buxom, well-coiffed blonde in her late fifties. She pulled alongside the man, stopped, rolled down her window and barked at him. He went over to her. She slapped some cash in his mitts and sped off. Surprised, he looked blankly at the bills, straightened his spine then went into a rage. "Bitch!" he yelled after her, then stuffed the cash in the busted base of a street lamp and stomped off, shaking his fists at the air.

"Meat for dinner!" I yelped, pulling curbside, salivating as I retrieved the alms.

And once, on an early Monday morning, I faked a cheery good-bye as I dropped off my son at the sitter's. Shedding pretense, I headed for the car. As I contemplated the bureaucratic dolor of the job I sweated blood for, my center of gravity went to my feet. I was in a bottomless depression.

"Nothing's that bad," he said. I looked up into smiling brown eyes. His hair was thick and curly. He was my height, Mexican, leaning into the stone facade of the storefront. He sported a brown leather aviator's jacket, right hand buried in one pocket, left hand grasping a can of malt liquor. I gave a little nod and kept walking. My depression began to lift.

More recent was the time outside the supermarket parking lot. I was driving the old car, the one suffering bald tires and twenty-eight years of abuse. As I climbed out, a young, orange-skinned Black guy walked toward me, rag and spray-bottle in hand.

"Wash your window, sistuh? One dollar."

"You see what I'm drivin', don't yah? Hell I'm after *your* job."

He broke into laughter. "Best one I've heard yet!" I laughed with him.

One afternoon, my son and I spotted the familiar panhandler who worked a spot off a downtown freeway exit at Wilshire. We started tittering at his get-up, the crutch under one arm, the cast on his leg, a bandage around his head and sunglasses.

"Lookathat! I bet he's fakin' it!"

As we rolled to a stop at the red light, I lowered the window and waved a dollar at him. He stepped off the curb, limped over and reached for it. I snatched it away.

"You can have it, if you let me touch your mascara," I sniggered as my son cupped his mouth to smother incredulous giggles. Our wily panhandler, who was also laughing, doffed the glasses. As I smeared the thick gooey blackness under his left eye, we burst into hysterics. I gave him the dollar and sped off.

At this moment another young man intrudes on my modest prosperity. I've just gone shopping and am unloading groceries. As I cross the street, bags in hand, he rises from my neighbor's stoop and comes toward me. I try not to look at him, but see every move as I set the bags down and unlock my door.

"Please," his English is broken, skin yellow, eyes like agates, hands gesturing at the bags of food. He's in navy denims and a T-shirt. He looks about twenty. "If you could give—some money?"

I reach into my jacket pocket. Abe Lincoln puts in an appearance. I give him the fiver. He looks at it. It's more than expected.

"Something for you—I can do?"

"No thanks, sweetheart," I say. "Go on and do what yah gotta."

He brought out the mother in me.

Sleepless in L.A.

FOUR-WALL FEVER STRIKES, arouses restlessness.

After sitting all day, the hunger to move around takes hold. Most places stop serving at 11 p.m. There's always Al's on one end of town or Ben Frank's on the other. Tripping through Troy's for a game of gin or darts is one schmooze possibility—so is chasing down hot, doughy dumplings at that quaintly grungy little Cantonese place in Chinatown, the one that never closes.

Along Beverly, down La Brea, up Vermont, and before you get to Beachwood off Franklin, there's always some funky little culture hang and/or bookstore hawking caffè lattes and cake—ripe for the aspiring screenwriter, venturesome novelist, gritty song-writer or ambiance-starved poet.

But who wants to sit on overstuffed sofas or high-tech bum-huggers and eat?

Perhaps drive somewhere, park, get out and take in the somber ugliness and dangerous beauty of local night life, the minute hand fiercely ticking toward 2 a.m. West L.A. maybe, Hollywood, Downtown? Doesn't much matter.

Along Alameda and cruising through Skid Row, the fires burn, small incendiaries that defy ordinance and cold. The move-ment of denizens is alternately listless or frenetic. Behind glass and steel skyrises housing corporate kingdoms are impoverished shooting galleries where hypodermics are brandished in full view of anyone driving the back alleys in search of parking. Someone under duress is getting his/her head broken open outside the lobby of a single-occupant residency hotel.

Fear mars the recession-scarred, post-riot terrain. At the mini-mart, all goods and gas are skittishly sold behind bulletproof glass. Nuisance shopping carts appear randomly off a freeway on-ramp, or lean haphazardly into a curb. Some are abandoned, awaiting recovery; others are loaded with the scavenged or recyclable finds of some fringe-dweller plowing through nearby trash bins.

Walking along Melrose, a foreboding night owl sits motionless in lotus position against a lamppost until "it" turns its head to reveal gigantic ghost eyes—dilated portals, hair fallen out under the rages of stress or chemotherapy. Unwashed sleepers snore on bus benches and in doorways.

Over off Fountain, near Ardmore, the observatory, glowing in an aureate nest of lights, blossoms up out of a polluted sea of roofs on blighted A-frames, apartment complexes and stucco courts.

In front of the Capitol Records building, two rock 'n roll taggers chalk their message across glossy stone. Up off Bronson and down along Hudson toward Seward, the gutters glitter with broken glass from stolen or vandalized vehicles. On the lot of a closed service station, there are kitschy neon signs for sale. They're perched on a coupe, the lone leather-jacketed salesman anxiously on the scope for drive-by cash.

Near where Ports used to be, along Santa Monica Boulevard, there's the flash of Spandex and lamé. Catch-action thickens as torsos and bottoms are revealed to potential consumers. On Franklin, a mutt's paw prints mark a previous path through once-wet cement—immortalized like a show-biz star.

Along the Strip, Gazzari's is boarded up, but the view of the southern horizon remains impressive. Bars cover the windows of the tattoo parlor, but the door is open and heavy-metal shreds the ears of passersby. Retooled classic cars glisten in the muted luxury of showroom light. As a band of head-bangers packs it up outside the Roxy, a spectre in his 60s begs for change to feed his children, clutching a small shopping bag and a teddy bear. Blocks before Holloway, there's a new viper's den for randy funk enthusiasts.

With these sights come smells—as invigorating as the aromas wafting from Thai restaurants or Texas barbecue stops, as nauseating as the smell of skunk road-kill; as revolting as the pungence of urine or the sweetish stench of puke.

Wish upon a star.

Wish away last call. Wish away the eternal wait for closed

things to open. Wish L.A. were lit around the clock like New York City or clockless like Vegas. Wish it had a political conscience like Chicago or D.C. Wish it had a heart—like San Francisco. Or a soul, like Atlanta.

Wish on.

A Valentine

O DEAR WONDERFUL WANDA,

(How do you like that for a first line?)

Dearest Wanda (*no line at all*),

I keep asking myself if it was real. I know it was, but in some ways it was so beautiful that I think, no... unreal.

I don't want to write about what happened then. I want to remember that, always.

What I want to make certain of is one thing: and that is, for as long as we know each other that it will always have been groovy between us.

In your letter, (*I'll get to the business in a... "beat"... briefly*) you say... "Hey, you know, I feel a special feeling for you. But I won't call it love."

I've read that back and forth in and out, for the last fifteen minutes and I think I know what you mean.

I'm a li'l bit different. I say, "Hey, you know, I have a special love for you. But I won't call it anything but a feeling."

I think it's possible to love for ten minutes straight, or two months, or ten years....

I loved you the minute I saw you, and it wasn't a thing of "love at first sight"... it was a pleasant combination of urges, lust, beautiful vibes, soulful eyes, wonderful lips, strength in your new beauty and love. I've left out a lot, but I'll save it 'til I see you.

Right now I'm like the man who, when he has money, presses his dollars... when he doesn't have any money, he presses his pants. I'm not doing either one....

I feel honored, having met you in the middle of your feelings for me and returned them, having held you and loved you, having stirred it around inside and discovered it was as good as I thought it would be. All of it. I hope you are under the impression that I'm talking about the goodness that we feel about people who've loved us without fear or reservation—those we were able to love back in kind.

That's what I'm trying to talk about.

By the time you receive this, you will know that I love you all over again. If you read this letter as carefully as I know you will, you'll know that the only reason I haven't been whispering into your ear is because I've been talking aloud to myself in the middle of the night....

Printed September 1996 in Santa Barbara
& Ann Arbor for the Black Sparrow Press by
Mackintosh Typography & Edwards Brothers Inc.
Text set in ITC New Baskerville by Words Worth.
Design by Barbara Martin.
This edition is published in paper wrappers;
there are 200 hardcover trade copies;
100 hardcover copies have been numbered & signed
by the author & 20 copies handbound in boards
by Earle Gray are lettered A-T & signed by the author.

PHOTO: Susan Carpendale

WANDA COLEMAN was born in 1946 and raised in the Los Angeles slum known as Watts, famed for its August 1965 Rebellion. Following this ethnic insurrection she joined a teenpost and a number of organizations set up to channel the "riotous" energies of young Black Americans into constructive modes. A struggling welfare mother, she was determined to become a writer. She has received literary fellowships from the National Endowment for the Arts and the Guggenheim Foundation for her poetry. She is the author of *Mad Dog Black Lady* (1979), *Imagoes* (1983), *Heavy Daughter Blues: Poems & Stories* 1968–1986 (1987), *A War of Eyes & Other Stories* (1988), *African Sleeping Sickness* (1990), *Hand Dance* (1993) and *Native in a Strange Land: Trials & Tremors* (1996), all published by Black Sparrow Press.